MALAYSIA'S WASTED DECADE

2004-2014

BY THE SAME AUTHOR

Liberating The Malay Mind (2013)

Moving Malaysia Forward (2008)

Towards A Competitive Malaysia: Development Challenges of the
21st Century (2006)

From Malaysia, With Love (2004)
(with Karen E. Musa)

Seeing Malaysia My Way (2003)

An Education System Worthy Of Malaysia (2003)

Malaysia in the Era of Globalization (2002)

The Malay Dilemma Revisited: Race Dynamics in Modern
Malaysia (1999)

MALAYSIA'S WASTED DECADE

2004-2014

The Toxic Triad of Abdullah, Najib, and

UMNO Leadership

M. Bakri Musa

Author of

The Malay Dilemma Revisited

Library of Congress Control Number: 2014914568

CreateSpace Independent Publishing Platform, North Charleston, SC

ISBN 13 978-1500776305

CONTENTS

Part III: The Labu and Labi Team of Najib and Muhyiddin

Introduction

Malaysia's longest-serving Prime Minister Mahathir Mohamad stunned his followers when he announced his resignation at his UMNO's (United Malay National Organization) Annual General Assembly in June 2002. He had been in office for over 22 years. His statement triggered a mass hysteria among his followers. Senior ministers and party leaders wept, and pandemonium broke out in the hall.

The scene resembled a chicken coop at dusk with the birds settling down in their comfort zone when suddenly their head rooster flew the coop, or attempted to. The cacophony settled down and calm returned only after senior leaders cajoled Mahathir to rescind his statement. He did not but instead agreed to delay his departure to October 31st the following year.

That collective hysteria and mass crying were reflective of how dependent UMNO members were on Mahathir. He was their messiah, and now he was abandoning them.

Mahathir anointed Abdullah Badawi as his successor, and five years later Najib Razak took over from Abdullah. The handover from Mahathir to Abdullah went smoothly, with both in their traditional attire of Malay *baju* and *samping sutra* smiling and shaking hands as they exchanged the instrument of office in front of the King. The next day Prime Minister Abdullah awarded both Mahathir and his wife the nation's highest honor, the Tunship.

The shift from Abdullah to Najib five years later also went smoothly, at least on the surface, with beaming smiles all around. Prime Minister Najib also awarded Abdullah his Tunship, as well as one to his new wife who had no discernible service to the nation. That seeming cordiality and civility however could not mask the earlier intrigue and shadow play engaged by both leaders.

Abdullah and Najib may have been consumed with their own shadow play nonetheless there was no mistaking who was the master puppeteer. Mahathir directly picked Abdullah, and then indirectly forced Abdullah to choose Najib.

Soon upon assuming office, Abdullah sought an electoral mandate and secured an overwhelming one in 2004, eclipsing and embarrassing Mahathir's less-than-stellar performance in 1999. Abdullah's boys (his advisers were all males) made sure that no one missed the comparison. Being amateurs and new to the game, they treated their victory as the ultimate trophy but failed to capitalize on it.

They, or rather their patron Abdullah, paid dearly for that. In the following election of 2008, his coalition suffered a humiliating setback. It was returned to power but with a hugely reduced majority at the federal level while losing five states to the opposition.

Mahathir saw his error with Abdullah soon after the latter took office. Even Abdullah's 2004 impressive electoral win did not persuade Mahathir otherwise. That victory however, blunted Mahathir's withering criticisms, reducing him to a grumpy old man. With Abdullah's subsequent electoral humiliation four years later, Mahathir was emboldened and his criticisms gained traction, amply aided by Abdullah's inept performance. His forced ignominious resignation in October 2009 gave way to Najib, with enthusiastic support from Mahathir, at least initially.

Mahathir is a poor judge of talent and character. His initial enthusiasm for Najib, as with Abdullah, was misplaced and soon soured.

When Najib subsequently suffered an even worse electoral humiliation than Abdullah in the May 2013 election, Mahathir ratcheted up his scorn for Najib, labeling him a "weak leader." He openly expressed his regret for his earlier support for Najib and publicly rebuked him. To date, a much older and less vigorous Mahathir has yet to be successful in undoing his error with Najib. Malaysia remains cursed with Najib's clueless and rudderless leadership.

Abdullah and Najib squandered Malaysia's precious first decade into the new millennium. It was a wasted if not lost decade. It would be academic to judge who is worse, Abdullah or Najib. When both scored "Fs", it matters less whether one is F minus and the other simply an F.

There is little prospect for change, at least until the next election due no later than mid 2018. Even if there were to be divine intervention, Najib's deputy, Muhyiddin, is no better. Malaysia is doomed; it cannot escape its present sorry trajectory.

If nations do not progress, then *ipso facto* it regresses. Human progress is neither automatic nor inevitable, noted Martin Luther King. Corruption in Malaysia is now approaching the "tipping point" where it would be irreversible and permanently cripple the nation *a la* Nigeria. Meanwhile religious fanaticism continues unabated, abetted by Najib and his deputy. That too may soon reach the point of no return when Malaysia would be another Pakistan. In fact, Malaysia's fate would be worse; a Nigeria and Pakistan combined.

Those two challenges are crippling enough but there are others, as with deteriorating institutions. In the judiciary even senior judges think that their job is to protect their paymaster, the government. Likewise, the Election Commission sees itself as an agency of the ruling Barisan coalition.

All these are obvious to ordinary citizens; they do not need reminders from august bodies like the UN. Its Human Development Index showed that Malaysia improved by 1.05 percent in the decade of 1980-90; and 1.12 from 1990-2000. During the decade 2000-13, it grew only half as much (0.58), justifying my calling it the wasted decade.

Alas, the UNHDP Index is buried amongst the tons of all-too-frequent glowing reports by foreign consultants and international bodies, all paid for handsomely by the government of Malaysia. It took a catastrophic tragedy as with the disappearance of Malaysia Airlines Flight 370 from Kuala Lumpur to Beijing on March 8, 2014 to expose on the world stage the nation's inattentive military radar operators and bumbling senior ministers. Malaysian leaders could not answer even simple questions from the families of the victims.

In fairness to Abdullah and Najib, the rot did not develop overnight. The Malaysia of today is still burdened by Mahathir's legacy, quite apart from his role in anointing Abdullah and Najib.

This is Malaysia, so the race factor is never far from the surface. Already Muhyiddin, Najib's deputy and presumptive successor, is threatening the nation with another "May 13," the horrific race riot of 1969. That is Muhyiddin, always looking back, never forward. His is the collective mindset and caliber of UMNO leadership, consumed with still fighting the last battle.

The issues they should be confronting are far different. Rampant corruption, deteriorating institutions, vicious religious extremism, and an entrenched rentier economy, among others, are what would doom Malaysia.

Although the racism and ethnic viruses can easily be reactivated (look at Northern Ireland and the Balkans), Malaysia has a low probability for another interracial conflagration of the 1969 variety despite attempts by the likes of Muhyiddin to scare citizens, especially non-Malays.

In an inaugural Millennium Essay for *The New Straits Times* (November 1999) I wrote, "The greatest threat to Malaysia's social stability is not *inter-racial* confrontation rather *intra-communal*, specifically among Malays." There are three potential fault lines along which Malays could fracture: religious, cultural, and socioeconomic. Conflict on any one is unlikely to trigger a severe crisis but a confluence of any two or all three could be cataclysmic.

Interracial conflict is bad, and Malaysians already had a taste of it many times. The May 13, 1969 incident was only the most bitter. Bad as it is, the intra-ethnic or intra-racial variety is worse. More Arabs have been killed by fellow Arabs than by the Israelis. The carnage of the 1956 Arab-Israeli War pales in comparison to the current intra-Arab strife in Syria and elsewhere.

Divisions between Malays and non-Malays are over tangible issues, as with scholarship quotas, employment preferences, and economic set-aside programs. Those are what Hirschmann referred to as "divisible conflicts," potentially solvable through negotiations. Differences within Malays on the other hand are over cultural values, theological beliefs, and way of life. These "indivisible conflicts" are more difficult if not impossible to resolve. If a pious kampong Malay feels that a proper Muslim woman must don her *hijab* while her urbane secular-minded sister disagrees, you cannot readily resolve that difference. A compromise as with donning half a *hijab* would not resolve it.

The first half of this wasted decade was helmed by Abdullah Badawi; he has now exited the stage before he could inflict even more damage. Today Malaysia is burdened with his successor, Najib Razak, who is equally intent in destroying the nation through his ineptness and willful neglect.

In my book *The Malay Dilemma Revisited* (1999) I wrote this of Abdullah. "He would be Malaysia's Jimmy Carter, an honorable enough man but a totally ineffectual leader." I was half right, in his being ineffectual. As for Najib, "[It] is difficult to evaluate as he carries the burden of his famous father . . . . [O]bjectively, it is hard to find Najib's mark."

Mahathir was still sharp and in power when I made those observations but he was too close to Abdullah and Najib to view them the way I did.

When Mahathir named Abdullah the country's eighth Deputy Prime Minister in 1998, the reaction was a yawn. Mahathir had had three previous deputies, and expectations were that his fourth would end up like the rest, being dumped soon and denied the top slot.

However, when Mahathir announced his sudden resignation, the realization set in that Abdullah Badawi would now succeed him. Like sheep, Malaysians accepted that and shifted allegiance to their new shepherd-to-be, and the accolades began pouring in. The man's apparent lack of gross flaws normally associated with politicians only increased his halo and quickly blotted out the more pertinent point that he lacked executive or leadership talent. The time too was opportune for Abdullah, for by this time the nation had grown weary of Mahathir. They wanted change and overlooked Abdullah's shortcomings. He also benefited from this cultural trait–

Malaysians are over generous with a new leader; they wanted him to succeed.

Despite the glowing praises, Abdullah Badawi was as hollow as a beetle-infested sago palm trunk. Many mistook him for a *samping sutra* (golden cummerbund) when he was but a common cotton *pelekat*. His leadership was detached, incompetent, and irrelevant. He was unfit to lead Malaysia.

Najib's early pronouncements upon assuming office in October 2009 made me question my initial skepticism of him. Alas, it did not take long for him to live up (or down) to my low expectations of him. Top-heavy Najib is busy spinning himself just to remain standing, and he confuses fast circular motion as rapid advancement.

The commentaries were written from January 2008 to December 2013, during the tenure of these two leaders. I have grouped them in four sections, each reflecting a different theme: Abdullah; Najib; UMNO (the dominant partner in the ruling Barisan Nasional coalition); and the Labu and Labi (the comedic team in P. Ramlees' movies) dysfunctional duo of Najib and Muhyiddin. To reflect the evolution of my thought, within each section I have arranged the essays chronologically.

I conclude on a cautionary note. Like its flagship Malaysia Airlines (formerly Malaysia Airline System or MAS–Malay word for gold), the country too has lost its luster. Formerly blue-chip MAS is now a penny stock; likewise Malaysia. My worse fear is that Malaysia would end up as a Pakistan and Nigeria combined, wrecked with religious intolerance and extremism while its economy and social structure crumbled under the weight of corruption.

I derive no pleasure in penning these critical commentaries. I would have preferred writing complimentary columns extolling the virtues and accomplishments of Malaysian leaders. At least then the citizens could benefit and I could glow in the reflected glory.

My two earlier volumes, *Seeing Malaysia My Way* (2004) and *Moving Malaysia Forward* (2008) contained my essays up to 2004 and from 2005 to 2008 respectively. I thank my readers for their comments. Space however does not permit me to include the perceptive responses and robust rebuttals here as I did in *Seeing Malaysia My Way*.

M. Bakri Musa
Morgan Hill, CA
December 2014

Part I

The Vacuous Abdullah Badawi

Believing Your Own Spin

To hear Prime Minister Abdullah tell it, his government is ahead that of Japan, Germany and United Kingdom in terms of efficiency. He based this apparently on his reading of the 2007 World Competitiveness Yearbook compiled by the Swiss Business School IMD.

The man can hardly stay awake long enough to flip through the thick volume much less read or comprehend it. When he made that assertion to the assembly of civil servants last Monday, January 28, 2008, he was merely uttering what his "bright boys" on his infamous "Fourth Floor" fed him.

That is scary. They are now beginning to believe their own self-created legend and swallowing their own spin. If they truly believe that the Malaysian government is ahead that of Germany, they must be hallucinating, a deranged state of mind brought on through their prolonged isolation from the real world.

Hallucinatory state by itself is not dangerous as long as you are fully aware of it. The danger comes when you believe it to be the reality. Indeed the definition of psychosis (or in layman's term, madness) is the inability to differentiate reality from delusion. When individuals begin acting on their hallucination, then all hell breaks loose. They would then pose an immediate danger not only to themselves but also to society, and they would have to be committed to "protective medical custody," the euphemism for the nut house.

Absurdity of the Claim

The absurdity of Abdullah's claim is apparent by the manner in which he made it. He chose his regular assembly of civil servants as the forum. This is his favorite mode of communication, a mass sermon. According to press reports, about 9,000 civil servants were "privileged" to hear that special sermon from their leader. That represents the top one percent of the service, the Secretary-Generals, Director-Generals, and important departmental heads.

Assume those top civil servants each make an average RM$15,000 per month (a very conservative estimate), and with the normal working day of seven hours and with 22 working days in a month, their time would be worth (or more accurately, cost the public) about RM100 per hour, at the minimum.

Abdullah took about an hour to deliver his speech. Of course those civil servants would have to arrive early and then linger behind to socialize, including taking the obligatory group pictures. They would have spent at a minimum two hours that morning just to listen to the Prime Minister's homilies.

By my calculation, that morning cost the government (the public really) in excess of RM1.8 million (RM100 per hour times 2 hours times 9,000 civil servants). In addition there would be the cost of using that massive auditorium and the video transmitting facilities so the speech could be beamed to the various state capitals. I have not included the costs of the time of those civil servants in the other cities tuned to their television screens.

The biggest cost however, is hidden. The whole government machinery was paralyzed that entire morning. No important decisions could be made that day as senior officers were out of their offices during the hour before, during and after the assembly. Where do you begin to quantify in monetary terms such a huge loss in productivity?

These giant assemblies are a favorite with Abdullah. He loves the captured, doting and uncritical audience. That gathering reminded me of my weekly school assemblies, with the pupils dutifully lining up in straight lines under the strict gaze of our prefects before we would march obediently into the school hall. Then after we were all seated, the teachers would stroll in, with the junior teachers leading with the senior ones following, desperately trying to put some gravitas to their steps.

Likewise with this assembly of civil servants; first to enter the auditorium would be the "Superscale G" officers, (the lowest of the senior ranks), followed by the F, E, and so on to A, meaning the Chief Secretaries and Director-Generals. Only after they were all settled down and after an appropriate silent waiting period would Abdullah make his imperious entry.

Everybody would of course then rise and the applause would be long, loud, and sustained. The little fellow would make his way to the stage in his usual plodding pace, nodding, grinning and shaking more than a few hands along the way, albeit not so regally. Up on stage he would continue his wide grin, lapping every moment of this effusive display of manufactured affection.

In scale and grandeur, such a show dwarfs what the North Koreans regularly put on for their "Beloved Leader." The mindset however, among leaders and followers alike, is the same in both Pyongyang and Putrajaya.

In this day and age, a more effective way of communicating, and considerably much cheaper at that, would have been for Abdullah to videotape his speech and webcast it. Then civil servants or members of the public could hear it on their own free time. Chief executives of large multinational corporations communicate to their far-flung employees that way, and it is very effective. Of course those civil servants would not like it. They relish those assemblies because they get to *ponteng* (escape) from their offices and chores.

Abdullah and his senior advisors are still stuck on the school assembly mode of communication. That reflects the "school boy" mentality of his advisors. It is also "efficiency," according to the wisdom of Abdullah and his advisers. Unfortunately this is the kind of operational details that are frequently missed by foreign observers.

Widespread Disregard of Evident Reality

The IMD Yearbook report on Malaysia looks too good to be true. No matter how meticulous their research, those academics would have a tough time convincing Malaysians, especially those who have had any dealings with their government. Yes, the Yearbook does say that based on certain specific criteria and prescribed framework, the Malaysian government is ahead that of Britain, Germany, and Japan. The big question is the relevance of those criteria and frameworks to everyday reality.

When something is too good to be true, chances are it is not. Regardless how impressive the credentials of their contributors, if their reports and findings have, in Lord Bauer's memorable phrase, "widespread disregard of evident reality," we must not believe them. This applies not only to economics but also to everything else in life.

Abdullah and his advisors are banking that the average Malaysian would not have access to the Yearbook. They are right. At nearly RM 3,000 per copy for the cheapest print edition, few if any library would acquire it. Consequently few Malaysians would have the opportunity to read the full report and scrutinize the criteria and framework. That is an important caveat.

I can credibly make the claim of being the best surgeon if I choose my framework carefully, as for example, being the best surgeon this side of Coyote Creek. I may be factually correct but the issue is the relevance of that claim.

Malaysia has been favorably cited lately by two well known international bodies. One was the earlier World Bank Report on our Higher Education, and now this IMD Yearbook on competitiveness. It is instructive that Malaysia had engaged both bodies to do significant consulting work.

May I suggest to all, especially foreign pundits and scholars, that the current circus that is the Royal Commission on the Lingam Tape gives a more realistic picture of the government machinery than the expensive IMD Yearbook. As for the World Bank Report on Higher Education, the government would have gotten the same ideas and recommendations by buying *and* reading my earlier book, *An Education System Worthy of Malaysia*. It would have been considerably cheaper too!

If Abdullah and his advisors were to treat the IMD's findings as an endorsement of their present policies, that would doom Malaysia to perpetual mediocrity.

February 3, 2008

The Tale of the Rattlesnake

Spring comes early to my part of California. Already there are exuberant splashes of dancing daffodils on the hillsides. Soon the colorful California poppies will pop up. With the weather becoming warmer, the rattlesnakes too will soon emerge from their winter slumber.

Talking of rattlesnakes, I am reminded of the story of the kind lady who saw one such weakling that was dying from the long cold winter. Taking pity on the poor critter, she took it home and nursed it back to health. One day while feeding the now robust creature, it took a swipe at her hand and bit her.

As she lay dying she asked the snake why it had done that. "You should have known better, lady! You knew I was a rattlesnake, you should have killed me back then!"

On March 8, 2008, Malaysia will have a general election, with Prime Minister Abdullah seeking a second term, having secured an overwhelming victory back in 2004. This will be the voters' collective judgment of what Abdullah did with that earlier mandate.

If Barisan Nasional were to retain its supra-majority and Abdullah remained as Prime Minister, rest assured that he would continue the pattern he set in his first term. He would once again reward his cronies and family members with sweetheart mega-billion contracts *sans* competition, just as he had done during his first term. His excuse then was that he did not know that he was doing it!

He will continue dozing off during meetings in the mistaken belief that Malaysians approve of his mediocre performances. Also, expect the bureaucracy to become even more bloated. This self-styled number one civil servant answer to every problem is to spend more money and employ more staff.

For Malays, expect more books on Islam to be banned and more raids by moral vigilante groups intent on keeping us on the "straight path." Expect this Imam of Islam Hadhari to lead even more prayers in public, with the television cameras rolling on, of course.

For non-Malays, expect more temples to be torn down to make way for "community development," more cash demands from their insatiably greedy Ali Baba partners, and more reasons to take their children out of national schools.

In short, Malaysians would be like that innocent lady who took pity on the emaciated rattlesnake. Malaysians took pity on Abdullah and gave him another chance. Unfortunately, true to form, this rattlesnake Abdullah Badawi will bite us back with a vengeance.

Who Should We Blame?

There is a little bit of that kind lady in all of us, of wanting to be helpful, and yes, to be forgiving. We want to give our leaders another chance. We believe in the basic goodness of our fellow human beings. We are generous and believe that goodwill begets more goodwill. In short, we are not rattlesnakes.

Unfortunately there is the small minority amongst us intent of being rattlers. No matter how kind we are to them, their basic instinct is to bite back.

When I find a rattlesnake near my house, I remove it away back to the hills. If it returns, then I will not hesitate to kill it. I give that critter only one chance; it is too dangerous to have a rattlesnake crawling around near my house.

Malaysians have been too kind and for too long to this rattlesnake of a leader, Abdullah Badawi. He interprets the huge mandate he received in 2004 not as a trust given by citizens to lead them to greater heights, but as a license to indulge his private fantasies. He is not at all embarrassed by being endlessly feted, with him and his adult family members jetting off to far away destinations in his newly-acquired (at taxpayers' expense) luxurious Airbus. Where and when did this grandson of a pious humble village imam acquire his extravagant tastes?

When Abdullah was appointed Deputy Prime Minister back in 1998, this is what I wrote in my book *The Malay Dilemma Revisited*: "Abdullah is not known for his intellect or sense of mission. Nor is he very inspiring . . . He would be Malaysia's Jimmy Carter, an honorable enough man but totally ineffective leader." I was wrong about the honorable part.

I also wrote, "Abdullah's only redeeming quality was his humility; a fine enough tribute for a friend but an overrated quality in a leader." As we now know, Abdullah has a lot to be humble about, to modify Churchill's quote.

Democracy – Self Correcting

The mistake Malaysians made was in giving the man that massive mandate in 2004, prompted no doubt by the kind lady instinct in us all. Unfortunately, it cemented in Abdullah the delusion that his many inadequacies were virtues. Our intellectuals and pundits too were also taken in, mistaking Abdullah's silence for substance and his humility for wisdom. Had Malaysians been less generous and our intellectuals more critical,

Abdullah would have a far less inflated sense of his own capabilities and virtues. Who knows, we might have been spared his vulgar excesses.

Even Prime Minister Mahathir was fooled by Abdullah to appoint him as Mahathir's successor. At least Mahathir recognized his error of judgment, albeit belatedly, and is now working hard to remedy his greatest mistake.

The beauty of democracy is that citizens can (or at least given a chance to) correct our collective mistakes, or even those of our leaders. In this upcoming election [March 8, 2008], voters in Kepala Batas could do a great national service if they were to boot Abdullah out. That would effectively remove him as Prime Minister. More significantly it would trigger a seismic shift in UMNO's leadership. With the party's ban on contesting top posts effectively circumvented, its members would get a chance to preview many other candidates.

If Kepala Batas voters were to shy away in exercising this historic opportunity, then Malaysians could still teach Abdullah a lesson by substantially reducing his coalition's victories. That would also trigger a challenge to his leadership and we would have the same effect as the first scenario.

We Malays have a saying that sometimes we have to be unkind in order to be kind. We may think that we are being kind by giving a five-ringgit note to a starving drug addict, but then he would just as quickly use that money to get his next fix.

In the social sciences there is the concept of an "enabler," specifically referring to the battered wife syndrome, of the wife whose toleration of her husband's abuses only encourages him to be even more abusive.

In this election voters will have to be cruel in order to be kind to our leaders, ourselves, and our nation. Malaysians must be wise enough not to be inadvertent enablers of corrupt and incompetent leaders. We must get rid of the rattlesnakes among our leaders before they bite us.

If Malaysians were to continue on with business as usual with this election, then we have only ourselves to blame. It would not be the fault of the rattlesnake if it were to bite us back, as surely it would.

March 2, 2008

[Addendum: That election returned Barisan to power but saw its worst electoral performance.]

Undur Lah, Pak Lah! (Part II)

Any other political leader whose party had been humiliated as UMNO was at this last election [March 8, 2008] would by now have tendered his resignation. Abdullah Badawi however, is slow on the uptake. He does not respond to subtle signals, even though there was nothing subtle about the voters' rejection of his leadership. The only way to get his attention would be to hit his thick skull with a two-by-four lumber, metaphorically-speaking of course.

At a press conference early this morning he declared, "I don't know who is being pressured, I'm not resigning." At best that reflects a leader who is totally out of touch with the harsh reality; at worse, the bravado of an idiot. With Abdullah, it is both.

If UMNO members do not complete what the voters had set out to do in this election – that is, get rid of Abdullah – then the next election would be even uglier. If former UMNO leader and Prime Minister Mahathir was accurate in his assessment that the party can no longer be reformed from within (a sentiment I share), then we are indeed watching the beginning of the end for UMNO. The implosion has begun.

Nothing is inevitable, however. This once proud party could indeed regain its luster and the citizens' confidence if it were to thoroughly cleanse itself. As with a fish, the rot begins at the head and spreads rapidly from there. Chop the head of an organization, and a fresh one will emerge, ready to take over, as with a hydra.

UMNO has that opportunity to do this soon. Its Supreme Council members must move forward the party's leadership conference that was postponed to this August. The council should also rescind its earlier "tradition" of there being no contest for its top posts. It should open up the process and loosen the rules. There is no need for a prospective candidate to line up support from umpteen divisions. To discourage frivolous candidates, institute the payment of deposits, as with the general elections.

Those two initiatives would immediately open up the field. UMNO could then preview more candidates instead of restricting itself to the same old tired faces. New faces of course would not guarantee change. We have already seen many young leaders in UMNO who are only too quick to learn and too eager to acquire the unsavory traits of their elders.

A New Dawn For Malaysia

As Anwar Ibrahim rightly observes, this election marks "a defining moment" in the history of the nation and the opening of "a new chapter." It is indeed a new dawn for Malaysia, a pivotal point in its politics. He can say that with considerable authority. More than any other person, Anwar was responsible for this remarkable reshaping of the Malaysian political landscape. He campaigned actively for his party even though he was not allowed to contest as a candidate.

He was also instrumental in aligning and galvanizing the opposition parties. Those parties had worked closely before in the 1999 and 2004 elections, but without Anwar's charisma and personal involvement they did not achieve much. Clearly the Anwar factor is real and remains formidable.

The academics will no doubt have their own voluminous analyses of this election, the most significant turning point in Malaysian politics. I wish only to highlight one positive and refreshing trend. This election saw all parties fielding many new young candidates. Two fresh talents deserve scrutiny for different reasons, but both reflect the greater political dynamics.

One is Nurul Izzah, Anwar's daughter who defeated Welfare Minister Shahrizat Jalil in the Lembah Pantai constituency which included the upscale community of Bangsar and the University of Malaya campus. Unlike many of her cabinet colleagues, Shahrizat was a competent minister. She also treated her novice political opponent with civility and respect, rare among UMNO politicians. They have a penchant for demonizing their opponents.

Nurul Izzah's considerable talent (she has a graduate degree from Johns Hopkins) and appeal aside, her victory reflects the waning support of UMNO among urban sophisticated voters.

On the other hand, the fate of another young candidate, Abdullah' son-in-law Khairy Jamaluddin, provides an amusing contrast. A year or two earlier Khairy, using the "protection" of his father-in-law, managed to ascend to the number two position in UMNO Youth *sans* any contest or election. This time he was catapulted to the hitherto safe rural parliamentary seat of Rembau. Despite being challenged by an unknown school teacher, Khairy managed only to squeak through. UMNO has problems even in the Malay heartland.

Obviously this Oxford graduate was attempting to ride on his father-in-law's coattail, except that Khairy made the mistake of not recognizing that his father-in-law had none; he was naked!

Non-political Lessons From This Election

For Malaysians who rely on the mainstream media and are guided by its opinion shapers, the results of this election shocked them. For those who follow the alternative media however, the results were what they had expected.

While the pundits in the mainstream media were all wet in their prognostications – they all confidently predicted a return of Barisan's supra-majority – Raja Petra of *Malaysia-Today* was spot-on in his overall predictions. He also predicted a significantly reduced majority for Abdullah and a greatly enhanced one for Najib.

Mainstream media readers may not have heard of "Chegu Bard" Badrul Hisham Shaharin, Khairy's political opponent in Rembau, but

'Netizens are very familiar with his name. They also contributed substantially towards his campaign through the Internet. Had indelible ink been used on voters to prevent repeat voting, or without the Elections Commission spare "empty" postal votes handy, Chegu Bard would have handily crushed Khairy.

More telling was this phenomenon. During and immediately after the election I had difficulty assessing both *Malaysiakini* and *Malaysia-Today*; their websites were swamped despite their having multiple mirror sites in anticipation for the increased visitors. When the authorities tried to block *Malaysiakini*'s website, it could still be accessed via its multiple mirror sites elsewhere.

In telling contrast, I had no problem at all accessing any of the mainstream media's websites. They were not inundated with readers and visitors. Being impatient, I visited their sites. Hungry for news, any news, I settled for the mediocre.

This election was more than a repudiation of Abdullah Badawi. It also repudiated the mainstream media and their pundits. Doing away with Abdullah is much more a doable task, not so their incompetent sycophantic media.

UMNO members must not shy away from doing the necessary dirty task at hand, getting rid of its leader Abdullah Badawi. If they fail to do that, then Malays should not hesitate in getting rid of UMNO.

March 8, 2008

[My earlier essay, "*Undur Lah Pak Lah*," posted on September 3, 2006, caused uproar in Parliament when Opposition MP Lim Kit Siang quoted from it.]

Get Rid of Abdullah and UMNO's Hang Tuahs

It is utterly reprehensible that Prime Minister Abdullah Badawi refuses to take responsibility for the debacle suffered by his party at the recent [2008] general elections. Even more despicable were his enablers in UMNO, its senior leaders who indulged him.

They all dutifully lined up peasant-like at Sri Perdana [official prime minister's residence] to pledge their personal loyalty to Abdullah the very next day following the electoral debacle. These latter day "Hang Tuahs" – individuals loyal to leaders but not to principles or the organization – included Najib Razak, Hishammuddin Hussein, and Rafidah Aziz.

They all obediently bowed down low and kissed the man's limp hand solemnly. Pathetic! When they should have been apprising their leader of the grim political reality, they instead stooped low to humor and flatter him. Those are the duties of court jesters, not ministers and senior advisors.

If these future leaders of UMNO cannot tell Abdullah the bad news to his face, how can we expect them to represent Malaysia in dealing with their even more assertive foreign counterparts? How could we entrust them with the fate of the nation? Are these "*lembik*" (limp) characters the future "brave" defenders of *Ketuanan Melayu*?

This whole crowd – and then some – must go. UMNO must get rid of not only Abdullah but also his entire retinue of enablers and latter-day Hang Tuahs. There is no alternative. The only choice is whether UMNO members do the dirty job themselves and on their own timetable, or watch voters do it for them. This election was merely a preview; the next time it would be even uglier.

Former Prime Minister Mahathir is wrong in saying that Abdullah destroyed UMNO. It was not only Abdullah who did it; he had his supporting cast of enablers.

It is not all doom and gloom, however. The party had faced many challenges in the past and had successfully overcome them. All it took was the courage of a few or even single individuals, as Mahathir did to the Tunku, the Father of Merdeka. Where are the young Mahathirs in today's UMNO?

As for Mahathir, he acknowledges his grave mistake in selecting Abdullah. Give Mahathir due credit, at least he recognizes his error and is trying his best to rectify it. He has demanded that Abdullah take full responsibility for this electoral debacle. Meaning, Abdullah should quit. Mahathir however, can only do so much. Besides, he has little or no stake in the future of UMNO except in so far as affecting his legacy.

Another party veteran, Tengku Razaleigh (Ku Li), also called for Abdullah to take full responsibility. It is a crying shame that with today's UMNO, only the old are leading the charge for change. That normally is the province of youth. This reflects how far UMNO has degenerated as an organization. It is not enough however for Tengku Razaleigh to give press statements to indicate his displeasure with Abdullah. Ku Li must lead the change and challenge Abdullah, as he (Ku Li) did earlier. Even if Tengku Razaleigh were to fail, he would still have paved the way for others to pursue the challenge.

Other senior UMNO members like Musa Hitam, Tengku Ahmad Rithaudeen and Sharir Samad must also step up to the plate and fulfill their responsibilities. They must help ease out Abdullah if for no other reason that the alternative would be too ugly to contemplate. I have no wish to see Abdullah publicly humiliated; enough that he would get out of the way. Let the old man enjoy his pension and new wife.

If those senior members abrogate their responsibilities, then it would be up to UMNO's Supreme Council members – the party's governing body – to take the initiative. At its next meeting they should pass a vote of no confidence in Abdullah. Even if unsuccessful, the message would have been delivered. Abdullah is a slow learner; it takes a while for a message to sink down in him.

Such a motion, even if unsuccessful, would pave the way for others to introduce similar resolutions at the upcoming party's general assembly. UMNO members at all levels must continue to put the heat on Abdullah and his coterie of enablers until he and they all quit in shame.

This coterie includes Najib Razak, all current UMNO vice-presidents, and leaders of its Youth, Wanita, Putera and Puteri wings. They are not leaders but enablers.

I do not share Mahathir's high opinion of Najib Razak. He has Hang Tuah's blind loyalty minus the bravery or charisma. His tenure as Defense Minister is best summarized by the unfolding saga of the Altantuya murder trial, a tale of intrigue, assassinations, and megabuck commissions.

Mahathir's confidence in Najib has less to do with his (Najib's) talent, more in Mahathir expressing his *terhutang budi* (gratitude) to Najib's father, Tun Razak, for having "rescued" Mahathir after he was expelled from the party. Najib without the famous "bin" after his name would be just another nondescript civil servant, perhaps a district officer back in his hometown. Tun Razak's other sons all have considerably more talent than

Najib. If Mahathir felt an obligation to the late Tun, he (Mahathir) should have groomed any one of the Tun's other sons.

Malays, and UMNO, have no shortage of talent. You just have to be more inclusive and exhaustive in the search, to cast the net deep and wide, and not be content with netting the fish that float by. Usually those are the rotting or nearly rotting ones. The vigorous specimens are out there swimming and enjoying the deep blue water. You have to make an effort to get them.

March 9, 2008

Still Blind to Reality

If Abdullah Badawi could not leverage the huge mandate he received in 2004 into effective leadership, there is little hope that he could do any better now that he had been severely mauled in the last election [2008]. Those who think otherwise are merely deluding themselves and engaging in wishful thinking.

UMNO leaders are afflicted by this collective blindness, a willful refusal to see or even acknowledge this evident reality; they are deluded and in mass denial. Meanwhile the likes of Najib Razak and Rafidah Aziz continue to grovel up to Abdullah; after all they serve at his pleasure. Najib in particular does not want to disturb the current pattern knowing full well that this would be Abdullah's last term and that Najib would take over after that. If Abdullah were to fumble now, there is no assurance that he would not take the whole crowd, including Najib, down with him.

What amazes me is to see the likes of Shahrir Samad trying to spin the recent electoral debacle into something other than that. He would like us to believe that it was a positive development; the "maturing" of Malaysian society as a consequence of Abdullah's "enlightened" leadership. The surprise was that he could utter that ridiculous claim with a straight face.

Maybe Shahrir felt beholden to Abdullah for having been selected as a parliamentary candidate. Shahrir must have remembered only too well the fate that befell lawyer Zaid Ibrahim. He was one of the few UMNO MPs who had the courage to criticize or at least disagree with Abdullah; consequently Abdullah dropped him as a candidate this time around.

Shahrir is drawing the wrong lesson. He should instead recall that Zaid's stock soared after he was dropped. He was, among other things, named one of Asia's top philanthropists. With UMNO thrashed, Zaid must thank his lucky stars to have been spared the electoral massacre in Kelantan. God works in wonderful ways!

Then there is the hogwash circulating that it was not poor Abdullah's fault for the electoral humiliation rather his advisors. How convenient! These Abdullah's apologists are beginning to believe their own spin. Abdullah's advisors reflect on him; like begets like, meaning, Abdullah has dumb advisors because he himself is dumb. Getting rid of his present advisors would not solve anything; he will get other even dumber ones.

It is not just voters who have passed judgment on Abdullah's leadership, so have investors. Trading on the KL stock market had to be temporarily suspended on the Monday following the election. Try spinning that!

It is well to remember that voters' judgment is based on Abdullah's past performance. Stock market sentiments reflect expectations. Investors are declaring that Abdullah's remaining as leader would be a disaster, and they are betting their money on that.

Lame Duck Prime Minister

What happens to Abdullah as a person does not interest me; my concern is with the fate of Malaysia. Abdullah is now a lame duck leader; the longer he hangs on, the more damage he would inflict on his party and country.

If Abdullah does not step down now, Malaysia will in effect have no chief executive. The whole cabinet and indeed the entire government machinery would be consumed with a leadership struggle, both overt and covert, right till the upcoming UMNO General Assembly this August. Nothing substantive would or could be done, not that Abdullah was an effective executive at the best of time. Everyone would be jockeying for position. It is this uncertainty that corrodes investor confidence.

The infighting has already begun. It started out small, naturally enough, in the tiny state of Perlis where there is now an ugly tussle for the chief minister's post. Soon the crisis will spread, of trying to find scapegoats for the party's humiliations and over the dwindling goodies. It will not be pretty.

Whatever economic, political and other gains that Abdullah's hacks and family members hope to gain by his stubbornly clinging on to power would vanish just as quickly as with his toppling. Remember how quickly they tried to humiliate Mahathir soon after he stepped down, and he was a very strong leader. He fought back. Abdullah is spineless; he could not even stand up to the chief minister of a tiny state like Perlis. Abdullah would be piled on so quickly and mercilessly once he is forced out such that even the likes of me would take pity on him.

New Political Dynamics

This election alters fundamentally the political dynamics at the federal, state, and most importantly, local levels. This harsh reality has yet to sink in on UMNO operatives. The loss of five states, especially the three most industrialized – Perak, Penang and Selangor – will have severe ramifications, far more than the loss of the two-third supra-majority in Parliament.

All the major economic initiatives previously announced by Abdullah (the various "development corridors" except perhaps for the Iskandar Project in Johore, a state still under UMNO control) would require agreement from the involved state governments. Now that those states are controlled by the opposition, approval would not be automatic.

While previous UMNO or Barisan chief ministers would readily *kow tow* to Abdullah (after all *he* appointed them), the likes of Khalid Ibrahim (Chief Minister of Selangor) or Lim Guan Eng (Penang) have no such deference. They would demand, among other things, that the various contracts be subjected to competitive bidding. That would dry up the hitherto steady stream of bounties that used to flow to UMNO cronies.

Those greedy UMNO fat cats would now be reduced to angry and hungry mangy felines, viciously fighting each other up for the dwindling scraps of morsels.

An UMNO Mat Deros (a state politician, former railway gate guard who now owns a huge mansion) who previously could bulldoze his way through the local council or state government merely by showing those cowed officials pictures of him performing *umrah* (minor Hajj) with Abdullah would now find the going rough. As for the real Mat Deros, now dead, watch his estate being saddled with unpaid assessments, plus penalties. It would not surprise me that the infamous mansion in Klang would be cited for non compliance with local building codes and thus had to be torn down.

Rest assured that all those powerful UMNO ministers and functionaries wishing to have their own mansions in the cities of the states now controlled by the opposition would no longer get sweetheart deals where valuable crown land would be handed to them at cut-rate prices, *a la* Mat Deros. They would then heap their frustrations on Abdullah. It would be tough on them and on Abdullah, but good for Malaysia. That is one positive development of this election.

March 16, 2008

Good Team, Bad Captain!

Among other things, in this [2008] election Malaysians have asserted in no uncertain terms that they do not approve of Abdullah's inept administration and his tolerance if not encouragement of corrupt and shady practices among those closest to him. In forming his new cabinet however, Abdullah once again demonstrated that he has learned nothing from the election debacle, his frequent declarations to the contrary notwithstanding.

While the addition of fresh talent in the persons of Amirsham Aziz and Zaid Ibrahim makes this a good cabinet, the retention of the same old tired faces as Syed Hamid, together with the inclusion of tainted characters like the "double Muhammad" Taib, smudges what otherwise would have been a tolerable team. It was, as the *Economist* noted, Abdullah's shuffling deckchairs on his personal *Titanic.*

This election did what Abdullah could not, that is, get rid of his deadwood ministers like Samy Vellu and incompetents like Zainuddin Maidin. Voters showed the way but Abdullah did not carry it further with his choice of new ministers. This good new team is cursed with the same old bad captain.

A team no matter how talented could not turn an incompetent captain into a good one. Neither would a prolonged "warm up" time accomplish much; a bad captain will still remain so. As one blogger cheekily noted, today even Abdullah's "*sign dah tak laku*" (signature is worthless, as on a bounced check), in reference to the Raja of Perlis ignoring Abdullah's choice for a Mentri Besar. As of my writing, the Sultan of Trengganu too is set to do likewise.

Abdullah's cabinet remains bloated with 33 ministers, including five in his own department. His "reform" consists of nothing more than changing faces. He fails to address more fundamental issues like whether any of those ministries are needed at all.

For example, what is glaringly obvious from this election is that the Ministry of Information has no credibility with Malaysians or foreign observers. It is nothing more than the propaganda arm of the ruling party, and an inept one at that. Replacing its minister would not alter that reality. In the Age of the Internet, this is one ministry Malaysia can do without. Abolishing it, together with other unneeded ministries like Sports, Tourism, and Federal Territory, among others, would shrink the cabinet and streamline the administration.

This huge cabinet is unwieldy. No meaningful or robust discussions could take place. Even if each minister were to speak for only a few minutes, cabinet meetings would stretch for hours.

Singapore's Lee Kuan Yew, who knows something about forming an effective cabinet and selecting capable ministers, once said that he would appoint only those for whom a cabinet appointment would mean a reduction in their personal earnings. This does not mean that Singapore pays its ministers miserly – on the contrary they are very well compensated – rather that those ministers have excelled elsewhere and thus are earning considerably more than ministers.

Only two of Abdullah's appointees, Amirsham and Zaid Ibrahim, meet Lee's stringent criterion. Long-serving former Trade Minister Rafidah Aziz would find few takers in the private sector for her talent. The only reason she remains calm after being fired is that she did not want to jeopardize her chance of being given plump directorships in the many Government-linked companies. Further, if she were to complain too loudly, the Anti Corruption Agency would suddenly become diligent in scrutinizing her old Approved Permits import files.

Blemishes and Kudos

Abdullah's commitment to combat corruption is made hollow by his bringing Muhammad Taib into the cabinet. He was the former Mentri Besar of Selangor who was caught at an Australian airport with literally millions in cash on his person. He was acquitted from the criminal charge on a technicality of not declaring the currency; he has yet to explain how he secured the loot in the first place.

If Abdullah has not asked Muhammad that pertinent question, then he (Abdullah) is derelict in his duties by not exercising due diligence in selecting his ministers. If Abdullah did ask and was satisfied with Muhammad's answer, then Abdullah owes the public to share that explanation. Failure to do so would make Abdullah's renewed calls to combat corruption more than hollow; it would be hypocritical.

Yes, that incident took place over a decade ago, old story, Muhammad would claim. However, there is no statute of limitation with criminal acts. Time does not make a corrupt act less so.

I applaud Zaid Ibrahim's appointment. He is one of the few who is independent minded and unafraid to challenge the leader, a rare quality especially among Malays. We are still feudalistic, blindly loyal to leaders regardless of circumstances. I also applaud him for his commitment to the rule of law. Also rare among Asian leaders and newly rich, Zaid is well known for his charity works. Forbes magazine recently listed him as one of Asia's top philanthropists.

Of interest here is that Zaid Ibrahim was only recently found guilty of "money politics" by UMNO's Disciplinary Committee, whose esteemed members included Zaki Azmi, now Court of Appeal President and second highest position in the judiciary. Zaid strenuously appealed his "conviction" right up to the President of UMNO, Abdullah, but to no avail. It reflects more on the credibility and prestige of that disciplinary committee (more correctly, the lack of both) that Abdullah would now appoint Zaid to the cabinet to be in charge of law and the judiciary!

I have the highest regard for Zaid's personal integrity and professional honor. I bring this up merely to demonstrate Abdullah's and also UMNO's hypocrisy towards disciplining its members. The fact that members of UMNO Disciplinary Committee would choose to remain silent on Zaid's appointment attests to the "seriousness" with which they executed their duties. Let us acknowledge openly what was previously simply alluded to, that disciplinary committee was nothing more than a kangaroo court, its deliberations not worth considering, not even by UMNO's president..

Zaid should consider his UMNO "conviction" a singular badge of honor. When knaves and crooks rule and do the judging, the virtuous and honorable would be considered criminals.

Presidential Power Versus Collective Cabinet

In the previous cabinet, Abdullah was also the Minister of Finance and of Internal Security. That would be a tough assignment for even the most accomplished executive. With Abdullah, well, the results were obvious; he was totally ineffective. He held the Finance portfolio only to ensure that his family and cronies would get plump government contracts and privatization projects. In the new cabinet, Abdullah still holds on to Finance but he has given up Internal Security.

Abdullah continues to have the five full and four deputy ministers in his department. He is developing a presidential-type administration in tandem with the customary collective cabinet responsibility. This could potentially give rise to unnecessary conflicts. Eliminating those positions would reduce the size of the cabinet and enhance its efficiency.

As a former civil servant Abdullah revels in the committee system. His answer to every problem is to appoint a committee; it is a sly way to duck responsibility. The executive talent of a leader is inversely related to his penchant for forming committees. Abdullah is "Exhibit A;" he has never seen a committee he does not like.

Therein lies the problem; Malaysia is being "committeed" to death. Malaysians cannot allow Abdullah to do that; he must be forced to step down now for the good of the country.

March 30, 2008

Abdullah Badawi As "Practice Prime Minister"

In his novel *Gadis Pantai* (The Girl From The Coast), Pramoedya Ananta Toer revealed a quaint custom in ancient Malay culture. That is where the would-be lord of the kampong upon reaching adulthood would grab the prettiest village virgin to be his "practice wife." Then when he becomes sufficiently well honed in his "husbandly" skills, or when he gets bored with her, he would toss her out like a piece of soiled rag. He with his now enhanced skills would go on to marry a lady of "proper" background.

Fate has gifted Malaysians with a "practice leader" in the person of Abdullah Badawi. He is so inept, so spineless, and so lacking in ability to make decisions that he practically invites scorn and contempt. Or in Tengku Razaleigh's words, Abdullah showed a "stunning ineptness in managing …

straightforward functions of government." Today even *kedai kopi* (coffeehouses) patrons are not hesitant in ridiculing Abdullah.

Some of the criticisms leveled at Abdullah are crude and clumsy, but then so would the village nobleman's initial experiences with his "practice wife." The concern is less with finesse and artistry, more with getting it done. With time and practice, rest assured things would only get better.

Once Malaysians have become accustomed to being critical of Abdullah and are unafraid to criticize or even challenge him, then we would toss him out, as the village nobleman would his "practice wife." Malaysians would then be ready for a proper leader.

Consequences of An Uncritical Citizenry

Fate had blessed Malaysia with capable leaders in the past. There was Tunku Abdul Rahman, Father of Independence, who led the country out of colonial rule without shedding a drop of blood. However, as Malaysians had not yet learned to be good followers, we were not sufficiently critical of him and he got carried away with being the "world's happiest prime minister" while letting problems fester until they blew up in his and our collective faces.

He was succeeded by the able Tun Razak, but his life was tragically cut short by cancer. As such he was spared from being spoiled by an adoring and uncritical populace. His reputation remains intact and unblemished.

His successor Hussein Onn may not have been the most capable but at least he knew his limitations. He was wise enough to voluntarily relinquish his post. He took his oath of office seriously. He was meticulous and unusually astute in the choice of his successor even though he had personal reservations about the man.

In Mahathir, Malaysians had a leader of exceptional brilliance, unorthodox convictions, and courageous innovations. He transformed Malaysia. Like any other mortal, he had his share of faults. Unfortunately his uncritical and unabashedly adoring followers were equally blind to his mistakes, thus preventing him from recognizing and rectifying them.

Had Malaysians generally and UMNO members specifically been more critical of Mahathir in his choice of a successor for example, the nation would have been spared the current political muddling.

This uncritical sheep-to-shepherd dynamics also characterizes other Asian and Third World societies. Indonesia was blessed with the charismatic and brilliant Sukarno. He united those polyglot islands into a cohesive nation while bravely taking on the Dutch colonialists at the same time. China has its Mao. However, as their uncritical followers did not rein in their leaders' initial excesses, those leaders got carried away.

Making Malaysians More Critical

Similarly, Malaysians are excessively deferential to their leaders, rarely challenging or even criticizing them. To their followers, these leaders are always clad in the finest fashion even when all they have on is nothing but a piece of tattered stained loincloth. The relationship is akin to that of a flock of sheep and its shepherd, of blind obedience.

That may be fine for docile sheep but it is hardly the recipe for a progressive and competitive society, or at least one that would merit the adjective "modern." In such societies leaders must be held accountable, and followers in turn must not hesitate to hold their leaders to exacting standards. This reciprocal relationship means that followers must be willing and not be fearful to criticize and challenge their leaders. That is the best way to ensure accountability. It would also discourage these leaders from being led astray by their blind ambition or abusing the trust we grant them.

Without being unduly Pollyannaish, the only way to make sense of the current political mess is to believe that this is part of a divine design, of Fate providing Malaysians with a "practice leader" in order to better prepare them for a real one in the future.

There are two towering personalities in the horizon that fit my characterization of a real leader: Anwar Ibrahim and Tengku Razaleigh (Ku Li). In their previous incarnations, these two have had their share of fawning followers who egged them on to make unwise decisions. For Anwar, it led to his prematurely challenging Mahathir. He (and us) knows only too well the disastrous consequences of that fateful decision. Tengku Razaleigh, again at the behest of his admiring supporters, left UMNO briefly to form Semangat Party.

The problem is not with Anwar or Ku Li challenging Mahathir, rather that we as a society have yet to deal with or learn the art of challenging and criticizing our leaders. Our standard response to dissatisfaction with our leaders is either to split the organization or riot in the streets. Enter Abdullah as "practice leader;" now we have learned at least not to riot, a significant advancement.

Anwar and Ku Li are now much wiser. They would be even better leaders if we let them be, meaning that we should not let our guards down lest they would be tempted to be led astray by their uncritical admirers.

I note a certain humility and magnanimity in both Anwar and Ku Li. To them, the travails and weaknesses of Abdullah Badawi truly pain them. To these two nationalists, challenging Abdullah is not a route for the fulfillment of their personal ambition, rather a patriot's obligation.

To young readers who may not yet quite grasp the "practice wife" concept, let me substitute a sports metaphor. Abdullah is a convenient punching bag for Malaysians to practice on how we should learn to handle future leaders. For now, his ineptness and incompetence make those lessons easy for us, though not for Abdullah.

In Pramoedya's novel, the young nameless lady who is the nobleman's "practice wife" returns to her village. Only through her inner strength and sterling character could she maintain her dignity and respect among her people.

When Abdullah gets tossed out, as inevitably he would, lacking strength of character, the public scorn heaped upon him would be merciless. Abdullah's predictable humiliation would not arouse any pity from me, but his destroying what was once a fine Malay institution – UMNO – would.

The only redeeming feature to the whole ugly saga would be that Abdullah would also bring down with him the "practice pundits" and "practice editors" in the mainstream media, as well as the "practice academics" and "practice intellectuals" in the universities.

April 6, 2008

Targeting The Biggest Ass

Johore UMNO leaders had told Prime Minister Abdullah that he must have a succession plan that is "structured, smooth and speedy." This "Three-S strategy" missed targeting the biggest ass of all, Abdullah himself. The initiative had more to do with saving Abdullah's "face" than with solving the grave problems confronting the party.

If UMNO members and leaders were serious, they would focus on getting this harsh and unadulterated message straight to Abdullah: He is unfit to lead the party and country. He has clearly demonstrated this through his deeds (or lack of them) and words. The man is a habitual liar; he cannot separate fact from fiction or distinguish reality from fantasy.

Abdullah's idea of taking responsibility for his party's electoral debacle is merely to utter that statement. He has no inkling of what it means to accept responsibility.

Abdullah's pleading that he is needed to "revive" the party is laughable and self serving. If he could not pilot his ship of state competently when it was calm, there is no hope that he would be any more capable now when it is stormy and threatening to get worse every day. Abdullah *is* the problem, and a very huge one at that. His moving out would be a big part of the solution. It would not solve everything of course, but it would remove a major impediment to finding the solution.

His "leadership" has been nothing more than endless sloganeering ("Work with me, not for me!"), like the leader caricatured in Shahnon Ahmad's short story, "*Ungkapan*" (Sloganeering).

Having grown accustomed to the perks and trappings of his office, Abdullah will not leave voluntarily, much less gracefully. He has to be literally dragged out. Subtleties and hints will not work on this man. He is too dense to read the signals. He is also insulated, surrounded by courtiers ever willing to spin bad news as otherwise.

Only Three Exit Strategies

There are only three ways to get rid of Abdullah. One is for him to be successfully challenged as party leader in the upcoming UMNO General Assembly in December [2008]; two, for a sufficient number of the ruling coalition members to vote with the opposition in a "no confidence" motion in Parliament; and three, through divine intervention, not inappropriate for a man who is never shy in parading his piety and religiosity.

Knowing the onerous obstacles placed in UMNO towards challengers, the first option is unlikely. Granted, Tengku Razaleigh – the only one to have come out publicly to challenge Abdullah – is a formidable challenger. More daunting however, is the cultural inertia of Malays, especially those in UMNO. They have yet to learn the essential lesson that challenges and competitions are healthy, not acts of treason or betrayal.

The second path is more realistic. The political resurgence of Anwar is real. Far from being the "Anwar who?" whom I caricatured only a few years ago, he is now increasingly viewed not only as the de facto leader of the opposition (even though he is not yet in Parliament) but rightly as Prime Minister-in-waiting.

Anwar will be able to contest a parliamentary seat once his statutory prohibition ends on April 14, 2008. A vacant seat will surely come up soon as Malaysia has a good track record of MPs dying in office or getting caught in some scandalous acts and thus having to resign. Failing that, one of the current MPs from his party could resign, not to pave the way for Anwar (though that would be the convenient and acceptable excuse) but because the job is not as glamorous or challenging as it is made out to be. Many of his party's MPs are successful, young and honest professionals; their "elevation" to the "Yang Berhormat" (Your Honorable) status cuts deeply into their income as well as career prospects.

As for divine intervention, that is beyond my purview. However, many a leader had used "medical" reasons as a convenient face-saving cover for resigning. Abdullah could always blame his hemorrhoids or narcolepsy (a pathologic tendency to doze off).

Abdullah Is *The* Problem

When Abdullah assumed office nearly five years ago, I was one of the few who were not enthused about his leadership potential. My conclusion was based on reviewing his performance as a minister. I predicted then that by the time Abdullah leaves office, Malaysians would be counting their blessings if he had not screwed up the country too much, and that the best we could hope for was for him to maintain the status quo.

Alas, I was wrong. My confidence in the maturity and resilience of Malaysians in not tolerating Abdullah's gross incompetence was misplaced. Malaysians are also incredibly generous as demonstrated by their giving the man a rousing endorsement in the 2004 election in the hope that it would give him the necessary boost and confidence to lead. Unfortunately that too could not override his basic ineptness.

In their collective wisdom, in this recent 2008 election Malaysians decided that it was not necessary to deal a crippling blow, only enough punch that would leave Abdullah and UMNO reeling, and in the process trigger an implosion in an already corrupt and dysfunctional organization.

Equally remarkable, Malaysians had also demonstrated that they were capable of executing peaceful political change. There was not even a hint of civil disorder following Barisan's loss of five states. Compare that to 1969 and the horror that followed when the ruling coalition lost only one state.

To be sure, had the election been conducted free and fair, with no stuffed postal ballots and with the use of indelible ink to prevent fraudulent voting, the ultimate message would have been delivered, and Abdullah and his ilk would have been kicked out.

Perhaps it was better this way. For had the Barisan Nasional been voted out, there would have been a dangerous political vacuum as none of the opposition parties could form a government. Their loose coalition, the Pakatan Rakyat (Citizens' Alliance) had yet to be ratified. Now having sensed that power is within their grasp, the opposition parties are ready and willing to sink their differences for a common cause. Meanwhile UMNO and its coalition partners are galloping fast towards their collective demise. Their course is irreversible.

Thankfully my earlier dire prediction on Abdullah was misplaced. He has not destroyed Malaysia, only UMNO and Barisan Nasional. Malaysians can all count their blessings for his legacy not being any worse.

April 20, 2008

Apportioning The Blame

It is tempting – and comforting – to blame everyone for the failure of Prime Minister Abdullah's leadership, or take the other extreme and heap the entire blame on the hapless man.

Both approaches would be inadequate if not wrong. The corollary to "everyone is at fault" is that no one is. That would be a collective "cop out," an abrogation of personal responsibility. Even if it were that rare instance where everyone is indeed responsible, there would still be the different degrees of culpability that would have to be acknowledged.

Blaming Abdullah entirely would also be inadequate. That would gloss over the glaring inadequacies of the system, like its lack of checks and balances.

When a Turkish Airline jet crashed over Paris in 1974 because its cargo door blew out, the blame was not put entirely on the sloppy mechanic – although his negligence was clearly the triggering event – rather on the design flaws that would not indicate when doors were not properly secured. Firing the poor mechanic (though that was done) would not prevent future similar accidents, but improving the design with better indicator lights did.

An insight from the science of failure analysis is that catastrophes are often not the result of a single major error, rather the cumulative effects of a series of minor mistakes each compounding the other until a critical stress point is reached when the whole system would blow up. We are all familiar with the story of losing the war for the want of a nail.

Triggering Event

We could usefully use failure analysis to examine Abdullah's tenure. The triggering event (the sloppy mechanic if you will) was Mahathir's selection of Abdullah back in 1998. Had Mahathir not done this, we would have been spared this disaster.

Malaysia however, cannot and should not be at the mercy of the mistake of any one individual no matter how high his position. Besides, blaming Mahathir alone would also not pass the philosophical test on the meaning of causation. We might as well blame Abdullah's mother if we were to pursue this line of logic, for had she not given birth to him, we would have been spared this debacle. We could go even earlier and blame Abdullah's father for the conception. There would be no end to the line of blame with that logic.

Certainly Mahathir should have been more prudent and sought wider counsel in selecting his deputy. He should have had the courage to break party tradition and go beyond the sitting vice presidents in selecting his successor. While Mahathir was clearly the triggering factor, I would apportion only 10 percent of the blame on him.

The Man Himself

When Abdullah was selected to assume the highest office in the land, he should have taken that responsibility seriously. This was not "just another promotion," as he put it, in the tradition of the civil service from where he came. Granted, the man lacks introspective instinct nonetheless he should have at least contemplated his abilities and be aware of his limitations.

When the distinguished editor Howard Raines was appointed to head the influential *New York Times*, he knew that he lacked executive and business experience. Consequently he enrolled in a brief graduate business program. When Tengku Razaleigh was approached by then Prime Minister Hussein Onn to be his deputy, the Tengku politely declined. He felt he could contribute more by being other than a Deputy Prime Minister. That is the mark of wisdom and self confidence.

When Hussein Onn felt that leading the country was way over his head, he did the honorable thing: He resigned. That too is the mark of a wise man.

Abdullah clearly lacks executive talent and economic nous; he owes it to himself and the nation to remedy those deficits. He could have had the services of the best minds if only he had been prudent in selecting his advisors, *a la* President Ronald Reagan. For these reasons I would apportion a greater blame – 20 percent – to Abdullah.

Editors, Pundits, Abdullah's Advisors as Culprits

Just as Abdullah has a duty to select competent advisors, they too owe a duty to him and the nation in properly advising him. They are advisors and counselors, not courtiers and cheerleaders. Abdullah has his wife and family members to do that for him. My admonition also goes to Abdullah's other official advisors like his ministers and UMNO Supreme Council members.

This duty to advise extends beyond those with appropriately designated titles. Editors and journalists as well as intellectuals and pundits, whom society has implicitly imposed a similar obligation, also have a sacred duty and a greater obligation to the public in serving as checks and balances on the leadership.

Veteran news anchor Walter Cronkite's critical comments on the Vietnam War were instrumental in President Johnson not seeking a second term. Had Malaysian editors and journalists acted less like lap dogs, Abdullah would not have dared stray far.

It is hilarious to see these editors of the mainstream media now clumsily trying to correct themselves. They are finding that ingrained habits are hard to break, especially bad ones.

If these editors had a fraction of the fearlessness of Raja Petra [Editor and owner of the highly popular online portal *Malaysia Today*], and intellectuals an iota of the integrity of Azmi Sharom [a University of Malaya law professor], we are more likely to get honest competent leaders, and keep them that way while they are in power.

Academics like Shamsul AB who are on the public payroll and pundits like Johan Jaafar who earn fat public pensions have a public duty not to debase themselves to be the administration's sycophants. They have to remain true to their vocation.

These folks as well as those boys on the infamous "Fourth Floor" must therefore shoulder their share of responsibility for Abdullah's failings. I would apportion 30 percent of the blame to them.

We Deserve Our Leaders

Abdullah would not have been the leader he is without his followers acquiescing to or permitting it. Had Malaysians not given Abdullah that overwhelming mandate in 2004 and instead adopted a more skeptical "Show me first!" attitude, his ego would not have been so inflated.

He would have a more realistic assessment of his capabilities; it would have also chastened his advisors.

Malaysians had plenty of opportunities to remind Abdullah of his shortcomings prior to the recent general election. The last one was the Ijok state by-election. The excesses of UMNO operatives during this last general election grew out of voters' tolerance of their earlier shenanigans.

We are responsible for the leaders we get. We must scrutinize our leaders' promises and hold them accountable. If we fail to do that, then we have only ourselves to blame for their straying. For these reasons I would apportion 40 percent of the blame on Malaysian voters.

While Mahathir's culpability is a miniscule 10 percent, nonetheless he has freely admitted to it. More importantly, he is trying his best to rectify it. Malaysians too are becoming more circumspect and taking their voting responsibilities seriously, as demonstrated by this recent election results.

Abdullah continues to blame others – party saboteurs, Anwar, Mahathir – everybody but himself for his leadership failure. His advisors as well as the pundits, editors and intellectuals have all remained uncharacteristically silent. They have yet to acknowledge much less rectify their mistakes.

The foregoing is not an accounting exercise rather a suggestion on how we should treat our leaders in future. The burden is particularly high for voters who are also commentators, editors, and intellectuals.

April 27, 2008

UMNO's Hang Tuah - Hang Jebat Dilemma

The furor over Tun Mahathir's quitting UMNO cannot hide an increasingly obvious and ugly reality: Abdullah's incompetence as Prime Minister. Ranting and raving against Mahathir will not alter this singular fact.

Only an ardent few – his family members, closest advisors, and those beholden to him – believe that Abdullah has executed the duties of his office diligently. These individuals will forever remain faithful to him even if he were to drive the country to ruins. Consider that Saddam Hussein and Shah Pahlavi still have their ardent admirers even to this day.

For others, their only excuse for wanting Abdullah to stay on is for "party unity."

Mahathir's poser to Abdullah's putative successor Najib Razak on whether he is loyal to UMNO or to Abdullah is a dilemma shared by all party members. Najib as well as all UMNO members would do well to re-read our classic Hang Tuah-Hang Jebat legend, and in particular ponder the fate of not only the two protagonists but also their sultan and the Melaka sultanate.

In 1987 when UMNO was split, a consequence of the Mahathir-Razaleigh rivalry, the party was weakened but it survived because it had a strong leader. Early in its history when its first president Datuk Onn left the party, the impact was minimal as the party was strong and it had a cadre of capable young leaders like Razak. This time however, both the party and its leader are weak.

If party members were to shy away from doing the dirty but necessary job of removing Abdullah from the leadership of UMNO, and thus the Prime Minister's office, then others would by default remove that office from him, and from UMNO. With every delay, Abdullah (and UMNO) gets weaker while Anwar Ibrahim (and his Pakatan Rakyat) becomes stronger.

Seeing Through Abdullah

Like Mahathir, most Malaysians believed in Abdullah, at least initially as evidenced by his overwhelming electoral victory in 2004. Four years later they too were disillusioned, just like Mahathir, although his started much earlier.

Some still believe (or more correctly, hope) that Abdullah could yet salvage his leadership. This hope for a miracle is misplaced. Incompetence cannot be readily remedied, especially in someone with a demonstrated flat learning curve. Besides, the highest office in the land cannot be used as a training ground. We cannot have an "intern" or "practice" Prime Minister; the stakes are just too great.

If Abdullah could not lead when he had a commanding mandate, what chance is there for him now that his hold is tenuous at best? He is already consumed with putting out political brush fires, distracting him from his most important task of leading the nation. Abdullah is now clearly damaged goods; Malaysia deserves better.

Only a tiny minority saw through Abdullah and recognized his emptiness right from the very beginning. It is more with sorrow than vindication that I admit to being in this group. I would have preferred to have been proven wrong.

I have never met Abdullah; my assessment of him is based entirely on his records and accomplishments, or lack thereof. Perhaps because of this I am not swayed by the man's put-on piety, seeming humility, or servile loyalty. Those attributes are held in high esteem in Malay culture, which may explain why many, including the shrewd Mahathir, overestimated Abdullah's ability.

Abdullah was a longtime civil servant, rising to Deputy Secretary-General in the Ministry of Culture, Youth and Sports before entering elective politics. Respectable enough achievement, but then that ministry is not exactly the hotbed for super-achievers.

Before being kicked out of the cabinet in 1987, a casualty of the Mahathir-Razaleigh rivalry of the time, Abdullah had served as Minister of Education, and later, of Defense. One is hard pressed to discern his legacy in both positions. A measure of his worth was that the best he could do outside of government was as a ticket agent – in his sister-in-law's travel agency! That was the private sector's valuation of his talent and experience, despite having served in the two most senior and prestigious portfolios.

Later when he re-ascended the UMNO hierarchy, Mahathir invited him back to serve as Foreign Minister and later, Home Affairs. In the latter position he was responsible for the police. Our current inept and corrupt-ridden police force is his legacy.

Mahathir's Mistake

You have to give credit to Mahathir. Not only did he admit to his colossal mistake in selecting Abdullah back in 1998, he is also making a vigorous effort to undo it. Admitting to or rectifying your error is a rare attribute among leaders.

Abdullah has yet to learn this essential lesson. That is, merely uttering that you are taking responsibility, as Abdullah did for his party's routing in the last election, is not enough; you have to act on it.

The current crisis in UMNO is not, as is widely commented upon, simply a battle between Abdullah and Mahathir. The fundamental issue is Abdullah's incompetence, and its impact on the nation.

Winning elections is a partial measure of effective leadership; it is not the only or full measure. Abdullah's predecessors Tunku Abdul Rahman and Hussein Onn were both successful at elections, yet when their leadership was found wanting they withdrew gracefully. Britain's Margaret Thatcher also had the grace to resign when support for her was declining even though she had led her party through three successive electoral victories.

Abdullah has neither the grace nor the competence of Thatcher. He is too *syok sendiri* (self indulgent) with the perks of his office, with its luxurious corporate jets and palatial mansion to even contemplate resigning. It is easy to be stubborn in such circumstances. Like a dumb mule surrounded by lush hay, Abdullah will not move. It will continue mindlessly chewing the cud, oblivious of the turmoil it caused. It is well to remember that a mule with too much hay will inevitably succumb to lethal gas bloat.

Many consider Mahathir's resigning from UMNO an irrational act as that would only hasten the ascent of his old nemesis, Anwar Ibrahim. Mahathir however, may be signaling something significant. He must believe (or have reasons to) that Anwar's chances are real and strong. By resigning now, Mahathir would be spared the fallout from UMNO's inevitable implosion. He could then with a smirk remind us, "I told you so, this Abdullah is a disaster!"

Many are wondering why Abdullah is not coming out swinging at his tormentors. There is a reason for Abdullah's reticence. His entanglement in the UN's Iraq Oil for Food Program scandal is only a hint and a glimpse.

I am reminded of J. Edgar Hoover, the longtime FBI director who was the most feared and powerful man in Washington, D.C., simply because he held so many secrets of important people. Nobody dared touch him for fear that he would spill the beans.

Mahathir was Prime Minister for over two decades. While not a shrewd observer of human behavior, he was a meticulous record keeper. Think of the many shenanigans committed at home and abroad by our sultans, ministers, and other senior officials that were simply hushed up, let alone prosecuted. Those who are tempted to sneer at the old statesman better have pristine personal and official backgrounds; otherwise they would be well advised to maintain their "elegant silence."

Notice Mahathir's immediate stinging riposte to Shahrir Samad's and Musa Hitam's criticisms of him recently. In so doing Mahathir sends a not-so-subtle message to his other detractors, including those on the Royal Commission on the Lingam Tape, that their stinking laundry too could be aired out for all to see and smell. As Prime Minister, Mahathir must have had more than his share of favor seekers, shameless flatterers, and the outright corrupt who groveled before him. He could easily expose them should they become too critical of him. If that is blackmail or vengeance, so be it.

I have a different take should Mahathir expose those dirty secrets. Far from being a blackmail or nasty vengeance, such ugly revelations could prove to be a necessary national catharsis. Much as I hate to see what would be revealed, it would be good to have all the rot finally out in the open. The hope is that the subsequent shame will effect some change.

As a former physician Mahathir knows only too well that the best if not only remedy for a long festering abscess is to lance it deep and wide, to let all that trapped putrid pus out and expose the wound to the sterilizing effect of sunshine. Only then could the healing begin. Were Mahathir to do that with the nation's abscess, we can all thank him. The man may yet make his greatest contributions *after* he retired!

May 18, 2008

Kosovo's Independence and Abdullah's Impotence

The inexplicable and highly noticeable silence of the Organization of Islamic Conference (OIC) to Kosovo's declaration of independence on February 17 reflects the organization's irrelevance in contemporary world affairs. It also reflects the impotence and incompetence of its leader, Abdullah Badawi. Not that we need yet another demonstration of his glaring deficiencies!

As an association of Islamic political entities, OIC should be concerned and engaged with Kosovo. This after all is an organization that counted the Palestinian Liberation Authority as its member even before there was a Palestinian state. More importantly, considering what the people of Kosovo suffered while under the rule of the dominant Serbs who were intent on "ethnic cleansing," international organizations like the OIC should take the lead in liberating Kosovo.

While secular (and non-Islamic) Western states like America and the EU are supportive of Kosovo's independence, the OIC chooses to remain silent, an irony that defies comprehension. OIC's silence and non-involvement means only one thing: It condones or at least remains blind to the demonstrated atrocities of the Serbs.

OIC specifically and the world generally should support Kosovo's independence even if the Serbs were Muslims and the Kosovans, Christians. Injustices and tyrannies recognize no religion or race; they should be universally condemned regardless of the race or religion of the oppressors and victims.

The largest Muslim country, Indonesia, joins China and Russia in opposing Kosovo's declaration of independence. They do so not on the merits or demerits of the issue rather because of their own fear of secessionist movements within their borders. They are assessing Kosovo based on their own selfish political considerations without any regard to the greater overriding humanitarian issues. China is burdened by problems in Tibet and elsewhere; Indonesia still has unresolved matters in Aceh.

Kosovo is not the only glaring blind spot for OIC. This organization under Abdullah Badawi's leadership is deaf to the crying tragedies plaguing the Muslim world. From the continuing humanitarian catastrophe in Darfur to the endless ravages of war in Afghanistan and Iraq, OIC's silence is reprehensible and morally indefensible. It goes contrary to everything our Holy Koran holds supreme, and to the teachings of our Prophet Muhammad, s.a.w.

An irony lost on the greater Muslim world is that most of the charitable and humanitarian relief works undertaken in Kosovo, Darfur and elsewhere in the Muslim world are being done by Western non-Islamic entities.

The Appropriate Lessons from the Balkans

Since Tito's death in 1980, the old Yugoslav Republic had been fractured, violently and repeatedly. China, Indonesia and others opposed to Kosovo's independence are drawing the wrong lessons from this.

Ethnic, religious, language, and cultural differences are not unique to the Balkans. Today as a result of globalization, and earlier through artificial drawings of political boundaries by colonial powers as well as mass migrations as a consequence of wars and economic dislocations, few countries have culturally or racially homogenous populations. Such diversities are fast becoming the global norm.

States that refuse or have yet to accept this reality are sitting on a political time bomb. They are the Yugoslavias of the future, their fate sealed in inevitable brutal Balkanization.

Those countries that tolerate–and merely tolerate–the diversity within their borders will survive, but only barely. Only those few enlightened nations whose wise leaders and citizens embrace this new reality of plurality and leverage it as an invaluable asset would thrive, and thrive well in this increasingly globalized world.

The lesson from the Balkans is not to try to homogenize or "purify" your society. The efficient and disciplined Germans tried it under Hitler, and they paid a horrific price on themselves as well as on their victims. Decades later and not far away, Milosevic and his band of bearded thugs too tried it in their own barbaric ways, and also ended with little success and much misery.

Like the old Yugoslavia, America and Canada too have many minority groups, including aboriginal natives who have yet to join the economic mainstream. America counts many prominent minorities among its elite. Indeed America is currently looking to vote for its first black president. That aside, visit Washington, DC, and you see many black and brown faces in Congress as well as in the permanent establishment. There is no secessionist sentiment in predominantly black Washington, DC, or the Virgin Islands. Indeed Hispanic Puerto Rico is clamoring to be the 51st state of the union.

Likewise Canada; it was once afflicted with a secessionist movement in its predominantly French province of Quebec. Today with the whole of Canada embracing bilingualism and biculturalism, as well as economic and other developments in Quebec, the once powerful Parti Quebecois that advocated for Quebec's separation from the rest of Canada is now an irrelevant force.

Then consider Canada's aboriginal populations. While Australia has merely apologized for the maltreatment of its first citizens, Canada has gone further. It has granted greater autonomy to its northern territories so that now Canada has legislative and other bodies run almost entirely by the native population. Rest assured that they have no desire to separate; they feel very much a part of greater Canada, and are very proud of it.

Yugoslavia was once united and peaceful under Tito's brand of communism. With the fall of communism and the emergence of democracy, the country quickly disintegrated, an irony and perversity not fully acknowledged. Milosevic may have given democracy a bad rap; more accurate however is that he and many other despotic leaders are merely wrapping themselves under the cloak of democracy and freedom. They view democracy not as a system that would guarantee freedom for their people rather as a license to inflict the tyranny of the majority upon the hapless minority. Their brand of democracy is nothing more than a pseudo sophisticated mob rule. Mob rule is still mob rule regardless whether it has been sanitized through the ballot box.

As per the Koran, human freedom is a God-given right. It is definitely not the gift from some enlightened colonialists or our benevolent leaders. It is ours to begin with, our inherent right. In a democracy we willingly give up part of that to the state for the common good, and only for the common good. We certainly do not give up our freedom so our leaders could oppress us. Only through freedom could humans come together. We cannot be coerced to do so; Tito's success was a mirage.

Malaysia is a plural society. The relevant lesson from the Balkans is that Malaysia should embrace and leverage its diversity to common advantage. Malaysia should look to successful plural societies like America and Canada. There is much that Malaysians can learn from these two countries. I just hope that Malaysia–its people and leaders–would draw the right lessons from the Balkans as well as from America and Canada.

It is already too late to demand this of our present generation of leaders as exemplified by Abdullah Badawi. However with the many new young faces as candidates from all parties in the upcoming general election, it is appropriate for us to ask them the lessons they have learned from

Kosovo. Even if they were to respond that they have never heard of Kosovo or the Balkans, that in itself would be highly revealing.

June 1, 2008

Long Goodbyes Are Only For Lovers

I do not know what to make of the standing ovation Prime Minister Abdullah received from UMNO members upon announcing his retirement on July 10, 2008. One thing was clear: there was no love lost between Abdullah and them. Likewise, despite the effusive tribute heaped upon Abdullah by his chosen successor Najib Razak on that same occasion, there was also no love lost between the two.

In announcing his resignation so far ahead, and thus ensuring a long drawn-out transition, Abdullah ignored a fundamental element in human (and also political) relationships. That is, long goodbyes are only for lovers! Abdullah should ponder the lyrics of the chorus line in Ronan Keating's song, "The Long Goodbye."

Come on baby, its over, let's face it!/ All that's happening here is a long goodbye.

While it may be sentimental (and hence tolerable) for lovers breaking up to have long goodbyes, however a protracted political transition would be disastrous for a nation. Far from clarifying the leadership crisis, it only compounds the uncertainty.

Let's face it. This belated 'love' between Abdullah and Najib will not last; neither will they, politically. The world of politics is like the animal world. When you are seen as weak, your predators will quickly pounce in for the kill. While it would be obscene to celebrate such an outcome, nonetheless it would be therapeutic for UMNO, Malays, and Malaysia.

That standing ovation after Abdullah made his announcement meant nothing except as an expression of common Malay courtesy. Perhaps by giving him that would encourage him to go further and announce an earlier exit. They would then continue giving him ever more enthusiastic ovations – thus calling for even more announcements – until he declared his withdrawal right away. At which point he would bring the house down.

The Limp and the Crippled

As perverse as it may seem, Abdullah's announcement was meant to reassure UMNO members as well as the public. The result was anything but; the speculations continued, only more intense and interesting.

In truth, the party and country would be better off without these two top leaders. This pact, conveniently arranged by the pair and purportedly "endorsed" by the party's Supreme Council, was meant to strengthen the top leadership by portraying a public picture of seeming unity.

The limp and the crippled clutching each other would not result in a steady standing couple, much less an ambulatory one. Far from giving strength to each other, the pair would succeed only in bringing the other down. No marks for guessing who is who here!

That Abdullah is a limp leader is now obvious; made more so by his coalition's recent electoral thumping. Yet there are still otherwise perceptive pundits who feel that if only those UMNO warlords and ministers would let him lead, Abdullah would do wonders!

If Abdullah had not shown his leadership talent by now, especially after he received that massive mandate in 2004, rest assured there is no talent, hidden or otherwise. Abdullah just does not have it; two more years would not miraculously produce one. The sooner he, UMNO, and the pundits accept this reality, the better it is for Malaysia.

Previously the pair was consumed with neutralizing each other. This desperate last minute union of convenience is brought on by fears that both would be wiped out by a third force.

Before that, Najib Razak, egged on by unconcealed endorsement from former Prime Minister Mahathir, had been making some uppity remarks on challenging Abdullah. Mahathir however now seems to be changing his tune; he has openly chided Najib for not standing up to Abdullah.

Najib's trajectory was also rudely interrupted by sordid revelations relating to the murder of the Mongolian model. One has it that Najib allegedly had an illicit sexual relationship with the victim; another, Najib's wife Rosmah was somehow involved in the murder itself. She has denied the allegation, but curiously has not seen fit to sue Raja Petra who made that serious allegation.

Najib denied "knowing" the model, a proclamation of innocence reminiscent of and equally unconvincing as President Clinton's "I did not have sexual relations with that woman!" statement. Najib may be flattered by this reference to President Clinton. Najib may be a Clinton in sexual morality but he lacks the latter's leadership brilliance.

Perhaps Najib, a consequence of his early British education, was using the word "knowing" in its narrow biblical sense as, "Joseph knew his wife, and she conceived." There was speculation that the murdered model was pregnant, with the fetus's paternal origin the subject of intense gossip.

Anwar Ibrahim has as usual read the political situation well. He has shrewdly aimed his guns not towards Abdullah but at Najib. He knows that Abdullah will implode sooner or later. Besides, Anwar's nemesis Mahathir is doing a pretty good job demolishing Abdullah. It is not that "the enemy of my enemy is my friend," rather if my enemies are bent on destroying each other, sit back and relish the scene!

Abdullah also faces a more formidable challenge from Tengku Razaleigh. The Tengku has been getting some traction in his attempt to challenge Abdullah.

Malaysian Politics Hitting New Bottom

With the series of sordid sexual allegations involving senior political figures, Malaysian politics seem determined to hit new bottom (pun intended) each time. The authorities and the public have been distracted by the salacious details, real and fantasized. Indeed, the police are now consumed with this prurient investigation, at the expense of fighting crime and corruption.

Malaysia's political problem is clear: It is UMNO, specifically its leadership, or lack of one. It is a problem because UMNO is the biggest party in the ruling coalition. UMNO is now rotten to the core.

It is instructive that the only fresh young talent attracted to UMNO these days are such characters as that college dropout Saiful Bukhari and the lost soul (politically) Ezam Noor, a former Anwar aide. Saiful received an endorsement from no less than Najib Razak, while Ezam was feted by Abdullah himself! Such low standards!

Saiful was the pretty boy who hitherto successfully passed himself off (at least to the gullible) as a "personal assistant" to Anwar Ibrahim. This young man is determined to bring Malaysian politics down to new bottoms, literally and figuratively!

Ezam Noor meanwhile successfully (he thinks) passed himself off as a pretentious warrior against official corruption. He also fancies himself as being oratorically-gifted, matching Barack Obama but without the intellect. Ezam's brain, judging by his utterances, could only be slightly bigger than that of a grasshopper, which may explain his frequent political hopping. Nonetheless that was enough to impress UMNO's top echelon.

Like Saiful, Ezam is threatening to reveal other sordid details involving Anwar Ibrahim. Rest assured that when Ezam does that, his standing in UMNO would be significantly enhanced. Such is the rot in UMNO.

Some sympathetic commentators (or perhaps they are just eager to ingratiate themselves to Abdullah) lay the blame for UMNO's problems on the party's "warlords" and its essential conservatism. If only the party would accept Abdullah's "reforms" and the warlords get out of his way, these pundits insist, then there would be a renaissance of the party and wondrous things would magically happen!

These pundits missed the point. Those warlords flourished precisely because of Abdullah's ineffectiveness. Far from embracing reform, Abdullah is the greatest obstacle towards it.

One badly needed reform is for the party to open up its election process by doing away with the current onerous nominating requirements. Do away with nomination quotas and you would invite more candidates.

That would be the only way to discover new talent. Abdullah however, is determined to keep this barrier, in fact anything that would help keep him in power. He is a Malaysian Mugabe in the making, if we let him be.

UMNO's Malignant Abscess

There is a malignant abscess in UMNO; it needs to be lanced and soon lest it metastasizes and kills the party corpus. The nidus of this putrefaction is the limp Abdullah and the crippled Najib. The pus had to be let out and the abscess flushed. The sooner this is done, the less complicated the surgery would be and the earlier the healing process could begin. The more swiftly the lancing is accomplished, the less pain (and mess) there would be.

The scalpel is now in the hands of UMNO Supreme Council. If it fails to exercise this solemn responsibility, then the tool would be quickly taken out of its hands and then given to the membership. If they too fail to use it, as by giving candidates like Tengku Razaleigh and others the necessary nominations to contest the party's elections or doing away completely with the quotas, then they too would also lose the privilege of using that knife.

The dye would be cast long before the party's elections in December. During July and August the party divisions will be selecting their delegates and choosing the party's nominees. If the members too become limp and crippled by the directive from above, and if they fail to exercise their independent judgment, that would seal the party's fate. This month and next will be their last chance to redeem the party they love.

Keadilan Wan Azizah's parliamentary "no confidence" vote against Abdullah scheduled for tomorrow [July 14] has little chance of success. Nonetheless it would serve as a warning thunderbolt, signaling the coming of a severe storm.

While the sound of a lightning bolt is a reliable predictor of an imminent storm, not so a standing ovation is of future endorsement.

July 13, 2008

Malicious Mindset and Perverted Priorities

The continuing furor over a college dropout's allegation that he had been sodomized by opposition leader Anwar Ibrahim reveals the malicious mindset and perverted priorities of the Abdullah Administration. It is also a gross perversion of justice.

Those who would have Anwar swear by the Koran and voluntarily donate his DNA to the police, whose reputation is only slightly less soiled than the criminals they apprehend, have it backwards. It is the norm of the civilized world that one is innocent till found guilty; it is for the state to prove its case beyond any reasonable doubt.

I can excuse law-illiterate Abdullah for not appreciating such nuances, but for his law-trained ministers like Rais Yatim and Syed Hamid not to know that is reprehensible. They are breaching their profession's ethics and ideals.

Besides, since when has our Koran been debased to a lie detector? If only the truth could thus be readily sought, we would not need expensive forensic investigations! Such naiveté!

What with the economic challenges, endemic corruption, and rampant crime in the country, our leaders' voyeuristic obsession on this alleged male-on-male *khalwat* represents gross misuse of scarce state resources and a flagrant perversion of priorities.

Perverted Priorities

In this 21st century, a charge of sodomy sounds so, well, medieval! To think that in Malaysia today that 'crime' carries a 20-year prison term! Perhaps some diligent law student could tell us the last time there was a sodomy trial in Malaysia. I am not counting the 1998 sham trial against Anwar Ibrahim that was subsequently overturned on appeal.

That charge was nothing more than a crude political maneuver to smear and silence the former Deputy Prime Minister. The glaringly shoddy forensic investigation and amateurish prosecution did not in the least embarrass the authorities. Nonetheless in the process Anwar suffered his infamous black eye as the result of being senselessly beaten while in custody by no less than the Chief of Police. The country however suffered an even more damaging black eye, figuratively speaking, from that sorry episode.

Many countries have repealed their sodomy laws. Even prudish Singapore reduced the penalty to a maximum of only two years, a far cry from Malaysia's 20! Such an enlightened attitude does not mean that society treats lightly or refuses to acknowledge male-on-male sexual assaults. Many jurisdictions have removed the gender specificity to the crime of rape, meaning it can be perpetrated by man on man. It would not surprise me that, like everything else, the Malaysian penal code has yet to be updated to recognize this new reality.

That said, unlike rape, which requires the legal determination of lack of consent, sodomy does not have that statutory burden, only that foreign sperms (or any tissue) were found in the victim's anus, a fact that could be established through forensic examination. That overrides the "he says, she says" (or in this case, 'he') argument. The authorities' long delay following completion of the forensic examination in Anwar's case signals something sinister.

In the context of modern criminal law, what the young man alleges is that he had been raped. Of course in conservative Muslim Malaysia, a rape charge does not quite have the same devastating political impact as that of sodomy. Indeed, in UMNO's upcoming party elections one of the candidates for Vice-President was once accused of raping an underage girl.

This sodomy investigation is less the seeking of justice for a 'soiled' pretty boy, as Abdullah would like us to believe, more an orchestrated political exercise in character assassination. The recent public opinion polls confirm this.

Meanwhile there are two statutory declarations linking Deputy Prime Minister Najib Razak and his wife Rosmah to the brutal murder of a Mongolian model, a translator in the scandalous multibillion dollar submarine deal with France. By whatever measure, the viciousness of the crime or the personalities implicated, these other two allegations are considerably more serious. You would not know that from the reactions (or lack thereof) of the officials.

In contrast, this sodomy allegation has been commented upon by ministers, senior officials, and Members of Parliament. Don't they have substantive matters to worry about? Even science-illiterate Abdullah has suddenly become an expert on DNA in forensic investigations!

Now we have evidence that another physician had also examined the young man and found no external indications of bodily injury. This fact was known to the police but it chose to ignore it, until the report was exposed by Raja Petra in his *Malaysia-Today*.

Although that first physician's assessment was not a formal forensic examination, nonetheless its negative clinical findings cannot be dismissed. Discrepancy between it and the subsequent official forensic examination must be explained. It throws reasonable doubt to the charge.

The story gets even more bizarre. The victim had a special "visit" with Deputy Prime Minister Najib Razak right after the alleged incident. Najib apparently took pity on this stranger. Such paternal concerns! Even more inexplicable is why Najib or his subordinates would allow such access to the prime minister by this nondescript political climber.

Serious Problems Neglected

There is no shortage of critical problems facing the country. Citizens' concerns are far from these sexual shenanigans, real or alleged, lurid or otherwise. They are too busy eking out their daily living. Our leaders' preoccupation with these silly things merely confirms the public's deepest suspicions of incompetence and omission at the highest levels.

Malaysians suffer daily through the rot of their institutions, as when they visit the land office to pay their assessments or see the dilapidation and neglect that is their children's schools. On the roads they are harassed by those menacing *Mat Rempits* while having to contend with those men in blue demanding their share of the "road toll."

Where are our leaders? Asleep at the wheel, and with Abdullah literally so! What with the upcoming UMNO elections in December, they would be even more distracted.

Tun Mahathir, hitherto a trenchant critic of Abdullah, unhesitatingly supports him in this latest action of prosecuting Anwar, dubbed Sodomy II, declaring that it is unlikely for Abdullah to be stupid enough to repeat his (Mahathir's) mistake of a decade ago with so-called Sodomy I. Mahathir deludes himself if he believes that Abdullah has now suddenly become smart or has his priorities right. Mahathir is also mistaken if he thinks that Anwar is as stupid as Abdullah to repeat or be caught with the same mistake.

Contrary to Mahathir's new-found assessment, Abdullah is as inept and incompetent now as he was before Saiful's statutory declaration. Abdullah will remain so until we get rid of him. Mahathir was wrong on Abdullah before (as he now readily admits); Mahathir is wrong on Abdullah now.

When Mahathir asserted that we must get rid of Abdullah for the good of the party and country, his message resonated with the masses. In supporting Abdullah's current foolish action on Sodomy II, Mahathir not only risks diluting his central message but also jeopardizes his last chance at remedying his earlier grievous error in anointing Abdullah.

With Abdullah asleep at the wheel, continue to expect the worse. As for this second sodomy charge, look ahead to the mainstream media to be filled with silly utterances of politicians and pundits, as well as prurient details of this slimy case. I for one do not look forward to the graphic description of the private anatomy of this pretty boy who started the ball (pardon me, *his* balls) rolling.

August 3, 2008

Malaysia's Leadership Now Just A Trinket

The latest UMNO shenanigans effectively reduced the party's (and thus the country's) leadership to a Sunday market trinket, to be haggled between a desperate discredited seller trying to get the best possible deal, and a bankrupt buyer who has only his father's famous name to offer as currency.

Tengku Razaleigh, in referring to the tussle between Abdullah Badawi and Najib Razak, said, "… [W]e are embarrassed at the sight of two grown men playing this endless children's game of 'yours and mine' with the most important responsibility in the land, oblivious of the law, oblivious to the damage they are doing to the nation." The prince's observation on the damage wrecked on Malaysia is spot on, declaring that Malaysia had been reduced to a banana republic and a laughing stock of the world.

What Abdullah and Najib do not realize is that the value of the trinket they are frantically bargaining over keeps dropping. While the two are consumed with striking a deal between them, they fail to notice that Anwar Ibrahim is on the sideline, ready and willing to take over, thus effectively reducing the two protagonists to irrelevance and their trinket, well, just that.

Meanwhile the important business of running the country is neglected. While the two leaders have been consumed with appeasing their respective followers, as well as engaging in hours of "four eyes only" meetings haggling over when, how, and at what price the trinket would be handed over, the nation's problems keep compounding, from the massive public health hazard of contaminated milk products imported from China to the American credit crunch that will soon spread around the world.

It is time to make these two characters irrelevant and let this desperate drowning duo strangle each other and sink to the bottom of the cesspool they have created for themselves.

The priority is to make sure that they do not drag the nation down with them. This responsibility falls heavily on those leaders of the opposition, in particular Anwar Ibrahim. He has to be ready to take over and make the necessary preparations now, especially with regards to policies and personnel.

The Price Keeps Dropping

Right after the March 8, 2008 electoral debacle, Abdullah declared that he still had the trust of the people. Then with confidence borne out of ignorance *a la* the village idiot, he asserted that he would serve his full second term. He even intimated that he might lead his coalition to its third electoral victory in 2013! Such detachment from reality!

It was merely out of courtesy (the trademark of our culture) and respect for the highest office of the land that Abdullah was not laughed off the stage. Unfortunately he mistook that as acceptance, if not rousing endorsement, aided by his cronies, advisers, and family members feeding his fantasy. The world knew better.

On the surface Abdullah did seem to have a mandate. After all, his coalition secured a comfortable though not the usual two-third majority in

Parliament. On closer scrutiny however, his Barisan coalition barely scrapped through the popular vote, while many of the seats won were only with the slimmest of majorities. That election also saw the loss of five states, including some of the most developed, repudiating Abdullah's leadership.

When the rumblings of discontent over his leadership became louder, especially after his coalition's thumping at the Permatang Pauh by-election, Abdullah was forced to lower his bid, but just a tad. He now thought he could satisfy his detractors by agreeing to hand over power by June 2010. He set it far enough ahead such that should circumstances shift, he could conveniently change his mind. Abdullah was counting that people would not see through his not-so-sly scheming.

Again he misjudged the public, and his party's mood.

Following a raucous September 2008 UMNO Supreme Council meeting in which a few finally caught on to the reality and spoke up, albeit tentatively and a little belatedly, Abdullah further lowered his asking price. Now he did not rule out on an earlier exit, clarifying that the June 2010 date was meant only to be the latest when he would quit. That pacified the dissidents, including the outspoken Muhyiddin Yassin and the hitherto "Iron Lady" Rafidah Aziz. They were an easily-mollified bunch.

Then following the gathering of his clan, and undoubtedly convinced once again by them, Abdullah backtracked. They prevailed upon him that his leadership was worth more and he should hold out for a better price. That triggered yet another volley of grumbling and dissatisfaction in UMNO.

At a special meeting of UMNO Supreme Council last week, presumably to discuss specifically the leadership transition, Abdullah was given an ultimatum. He must decide by October 9, 2008 on whether to defend his leadership. The alternative presumably would be to quit.

To an average observer with a modicum of commonsense, that was just another nice way for the council to say, in the grand Asian tradition of "saving face," that it no longer had confidence in Abdullah. He however is thick-skulled and a tad slow on the uptake. Besides, with another round of meetings with his clan, they convinced him that indeed was not the intent of the council. "Flip-flop" Abdullah listens to whoever has his ear last.

More to the point, that council's decision was meaningless. If Abdullah were to decide not to defend his position at the now-postponed UMNO convention, the country would still be faced with a leadership crisis and uncertainty for the next six months. Everyone would be consumed with positioning themselves. No effective government work would be done as every UMNO politician would be busy politicking.

On the other hand if he decided to cling on, it would still create a leadership uncertainty, and there would still be heavy intrigue and relentless campaigning. Nothing would have changed and the nation's business would still be unattended.

Abdullah had again abused the traditional Malay culture of *halus*, the subtle way. The gullible Muhyiddin went so far as to describe Abdullah's latest "decision" as "magnanimous!" No word from the "Iron Lady." As I said, they are easily satisfied. I wonder how long before UMNO Supreme Council members realize that they had once again been had by Abdullah.

As for Najib, he is burdened with his own considerable baggage. He would like that trinket be handed over to him as if it were his due, and without contest, all in the name of party unity of course. Contest means having to scrutinize his record, which is not pretty. It is in fact sordid.

If only there were some *jantans* (males) in UMNO Supreme Council, they would have long ago given Abdullah an ultimatum. Resign or we push for a "no confidence" vote! That is the only language Abdullah understands: direct and brutal. There cannot be any subtlety or he will pretend to miss it.

It does not take a *jantan* to do that, only some responsible adults concerned about the lack of leadership and the country being left adrift. Absent that, rest assured that come October 9, Abdullah will again waffle, and UMNO Supreme Council will have to find yet another face-saving device to spare some modicum of respect to its leader who clearly no longer deserves any.

I could not care less about those UMNO Supreme Council members except that they are also the leaders of our country. That is the scary part. If they cannot stand up to a limp Abdullah Badawi, how can we expect them to face up to a President Bush, China's Hu, or even Singapore's Lee? That should terrify the heck out of all Malaysians.

Meanwhile Malaysians are reduced to watching the bizarre haggling over an increasingly worthless trinket between their two top but desperate leaders. We all should be embarrassed by that, not just Tengku Razaleigh.

October 5, 2008

Abdullah's Pivotal "Non-Decision"

There are three possible decisions that Abdullah Badawi could make on or by October 9, 2008, ahead of his party's divisional meetings. One, he could remain stubborn and defend his post; two, announce his resignation; and three, waffle and leave it up in the air, effectively a "non-decision."

This third option would be more in character with him. Throughout his tenure Abdullah has shown a singular inability to make even the simplest decisions. He would defer them until the last minute when decisions would be forced upon him as the other choices would have been effectively taken away from him by changed circumstances.

With the third choice Abdullah, on advice from his "bright" advisors, would of course frame or "spin" it not as a "non-decision" rather dresses it up in a language more in tune with our culture. He would for example "leave his fate to Allah," or for his "party members to decide." This would be a classic Abdullah's non-decision and "flip-flop."

This option is also nothing more than a diluted form or an attempt for a more acceptable and less confrontational version of the first choice. Former Prime Minister Mahathir, who knows a bit more about Abdullah, predicted that Abdullah would not give up his position. Mahathir would be wrong if he were to think that Abdullah would boldly declare his intention to stay on, that is, as with the first option.

That first option would be out of character for Abdullah as it would mean an inevitable confrontation with his party leaders, specifically UMNO Supreme Council members who had earlier given him the ultimatum. If there is any certainty about Abdullah, it is that he would do anything to avoid a confrontation, especially with his party members.

That has been the bane of his administration. Abdullah came in boldly proclaiming to end corruption. With the first resistance from UMNO warlords used to plump government contracts *sans* competition, he waffled. Likewise with his "determination" to set up the much-needed Police Commission. That project is still in the air years later because of persistent opposition by senior leadership in the police force.

The decision that millions of Malaysians are hoping for is for Abdullah to gracefully announce his resignation. Were he to do that, it would give all his critics including severe ones like me a chance to finally praise the man. It would certainly be a brave decision from him. It would portray him as a leader who has the interest of the nation at heart, of a leader who puts the future of Malaysia ahead that of his own, as well of his family's and cronies' ambitions.

This painful decision could only come after the most difficult self-introspection. More significantly, it would require him to dismiss the advice of those closest to him. For this reason I believe that this would not be the decision he would make this week.

On a practical level, it would also mean Abdullah giving up those luxurious perks of his office that he has become accustomed to, if not relished. It is more than just having an opulent corporate jet at his disposal; it is all the attention and adulation he is currently getting from his staff, ministers, civil servants, and finally, the people (or some of them). I recently saw a picture of Rais Yatim, one of Abdullah's senior ministers, deferentially bowing low towards Abdullah while kissing his hand, peasant-style. Heavy stuff!

More to the point, as Henry Kissinger once observed, power is the most powerful aphrodisiac. With a new wife (albeit a divorcee) at his side, and with Abdullah in his late 60s, that is not a minor consideration.

At a more profound level, by resigning now Abdullah would go on record as being the shortest serving Prime Minister of Malaysia. He is mindful of the accompanying opinion that invariably would be associated with that, of being the least effective leader of the country. I am certain his advisors, and others whose fate is tied to him, would not too subtly remind Abdullah of those realities in an attempt to dissuade him from resigning.

Gracefully resigning now would require much of Abdullah. It would require of him to acknowledge the worsening situation in the nation as a consequence of his ineffective leadership. Not many of us are courageous enough to face up to our own limitations. This task is made that much more difficult as there would be plenty of folks around him and whom he holds dear telling him otherwise.

Self-examination and serious introspection are not and have never been Abdullah's strong suits. Do not expect him to exercise this option.

Consequences of "Non-Decision"

Abdullah and his advisors will, as usual, be oblivious of the devastating consequences of his hanging on. For UMNO, it would mean further turmoil and fractious upcoming divisional meetings and the twice-postponed General Assembly; for the nation, continued rapid decline.

The implosion of UMNO is inevitable; Abdullah's hanging on would only hasten this. The decline of UMNO as an institution is not something I would celebrate, notwithstanding the party's many detractors. Quite apart from it being one of the most enduring political parties, having been in power continuously for well over half a century – a record unmatched anywhere – it is also one of the few successful modern *Malay* institutions.

UMNO is still the largest Malay party with the strongest grassroots organizations. While not belittling the opposition's remarkable achievements in attracting young Malaysians, especially Malays, UMNO still has many capable leaders despite the fact that they have been eclipsed by the more numerous corrupt and ineffectual ones.

UMNO's accomplishments are many and should not be belittled. It was instrumental in successfully leading the nation to independence, of besting a domestic communist insurgency, an achievement that has yet to be replicated anywhere else, and an earlier enlightened development policy of emphasizing growth with equity, now accepted as mainstream economic wisdom.

If that reads like I am writing an obituary for UMNO, it is, and not a premature one at that!

The fact that these achievements have been corroded and corrupted by later leaders, especially during Abdullah's tenure, does not in any way diminish their luster. Instead those achievements should inspire subsequent leaders and challenge them to exceed those high expectations.

The reality under Abdullah is ugly. While his apologists would claim that the present climate of political "openness" is Abdullah's finest legacy; in fact he was a bystander. The present openness has more to do with technology, in particular the Internet, than with Abdullah's stated mission.

As for Abdullah's role in this new openness, just ask the likes of Raja Petra Kamarudin, the "Hindraf Five," and hundreds others incarcerated without trial under the Internal Security Act during Abdullah's tenure. That is Abdullah's real legacy, and the reason I do not look forward to this week when he will announce that he will *not* vacate his office.

October 5, 2008

Wise Decision And A Class Act

Prime Minister Abdullah's decision this week to resign is wise. That decision is good for him, his party, and most of all, the nation. I am certain it was not easy for him to reach that decision but in the end he did it, "guided by my conscience" and placing "the interests of the nation above all else."

I applaud him, especially considering the intense last minute pleas by his many well-meaning supporters. It was a decision that was not expected by many, yours truly included. This is one instance where I am only too happy to acknowledge my misjudgment of the man on this point. [See my earlier commentary.]

Abdullah's plaintive admission, "I know I've not been doing well; it's time for someone else to take over," must come only after the most difficult introspection. To admit to one's limitations is never easy, especially for a leader, as there are always supplicants and subordinates who are only too willing to filter the harsh reality. Some leaders never get it at all. Saddam Hussein went to the gallows still believing that he was Allah's gift to the Arabs.

I applaud Abdullah's wise decision for another important reason. I never underestimate the potential multiplier effect of a single good decision. Properly seized upon, it will lead to many positive consequences. Already judging from his resignation statement, Abdullah is now all the more committed to reforming the anti-corruption agency and the process of judicial appointments, among others.

Freed from the burden of his political future, and fully aware that these last few months could well determine his legacy, I hope Abdullah may be more focused.

Dignified Statement

Abdullah already has set a standard of sorts in the dignified manner in which he announced his stepping down. He made sure that his cabinet colleagues and fellow leaders in the Barisan Nasional coalition hear of his decision first, in private, and directly from him.

It was a formal affair when he made his statement, surrounded by his cabinet colleagues and fellow UMNO leaders. He also read from a prepared text; this was not the occasion to ad lib. His tone was proper; his body language and emotions, appropriate. He did not blame anyone, nor did he express regret. There was no hint of personal disappointment or a sense of being betrayed. Abdullah gave proper due to the seriousness of the occasion.

As well he should. The country has been good to him; he made it to the top, a privilege granted only to a fortunate few.

The content of his announcement may have surprised many, but not its timing. There was no unexpected statement that would shock his audience or move them to public hysteria. Nor was there uncontrolled sobbing among his supporters, as with the embarrassing public spectacle that accompanied Mahathir's announcement of his retirement.

When there are no public tears, then the question whether those public displays of emotions are genuine does not arise. As we now know from subsequent events, those earlier hysterical displays of affection shown by the likes of Rafidah Aziz during Mahathir's announcement of his retirement were a fraud. Those histrionics were more for public consumption rather than genuine expressions from the heart.

In his resignation statement, Abdullah wisely avoided anointing his successor. He expressed only the hope that Najib would take over, and reemphasized that point in case it was missed. This was not a lukewarm endorsement for Najib or an attempt at getting even with him, rather Abdullah's correct reading of the constitution as well as his party's rulebook.

The leadership of Malaysia has to be *earned*. It is not a private heirloom to be passed on to a member of the next generation who strikes your fancy. Abdullah is correct in reminding everyone that Najib first has to win UMNO's presidency.

Abdullah showed great wisdom in not being presumptuous by even hinting who Najib should pick as his deputy should he win UMNO's presidency.

Abdullah's Five Goals

Abdullah articulated five goals he wished to accomplish in the remaining few months of his tenure. I would be satisfied if he could accomplish two, or at most three. Apart from strengthening the Anti-Corruption Agency and setting up the Judicial Appointment Commission,

Malaysians would be satisfied if he were to establish an effective social safety net.

Those three objectives are not mutually exclusive. On the contrary, they are closely related. If we have a judicial system that has the respect and confidence of the people, that would go a long way towards reducing corruption. Eradicate corruption and there would be enough resources to devote to the needy. We have currently wonderful programs (at least they are on paper) for the poor but because of endemic corruption and abusive political patronage, those programs suffer through considerable leakages.

There is one major reform, supported by many in UMNO, which Abdullah could initiate. That is, remove the current onerous burden placed on challengers to senior party leaders. Relax the rules such that anyone with the minimal number of nominations by individuals, not divisions, could compete. When no candidate could secure a majority vote, have a run-off election between the top two vote getters.

Abdullah calls for a convention of his Barisan coalition parties "to improve inter-racial and inter-religious relations." I respectfully suggest a more modest and readily achievable goal: first focus on improving UMNO. Leave the coalition alone. A clean, strong and effective UMNO will mean an equally clean, strong and effective Barisan.

Such a simple and easily implemented reform initiative to his party would dent the corrosive powers of the party's warlords that have created the cesspool of money politics. By removing the current onerous nominating barrier, the divisional meetings currently underway this month would become mute, at least as far as nominating candidates are concerned. Perhaps then those meetings could become more meaningful with members using these opportunities to discuss substantive policy matters instead of trying to create camps around personalities. That would also elevate the deliberative levels of those meetings to the benefit of the members and the party.

Only by opening up the nominating process and encouraging as wide a field of candidates as possible could UMNO attract and produce its own Barack Obama. All Malaysians, not just UMNO members, would then benefit.

Those four objectives, three for the nation and one for UMNO, are well within Abdullah's reach. Focus on them, and Abdullah would be able to redeem his leadership. That would be a legacy worth striving for.

October 12, 2008

Part II

The Rudderless Najib Razak

Exposing Our Leaders To Greater Competition

The recent [December 29, 2008] installation of Tunku Muhriz as the 11th Yang Di Pertuan Besar (Yam Tuan) of Negri Sembilan (the equivalent of a sultan in the other states) illustrates one important point. When the top position is not automatically handed down to the putative Number Two and instead you widen your choice, you are more likely to end up with a far superior candidate.

The consensus among the rakyat as well as the establishment is that Muhriz is a far superior candidate, and a better person to boot, than the other contenders, the three sons of the just-deceased Yam Tuan, Tuanku Jaafar.

It is too late now for Jaafar's three adult sons to appreciate and benefit from the wisdom of my observation. It is hard to learn as an adult the lessons you should have learned as a youngster.

Tunku Naquiyuddin, Jaafar's oldest son, must have felt the sting the most. After all, his father had named him Regent, or acting Yam Tuan, on a number of occasions. Naquiyuddin must have felt that the throne should rightly be his. Indeed he had already begun acting as the Yam Tuan, as he did recently when he called for restoring the sultans' absolute royal immunity. At the personal level, he was already behaving only too well as a feudal king.

As for Muhriz, he had learned his lesson well, and very much earlier on too, way back in 1967 when the *Undangs* (Territorial Chiefs) bypassed him to pick his father's half-brother Tuanku Jaafar as the 10th Yam Tuan to succeed Muhriz's father, Tuanku Munawir. Sensing that the royal throne would not be his or his family any more, he wisely prepared himself for life in the real world outside the palace. By all measures he has done well, having obtained a law degree and acquitting himself credibly in the private sector.

He has also imparted those valuable lessons onto his children. They too have done well academically and personally *sans* their royal titles, making their achievements that much more credible and praiseworthy.

The Badawi Disaster

The wisdom of my observation is universal. Note the disaster when Deputy Prime Minister Abdullah Badawi automatically assumed the top slot upon the retirement of Dr. Mahathir. Had Mahathir widened the choice of candidates to succeed him, Malaysia would have been spared the incompetence of Abdullah Badawi.

This pattern of the number two automatically becoming number one is standard practice in the Malaysian civil service. Those senior civil servants behave like airplanes stacked at a busy airport, each patiently waiting his turn and not daring to upset the established pattern lest it would threaten his position and prospect.

I have seen this pattern broken only rarely, as in the early 1960s when Dr. Majid Ismail, then an orthopedic consultant, was tapped to be the Director-General of Health, bypassing many senior medical bureaucrats. He upset the entire hierarchy at the Ministry of Health. Majid later distinguished himself as one of the most farsighted and enlightened health policymakers. Today that Ministry remains one of the few that do not hew to the strict "*tunggu geleran*" (waiting your turn) pattern of the civil service. It is thus not a surprise that it is one of the more professionally-run ministries.

Come this March [2009] with the current number two Najib Razak automatically assuming the number one position with Abdullah leaving office, Malaysia risks repeating the same mistake. There will be no contest to select the best candidate for the top slot. UMNO in its wisdom has adopted rules and traditions that stymied competition especially for the top post.

Back to Muhriz, he too was the crown prince, heir apparent to the throne, when his father was Yam Tuan. Yet that did not help him when his father Munawir died in 1967; the four *Undangs* in their wisdom bypassed Muhriz.

The public reason given back in 1967 was that Muhriz was too young—he was only 18 then—to be Yam Tuan. Additionally, the political establishment then led by Prime Minister Tunku Abdul Rahman lobbied the *Undangs* hard for Tuanku Jaafar, believing that he (and his family) would be sympathetic to UMNO.

Fast forward to 2008, despite being a crown prince and appointed Regent many times, the *Undangs* voted to deny Naquiyuddin the throne. They had their reasons which of course were not disclosed; nonetheless their decision was well received, especially by the public.

Tunku Munawir died at the relatively young age of 47 from what we would term today as "lifestyle diseases." The *Undangs* were concerned that the young Muhriz would follow in his father's footsteps, in the village tradition of *bapak burek, anak rentik* (fig: like father, like son).

As it turned out, Muhriz was anything but his father, both in personality and accomplishments. Nevertheless like many, I do not fault the *Undangs* for their decision back in 1967. By any objective criterion, picking

Jaafar, a British-trained diplomat, was a wise move. Muhriz on the other hand was barely out of high school then.

Today's *Undangs* are a far different breed from their predecessors of a mere generation ago. The position of *Undang* is also hereditary but not in a strict linear fashion, just like that of the Yam Tuan. The various clan chiefs would gather and pick from among the many entitled to be *Undang*, just as the *Undangs* would pick the Yam Tuan from among the many eligible princes. A primordial form of democracy and representative government as it were.

Following my theory, the caliber of *Undangs* should improve because of the competition among the eligible contenders. Yet we have the perverse situation today where the present generation of *Undangs* being even more poorly educated and of lower caliber than their predecessors. While a generation ago we had a lawyer and a university graduate among the *Undangs*, today we have a former utility meter reader and a *petai* seller.

Despite the erosion in the personal caliber of today's *Undangs* they were able collectively to come to a wise decision; the institution delivered. This demonstrates the vital role of institutions.

The aberration that is today's *Undangs* is the exception that proves my theory. Because the state had an intact institution and process in place, the right decision was made, overcoming the deficiencies in personnel. Imagine if these *Undangs* were more competent and less corrupt! Strong institutions manned by equally strong personalities do wonders for society; strong institutions but with poor personnel could also deliver–sometimes–as demonstrated by today's *Undangs*. Weak institutions with weak personnel are not the worst. The tragedy would be weak institutions helmed by strong-willed evil people.

Najib's Dangerous Mindset

The experience with the Negri Sembilan royal selection process illustrates the wisdom of exposing leaders to continuous competition, and of having the right institutions and processes in place to ensure that. That is the best if not only way to hold these leaders accountable. The biggest mistake would be to make them "President for Life" or heap some such similar honors upon them. Such excessive accolades are what corrupted otherwise sensible leaders. Even once wise and patriotic leaders like Sukarno ultimately succumbed to and became a tyrant simply because he was not held accountable or subjected to rigorous checks and balances by their followers.

UMNO once had the fine tradition where its leaders were routinely subjected to regular challenges. Even such venerable leaders as *Bapak Merdeka* Tunku Abdul Rahman were not spared. Today we look askance at such once brave figures as Sulaiman Palestin who would not hesitate to challenge any leader regardless how popular he was at the time. In contrast, today's UMNO leaders are given a free pass, in a misguided quest for "party unity."

Only through such constant competitions could we "toughen up" our leaders. During the recent American Presidential primary season, many members of the Democratic Party were upset that Candidate Hilary Clinton would not give up her race earlier and let the leading candidate Barrack Obama be declared the nominee sooner. As it turned out, the long primary was beneficial to Obama as it toughened him up such that he could easily withstand the subsequent onslaughts from his Republican opponent.

UMNO is making a terrible mistake in letting Najib Razak take over the top slot without subjecting him to a tough campaign. Such grueling leadership competitions are necessary for "baptizing" a leader. It would sharpen his leadership skills as well as let party members and voters preview his abilities.

Because he was not subjected to any competition, Najib Razak now feels that the country owes him the Prime Minister's office by virtue of his being the son of the much-revered Tun Razak. That is a dangerous mindset for anyone, especially a leader, to have. Ultimately it is the citizens who would bear the burden of such hubris in our leaders.

The many effusive comments about Tunku Muhriz now would not easily go to his head. Having once been bypassed for the top slot, Muhriz is fully aware that he could only secure his position by doing an excellent job and diligently attending to his royal duties. In contrast, Najib Razak has had an easy ride all along; he has yet to learn this important lesson.

January 8, 2009

UMNO's Reform Must Begin With Najib Razak

It is not enough for Najib Razak and other UMNO leaders to lament the loss of their party's "wow" factor, or for them to endlessly exhort the party faithful to "re-invent" and "re-brand" their organization. Reform is like sex;

merely talking about it is not enough, for without the necessary accompanying actions it only increases your frustration.

To regain voters' confidence, the change in UMNO must begin with its top leaders, specifically Najib. He has to demonstrate it through his actions; anything less and he risks frustrating voters and replicating the electoral disasters of Permatang Pauh and Kuala Trengganu.

First and foremost Najib must legitimize his rise to the party's top position. Being "promoted" by Abdullah Badawi is no endorsement, being that he (Abdullah) is a discredited leader. Likewise, being nominated unopposed is no ratification either, especially when the process is hopelessly riddled with "money politics," otherwise known as corruption.

Second, Najib must display some sense of enlightened leadership. For example, expending his precious time and political capital by intensively campaigning in a by-election that in his own words "would not alter the nation's political landscape" was neither necessary nor prudent. With the nation facing many critical crises, he should focus on more substantive matters.

Last, Najib must demonstrate that he has the personal qualities and moral integrity to lead the nation. Merely denying that he had nothing to do with Saiful Bukhari, that college dropout who alleged that he had been sodomized by opposition leader Anwar Ibrahim, or that Najib knew nothing of the brutal murder of that Mongolian model Altantuya and the attendant involvement of his hitherto closest advisor Razak Baginda, is not enough. The public deserves better; it demands a more thorough accounting.

Until then, any utterance by Najib about reforming UMNO will ring hollow and serves only to frustrate voters by unnecessarily raising their expectations. That is dangerous.

Legitimizing Najib's Leadership

Najib's only claim to his party's leadership is that he is currently unopposed. Where the process is open and transparent, being unopposed signifies unanimous approval. That is certainly any leader's dream and rightful claim of legitimacy.

UMNO's nominating process however, is deeply flawed, apart from being corrupt. The "unanimous" choice of Najib is anything but. The process is hollow and meaningless. With "money politics" rampant, Najib's nomination "victory" is irredeemably tainted.

The current nominating process is designed specifically to discourage or more correctly, prevent challengers. It is not a genuine contest. Requiring candidates be nominated by at least 30 percent of the party's 191 divisions effectively means that at most there can only be three nominees. That is an unnecessary barrier, meant not to get the best talent but to protect the incumbent.

This requirement was put in place only 20 years ago, following the bitter and divisive Mahathir-Tengku Razaleigh rivalry. Before that, and for the first 40 years of UMNO's existence, its leaders including Bapak Merdeka (Father of Independence), Tunku Abdul Rahman, and the much-revered Tun Razak (Najib's father) were routinely challenged at the party's leadership convention.

The party can do without this burdensome nomination "quota rule" as well as the equally damaging no-challenge "tradition" for its two top positions. The party's Supreme Council should override both. While many of its senior members are in favor of dumping this onerous rule, Najib remains "neutral." That is not the mark of someone confident of his leadership ability.

If Najib were to introduce a motion at the next Supreme Council meeting to remove this "quota rule," that would greatly enhance his legitimacy even if the Council were to vote against it. If the Council were to vote for it, then the party would benefit by opening up the process and the delegates getting to preview many more potential candidates.

Such an open process would also effectively blunt the current corrosive influence of "money politics" as there would be no need to bribe divisional leaders in order to secure your nomination. At the party's elections, with over 2,000 delegates, it would be difficult if not impossible to bribe them all. You could influence them only with your ideas and talent, as it should be.

Removing the quota would of course invite challengers to Najib. Tengku Razaleigh would definitely be one; there may be others. There would also be additional candidates for all the other positions.

If Najib were to survive a challenge from Tengku Razaleigh for example, Najib's stature and legitimacy would be greatly enhanced. That would effectively shut up his many critics.

Of course Najib could lose, and with that, his political career. That may explain his reluctance to tamper with the current quota rules which work in his favor. While such a maneuver would secure his immediate political survival, he would critically jeopardize his party's chance in the next national elections. Presently many, and not just those outside of UMNO and Barisan, question his ability and legitimacy. In supporting the current restrictive nomination rule, Najib sacrifices his party's future for his short-term political survival.

Articulating His Vision

Even if Najib were to prevail in an open contest, he still needs to articulate his vision for the nation. He has to convince Malaysians that he has "the right stuff." He has to give them his personal manifesto, as it were, and he should do that now before his party's convention in March. For come the general election he would be preoccupied with rallying his troops.

The prevailing perception is that Najib owes his current position merely by being the son of a famous father. To non-Malays specifically, Najib has yet to erase the ugly image of his keris-taunting antics of his UMNO Youth days. Additionally his career, while long, is very narrow; he spent his entire adult life in government, getting his paycheck from taxpayers.

Like his immediate predecessor Abdullah Badawi, there is nothing substantive to Najib's career in politics despite his overflowing resume. His tenure as Defense Minister was marked by the collapse of the Pularek Naval Base just before its official opening, the gross breach of security by the Al Muanah gang at the Grik Army base in Perak, and the now evolving scandal with the French submarine purchase. As for his legacy as Education Minister, good luck in discerning that.

Now as Finance Minister, he remains disturbingly quiet; he has nothing to offer on how to solve the grave economic challenges facing the nation except to issue bland, meaningless reassurances.

In contrast, Tengku Razaleigh bravely outlined his views of the current economic crisis and his bold strategies to deal with it. Compared to the towering leadership of the Tengku, Najib looks like a novice Boy Scout troop leader constantly looking to his manual on how to lead.

Demonstrating His Integrity

To demonstrate his integrity, Najib must clarify the many sordid allegations and rumors implicating him. Bland denials alone are not enough. The most damaging and one that requires the most detailed explanation is his role in (if any) or knowledge of the murder of the Mongolian model, and the involvement of his confidant Razak Baginda. That Razak Baginda was acquitted does not clear the matter. There remains the involvement of Najib's close security guards.

The accusations leveled at Najib are too detailed (including specific SMS texts and cell phone numbers) that they demand a more complete explanation from him. Hiding behind client-attorney privilege as Najib did in trying to dismiss the many SMS between him and Shafie Abdullah, the attorney who was at the time representing Razak Baginda, is inappropriate. For one, Najib was not Shafie's client, then or now. For another, such a "cover" would not sell in the court of public opinion.

Those details of the Altantuya murder, as well as the sordid mess of the Saiful Bukhari sodomy allegation, will eventually be revealed bit by bit in their respective criminal trials. A full disclosure now by Najib would help preempt the inevitable excruciating and embarrassing details.

Najib Razak may become the leader of UMNO and thus Malaysia's next Prime Minister come this March without bothering to address these three issues. However, the next General Elections will be less than 48 months away after he becomes Prime Minister. If not addressed frontally and openly now, these questions about his ability, integrity and legitimacy would only get worse. Yes, Najib may get his wish, but he could also end up being the nation's shortest-serving leader, for come the next national election, Najib and UMNO could be buried.

That would be quite a legacy for the son of a great patriot. Perversely then, Najib's political demise would of necessity trigger and be instrumental in UMNO's reform. By that time it may be too late to alter UMNO's fate, but at least he would have been instrumental in effecting something productive.

January 25, 2009

The Monkey Handler

In the few months that he has before assuming office I would have expected Prime Minister-in-waiting Najib Razak to be focused on forming his new leadership team and formulating major policies. Instead there he was in Perak smirking with renegade state politicians who had crossed over to his Barisan coalition. Najib looked like a mischievous monkey handler who had successfully enticed a couple of wily *monyets* (monkeys) from the neighbor's coconut tree to his.

In these perilous times Najib is more a slimy political operative consumed with concocting shady backroom deals than a national leader ready to steer the nation through tough economic and other challenges. This latest and unneeded upheaval in Perak only adds to Malaysia's already muddled political climate, and comes at a time when the nation can ill afford this distraction. Najib is oblivious of the evolving global economic disaster and its inevitable impact on Malaysia.

After finishing his latest act in Perak, Najib stayed away. The monkey handler's interest, like that of the monkeys they keep, is only in creating mischief. Once that is achieved, then he leaves to escape getting entangled.

Najib had planned to join in the Chinese New Year celebration in Ipoh to soak in what he expected would be a sea of public applause to his latest monkey act. Instead because of the unanticipated sea change in public mood, Najib wisely skipped the event. At least he knew when and where he would no longer be welcomed.

Najib should remember that Abdullah Badawi rode into office with the highest approval rating, and an untainted "Mr. Clean" image to boot. Today, less than five years later, Abdullah is being pushed out of office, and his legacy is anything but clean. Najib has yet to assume office and already his approval rating is under 50 percent, and his public image severely tainted by assorted sordid scandals. His public portraits are now being used for stomping on by muddy shoes. Rest assured that these are only the beginning.

A Chinese proverb has it that it takes three generations to destroy an enterprise. The first starts it; the second builds on it; while the pampered third squanders it. Najib Razak is determined to truncate that process. He is set to destroy a once proud and successful organization—UMNO—which his late father was so instrumental in starting and building. Najib will bring UMNO down with him, as prophesied by some ancient soothsayer's

"RAHMAN" theory of leadership, Rahman being the acronym (and a common Malay name) made up of the first initials of all UMNO prime ministers, with N for Najib being the last. The challenge is to ensure that UMNO's inevitable implosion under Najib would not also take Malaysia down with it.

Our Cultural Burden

If not for his family and political pedigree, Najib Razak would today be like thousands of other Malays with similar qualifications, nothing more than a mid-level functionary in the civil service or one of the many Government-linked companies. He was just old enough when his father died to benefit from the generosities and tributes of a nation in need to express them to a great patriot that was his father. Remembering the father's many great deeds, the nation could not do enough for his son; hence Najib's meteoric rise.

The dilemma with having your path smoothed out for you is that once you reach the top, there is no one there to grease the trail ahead. From then on you are on your own, and you are ill prepared.

It is also the Malay cultural tradition that such generosities and tributes are showered almost exclusively upon the first-born son. The assumption is that he is the carrier of the father's traits. This of course is not unique to Malay culture; nor is there a biological basis to that belief.

I wish we had not been slaves to our culture. By all means shower our gratitude to the late Tun Razak's family, but then let us be more prudent and choose the smartest or most promising from among his five children to groom, and not necessarily only the first born.

Tun Razak's other sons are way head-and-shoulders above Najib. The youngest, Nazir, is a banker. Even though he is not a politician, nonetheless his public utterances reflect not only a first-rate mind but also someone very much aware of the many challenges facing the nation. He has put forth novel ideas on solving them. Unfortunately, Najib is culturally constrained from taking advice from his youngest brother Nazir.

Last year Nazir suggested granting amnesty to corrupt individuals in return for their confessions and making good their loot, prior to implementing tougher laws. A radical idea with considerable merit! At the very least we would get a grasp of the magnitude of the problem and its infinite manifestations. That could help us design better laws and ways to combat the scourge.

Recently Nazir chastised the leadership for not going beyond orthodox fiscal stimulus and monetary measures to meet the current economic crisis. He suggested re-examining the New Economic Policy, with particular reference to minimizing its drag on the economy. He also called for greater collaborations with the emerging giant economies in the region, specifically China, India, and the Middle East. Most of all I like his idea of attracting foreign talents, especially into the education sector.

These are the kinds of innovative thinking we yearn from our leaders, not their endless monkeying with fence-hopping politicians. In chastising the "leadership," Nazir has shown that he is not constrained by our cultural norms.

The Monkey Story

There was this story of a peddler of hats who one day fell asleep under a tree in the heat of the day. When he woke up, his hats were all gone except for the one on his head. On looking up he saw the monkeys in the tree with hats. The peddler tried all manner of tricks to induce those monkeys to part with their newfound toys, but to no avail. In disgust he threw his hat to the ground and stomped off. In the finest "monkey see, monkey do" mode, the apes did the same, and that was how the peddler recovered his merchandise.

A generation later it was the peddler's son who fell asleep under the same tree. He too lost his hats to the monkeys. Remembering the lesson imparted from his father, the young man threw his hat to the ground in mocked anger. At which point the monkeys laughed at him. "You are not getting your hats back," they mocked him. "We learned your trick from *our* fathers!"

When Najib enticed those political monkeys in Perak to switch to Barisan, he stole a play from Anwar Ibrahim's game book. Anwar may rightly feel flattered by Najib's imitating, or more correctly, aping him. However, like the hat-peddler's son, Najib may have learned his lesson well but what he may not realize is that those political monkeys too had learned theirs! They are making a monkey out of Najib.

When you have a bunch of monkeys and an equally mischievous as well as irresponsible handler, there is no telling what lasting damage they could inflict. It is time to let Najib out of his monkey business and free those *monyet* under his keep, to once again roam in the jungle where they belong. If out of habit they still hang around waiting for their bananas and making a pest of themselves, then we should kill a rooster or two. That would scare away those monkeys, as per an ancient Chinese wisdom.

February 8, 2009

The Last UMNO Prime Minister

Newly-sworn Prime Minister Najib created buzz when he released 13 prisoners detained under the Internal Security Act (ISA) and lifted the ban on *Harakah* and *Suara Keadilan*, publications of the opposition parties. He also promised "a comprehensive review" of the ISA, a statute long abused to silence the government's critics. Malaysians long yearning for change applauded him. There were skeptics, of course.

Alas that was last week. This week the hopes of those citizens were cruelly crushed when they saw the real Najib with the announcement of his new cabinet. Far from being a team that would wow Malaysians, Najib's cabinet was, as Tunku Aziz put it, "a team of recycled political expendables." And a bloated one at that! Those skeptics were right; Najib's earlier act was nothing but a big and cruel tease.

This roster of "political expendables" was the best that the man could offer, from a leader who only a week earlier warned his party that it should "*ubah atau rebah*" (change or be crushed). When given the ultimate freedom to choose his own team, Najib stuck to the tried and true, or what he thought to be so. This was Najib's brave version of "*Berani Berubah!*" (Dare to Change!)

Najib is incapable of change; there is nothing in him to suggest otherwise. He could not even recognize the need for one, much less respond to it. Change would be totally out of character for the man. Far from welcoming or be invigorated by it, change threatens him.

Unfortunately for Najib, Malaysia has changed. Incapable of responding to it, he is doomed come this next general election. He will be our shortest-serving chief executive, our Gerald Ford. President Ford was the only unelected American President who assumed office following Nixon's forced resignation over the Watergate scandal. Like Ford, Najib too was not elected to the highest office. Ford was subsequently rejected by voters; the same fate awaits Najib.

For Malaysia, that would truly be a wasted decade, with the first half already squandered by Najib's predecessor, Abdullah Badawi.

The True Najib

Najib is the obedient first son, the loyal subordinate, and the traditionalist aristocrat. He inherited even his father's ancient tribal title, Orang Kaya Indera Shahbandar. How quaint in this 21st Century! His career path has been straight and narrow, on a track that had been conveniently laid down for him by others who felt indebted or grateful to his illustrious father.

Najib has never shown a talent or disposition for striking new paths. Even his ascendance to the Prime Minister's office was paved by others, in particular Mahathir and Muhyiddin Yassin. Najib must remember that a favor offered is a favor owed.

Just as he was the obedient son, Najib was also the dutiful and loyal subordinate. His blind obedience to Abdullah Badawi drew the wrath of Mahathir. As for experience, Najib has been dependent on paychecks from the public purse all his adult life. He never had to meet a payroll; he has no idea of the trials and challenges of that endeavor; nor does he appreciate the sense of accomplishments and independence of those who have.

This is not the profile of a leader capable of making radical changes that Malaysia so desperately needs.

The track Najib is on now ends at his office. Ahead, for him and the nation, is uncharted territory, with steep hills to climb and wide canyons to traverse. Turning back is not an option, as that path so carefully crafted by earlier leaders is now destroyed for lack of maintenance and prudent use.

That Najib is now portrayed as an agent for change is more a tribute to his highly-paid public relations operatives and the all-too-eager-to-please toadies in the mainstream media. However, you could pedal a dud only for so long; sooner or later the ugly reality would emerge and the delusion be busted.

When that inevitability happens, beware! Voters react with vengeance when they feel that they have been hoodwinked by their leaders. Ask Abdullah. The by-election results since the last general elections are portends for Najib and his party.

Totally Inept and Inadequately Prepared

Najib assembled his cabinet only last week. Even then he spent that limited time talking with leaders of his Barisan coalition instead of with potential candidates. He is clearly being negligent. He knew he would be Prime Minister many months ago; he should have been interviewing and short-listing candidates all along. Being unopposed as president of UMNO and thus freed from having to campaign for it, he had plenty of time to preview his cabinet choices prior to last week.

I am particularly perturbed by his choice of a deputy. Did Najib have a private session with Muhyiddin before selecting him? Nowhere is it written that UMNO Deputy President should also be the Deputy Prime Minister. Najib is being trapped by tradition.

Najib should have done a "Khairy Jamaluddin" on Muhyiddin, that is, keep him out of the cabinet and make him focus on rebuilding the party. God knows, UMNO needs intensive rehabilitation as much as its Youth wing, if not more so. Dispensing with Muhyiddin would strengthen Najib's image as a reformer, quite apart from taking the sting out of having singly excluded Khairy from the cabinet.

Najib gave the very important Education portfolio to Muhyiddin. Is Najib assured that Muhyiddin agrees with him on major policy issues, in particular the highly contentious matter of continuing the teaching of science and mathematics in English? Muhyiddin is unusually quiet on this matter.

It is equally hard to be enthusiastic on the rest of Najib's team. This is what happens when you choose your cabinet based on pleasing others, especially those whom you owe favors.

Najib struggled to get his team, just like Abdullah and Mahathir before him. Like them, he too found the pickings slim as he fished only in the same polluted and shallow puddle of UMNO and Barisan. He did not have the courage to venture beyond.

Najib unwittingly revealed much in his first few days as Prime Minister. Thanks to his PR team, Najib managed to sound very positive with his promise of "a comprehensive review" of the ISA. That sent orgies of praise for the man in the mainstream media and elsewhere. The more perceptive (or skeptical) would note that he specifically did not mention anything about repealing it.

Then there was his announcement on the release of the 13 ISA prisoners "with immediate effect." In Najib's lexicon, "with immediate effect" means at least three days later! This shows how much he is in tune with the actual workings of the civil service.

If I had been Najib's communications director, this is what I would have done. Knowing how easily our civil servants could screw things up, I would first check with the Home Ministry, specifically the Chief of Police and Prison Director, to arrange for the release of the prisoners. Send them to the nearby rest house at government expense if their families were not yet ready to receive them. I would then alert television stations and other news media so they would be there to cover it.

Only after assuring myself that all those meticulous preparations are in place would I have Najib make his announcement. Imagine what the dramatic impact would be with the split screens on the nation's television showing the prisoners being released as he made the announcement. It would also showcase the crispness of Najib's new administration. Had he done so, he would have been spared the embarrassment of his orders being delayed for days because of–you guessed it–the paperwork.

On the day Najib announced his new cabinet, the judge in the long-running Mongolian model murder trial rendered his judgment. Najib had been trying hard to ignore the grizzly tragedy, but it kept cropping up at the most inopportune time. His strategy is to stonewall, banking that the success of his policies would make citizens forget the gruesome crime.

Najib is mistaken in this. Even if his ethics were beyond reproach, Najib would find his policies a tough sell. Conversely, if he could clear up those sordid allegations (assuming of course he is innocent, a huge supposition) he would find that with his personal credibility now enhanced, the public would more likely buy into his policies. Stonewalling is no strategy.

Najib is doomed to be the last UMNO Prime Minister. He will not even be a "one-termer." He will go down in history as our shortest-serving Prime Minister. Worse, it will be recorded for posterity that he was the Malay leader who brought down a once glorious organization, UMNO, an institution his late father was so instrumental in setting up. All destroyed in just two generations; the first to build it, the second to destroy. Truly a very Malay story!

For those who warmly applauded Najib on his first few days in office thinking that this was the dawn of a new day for the nation, I hope they would translate their disappointment into effective action. Deliver to Najib his own KPI (Key Performance Index) at the next general election, less than four years away, plenty of time to lay and grease the track for Najib's (and UMNO's) exit.

April 13, 2009

Only A Good Beginning

Prime Minister Najib's liberalizing segments of the service sector is a good start. However, it is merely good but not excellent, and only a beginning but not the total solution. A half-cooked meal is often not only inedible but could also poison you; likewise, a half-baked solution is not only unworkable but could also be counterproductive.

For Najib to have an excellent and comprehensive solution would require him to address the more difficult underlying issue of what prompted the instituting of quotas in the first place. Unless that is resolved, his new policy will not be politically sustainable regardless how eminently sensible it is economically. Eliminate the need for quotas and Najib would be able to liberalize not only the whole service sector but also the entire economy, if not every facet of Malaysian life. That would bring his "1Malaysia" aspiration that much closer.

However, if he fails to resolve the fundamental problem of what necessitated the quotas, he would only trigger a severe backlash among Malays, the bulk if not his only base of support. Were that to happen, he would worsen race relations; the half-cooked meal being a poison.

Already we are seeing some interesting and unlikely coalition of opposing forces. The Bar Council, the self-styled champion against discrimination and a vociferous and relentless opponent of Malay "special privileges," suddenly became very protective of its members' interests when the government tried to liberalize the profession by allowing the entry of foreign law firms.

The objective of reform is to enhance Malaysia's competitiveness. Malaysia cannot be, unless Malays who constitute the bulk of the population are also competitive. Enhance Malay competitiveness and you also enhance the nation's.

This being Malaysia, with its "monkey see and monkey do" culture, Najib's half-baked move will be echoed by others eager to imitate and flatter him. We already have one monkey in the person of Khir Toyo, the discredited former Mentri Besar of Selangor, now suddenly discovering the "reform" religion. Rest assured that these guys are merely mouthing what is popular (or think is popular); they have no clue of the profound implications or associated difficulties.

Quotas were instituted to dismantle "the identification of race with economic activities," in the eloquent phrase of the New Economic Policy. I would have expected that after nearly 40 years, the announcement of the lifting of quotas of a small segment of the service sector would have been greeted with unbridled joy. That it was not points to potential troubles ahead. Najib ignores this at his peril as his hold on power is at best tenuous.

The right response is not to suspend the liberalization process rather to address its opponents' concerns. The first step involves answering the basic question of why, *sans* quotas, there were so few Malays in that sector. If there were but they had no sustaining power, the next line of inquiry should be to focus on why those Malays were not competitive.

Next would be to examine the failures of the current quota system. Why does it fail to nurture a class of enterprising Malays? It could be that the current policy perversely encourages the emergence of pseudo entrepreneurs and ersatz capitalists, thus oppressing the genuine variety, much like *lallang* (a tenacious weed) to *lengkuas* (spicy tuber root).

Unless answers are found to these questions, we are guaranteed to muddle through yet another half-baked solution. I have yet to hear sensible discussions from our leaders on these fundamental problems.

The key to making Malays (or any group for that matter) competitive is in revamping the schools and universities, and altering the reward system so as to encourage genuine entrepreneurs and risk-takers but discourage the rent-seekers and economic parasites.

Revamp The Education System

Graduates of Malaysian schools and universities have limited language abilities, abysmal quantitative competence, and poor critical thinking, skills needed in the marketplace.

Take language skills. There is only one "official" language in the marketplace, and that is the language of your customers. Those Chinese hawkers peddling their goods in the kampongs intuitively know this. That is why they speak fluent Malay.

The bulk of our customers speak English. This applies to our domestic as well as foreign markets. Hence fluency in that language is essential, especially in the service sector. This is where Malays are sorely lacking. We have erroneously and successfully indoctrinated our young, and also ourselves that learning another language (especially English, the language of our former colonizer) equals contempt of our own.

The average non-Malay already speaks three languages: their mother tongue, Malay, and English. The majority of Malays however are monolingual, only Malay. This did not happen by accident; our education system deliberately created this sorry mess.

Language skill is a good beginning, but by itself is not enough. To be a successful entrepreneur one must be able to manage risk. This requires an ability to quantify it. A business plan is nothing more than a formalization of your assessments and assumptions of those risks.

A project that would be economically viable when the cost of borrowed funds is 5 percent would not be so if it were to double. Likewise, a profit margin of 1-2 percent may be generous where the turnover is fast and high as with a retail store, but not when the volume is low. To evaluate all these would require some mathematical skills.

One does not need higher mathematics to be successful. Indeed the current meltdown of Western financial firms is attributed in part to their uncalled for faith and reliance on higher mathematics. You do however have to appreciate the difference, for example, between simple versus compound rates, or when the interest rates are calculated (daily, weekly, monthly, or annually), and whether based on the original principle or declining balance.

In my earlier book *An Education System Worthy of Malaysia*, I suggested innovations in our schools so they would produce graduates who are trilingual (Malay, English, and Arabic), and have high mathematical skills as well as enhanced science literacy. In some instances, I suggested bringing back the old English-medium schools, especially in rural areas. Currently those kampong students are the weakest academically and least prepared for the marketplace. More significantly, they are mostly Malays.

I also suggested reforming the undergraduate years so students would be exposed to broad-based liberal education regardless of their ultimate career choices. These reforms in education must go in tandem with if not precede our opening up the economy lest we would return to the bad old days of identifying race with economic activities.

Alter The Rewards System

After preparing the young rigorously through better schools, then we must align our cultural values, in particular the reward system, so as to encourage our young to be entrepreneurs and risk-takers.

Consider Malay cultural attitude towards failure. In Silicon Valley, California, a bankrupt entrepreneur wears his failure as a badge of honor, as a war hero would his battle scars, and moves on. To him, failure is a learning experience. In Malay culture, a failed businessman is viewed with contempt. Worse, he is seen as a caricature of the collective weakness of his race and forever stereotyped as well as stigmatized.

There must be a healthy attitude towards failure, to view it not as a reflection of a moral defect in our national character but part and parcel of the entrepreneurial process and indeed of capitalism. Hence bankruptcy courts are an integral part of capitalism, Schumpeter's "creative destruction" formalized.

To be sure, entrepreneurs have their own value system. To them, the success of their ventures is reward enough. Their satisfied customers are the rewards, expressed in the profits of their enterprises. However in honoring those successful businessmen and women, we align the social reward system so as to encourage others to be entrepreneurs and risk-takers.

The remarkable observation on successful entrepreneurs in America is that the ordinary citizen does not begrudge their wealth. On the contrary, they are role models. When we think of Bill Gates, we think of his many wonderful inventions to make our work more productive; his fabulous wealth is seen as well deserved and just rewards.

On the other hand, ordinary citizens have nothing but contempt for Malay billionaires. It is not so much their obscenely ostentatious lifestyles that offend us, rather we could not think of any useful service or product that they have produced that had improved our lives. Their wealth comes through their rent-seeking activities, not economic creations. They are parasites sucking the life out of our economy.

In the same vein there is similar contempt in America today for those highly-compensated financiers for their shenanigan "financial engineering" while we suffer through the destructions they wreck.

Peruse the list of honorees of Malaysian royal awards (focusing only on Malays); the overwhelming majority of them are civil servants and politicians. It is rare for Malay businessmen and entrepreneurs (those rent-seekers excepted) to be honored. As for the genuine creative producers like artists and scientists, they are never on the list.

The royal honors list is one measure; examine the list of beneficiaries of our generous loan programs disbursed by MARA and other public agencies, or the allocations of import permits and company shares. Rarely are those subsidized loans given to those who have completed their apprenticeship programs so they could start their own small enterprises. None of our agricultural graduates get loans or land grants to start their farms. Instead mega-million grants and valuable state land are given away to the politically well-connected who then just as quickly sublease them for hefty fees in the typical economically unproductive and socially destructive "Ali Baba" schemes.

Failure to revamp education and realign the reward system, liberalizing the economy would only aggravate existing inequities, bringing us back to those ugly pre-NEP days. That would not be good economically, politically, or socially. We paid dearly for that error in 1969; it would be folly to repeat it.

April 20, 2009

Walkabout Versus *Makan Angin* Management

It is commendable that Prime Minister Najib is periodically leaving his air-conditioned office to experience firsthand what ordinary Malaysians have to endure in their daily lives. Last week saw him riding the Light Rail Transit; the week before, strolling down Petaling Street. All these so he could "understand the pulse of the people."

Najib would like us to compare him to his late father with the latter's legendary working visits to the various "Operations Room" throughout the country to monitor development projects. Whether Najib would prove to be like his father or closer to Abdullah Badawi remains to be seen.

Recall that Abdullah too made frequent well-publicized visits to various governmental agencies. Once he visited the Immigration Department, notorious for its less-than-stellar public service. After a brief tour he announced that all the agency's problems had been solved, a miracle brought on by his impromptu visit. The sorry part was that Abdullah believed his pronouncement; Malaysians were of course much wiser.

At least thus far Najib had the sense not to wear a three-piece dark suit like Abdullah did on his walkabouts. Instead Najib opted for the more casual batik attire. While Abdullah appeared formal and imperious, like a sultan slumming, Najib was more like someone out for an evening stroll, *jalan jalan* (leisurely stroll) or *makan angin* (lit. eat wind). Regardless, both Najib and Abdullah looked like they were not attired ready for serious work.

Emulate His Father

I suggest that Najib (or his aides) look at the archives of Filem Negara to see how his father did it. The image we have of Tun Razak was of a leader who was serious, brooked no nonsense, and most of all ready to do some heavy lifting. It was not just an image. As many who had worked with him would attest, that was also very much the reality.

The Tun did it long before Tom Peters and Robert Waterman popularized the term "managing by wandering about" in their bestseller, *In Search of Excellence*. Never mind that twenty years later Peters would confess that he faked the whole data on which their book was based, or that many of the "excellent" companies he cited no longer existed! Later, the movie *Crocodile Dundee* brought to the American mainstream the Australian Aborigine's expression "walkabout."

A prominent feature of the late Tun's walkabouts was that they were working visits, not "photo ops" designed for the day's prime news cycle. The Tun's trademark gear was his bush jacket, not dark suits or casual batik. Aware of the blasting heat of the tropical sun, the Tun often wore a hat or carried an umbrella. The Malaysian sun is still as hot today even though I do not see our leaders appropriately attired on their various "official" visits.

Tun Razak's frequent field visits were focused. He would first hear the official briefings and then visit the various projects. Woe to the official whose glowing reports did not match the reality! Those visits were also opportunities for junior officers to show their stuff. The late Tun effectively used those trips to scout for promising talent.

How does Razak Junior measure up? Too soon to tell, but I wish that he would dispense with his colorful batik shirts and three-piece dark suits, have a more purposeful stride, and do away with the media hype. He should also severely trim his entourage, to a security person, a secretary to jot notes, and the head of the visited department.

I would also like him to be more prepared. Surely he did not need to visit the LRT station to know that our commuter trains are overcrowded and frequently late. What he should have done instead was to query the managers as to the steps they were taking to rectify the problems, and how the government could help.

A Short Reading List for Najib

Compared to his predecessor, Najib has one positive attribute; he is an avid reader. I suggest that he read how some great leaders did it. From our own tradition he could read the various celebrated accounts of the night-time walkabouts of our second Caliph, Omar (May Allah be pleased with him!), a legendary ruler. Closer to home, Najib could emulate his father. Unfortunately not much has been written by Tun's contemporaries on his unique management style; Najib would have to rely on Filem Negara's archives.

There are two books that I would recommend for Najib in developing his own walkabout management. One is Robert Townsend's *Up the Organization*, first published in 1970. Townsend was head of Avis Corporation, the car rental company whose advertising jingle, "We're Number Two; We Try Harder!" changed the fortune of the company.

Townsend related how whenever he was out visiting the various franchises he would phone his headquarters incognito to see how his staff would handle customers' queries. This was of course long before the days of outsourcing where such complaints would be routed to service centers in India. Townsend would also go to the local counters to experience the services his customers were receiving, or not receiving! When he found that wanting, he did not harangue the poor receptionists but would bring the matter up with their local managers.

The other book is Jack Welch's *Jack: Straight From The Gut*, co-written with John Byrne. Welch was the legendary CEO of the giant conglomerate GE Corporation. Under his leadership, GE's revenues increased five-fold and market value, 30 times.

On his frequent visits to the periphery, Welch would ask the local managers to name three or four of their promising subordinates. He would then meet them privately to get a firsthand assessment. Following that he would ask their managers what they were doing to groom the promising talents they have under them.

Welch went further. Whenever promising young talents were identified, they were "fast tracked." He would also make sure that their immediate superiors would also be appropriately recognized and rewarded for having played an important role in spotting and developing those promising candidates. Were Najib to do that, he would help reduce the pernicious habit endemic in our civil service where promising young subordinates would be banished to the *ulus* so they would not pose a threat to their superiors.

Najib should also adopt one of Welch's favorite practices. He would spend one whole morning addressing about 70 of GE's "fast tracked" managers attending a three-week development course at the company's "university" at Croton-on-Hudson, New York. Those were no cheerleading or pep rallies, he would challenge those future leaders, inspire them, and most all get fresh ideas from them. It was his relished assignment, one he rarely missed.

Likewise Najib should regularly visit INTAN [training center for civil servants] and challenge those young officers. Get them before they become corrupted by the corrosive civil service culture.

I would also suggest Najib heed one of Welch's more brutal practices, weeding out the bottom ten percent "underperformers" every year. Were Najib to do that, he would reduce the terrible bloat of the civil service and greatly enhance its efficiency.

I would not advise Najib to emulate another celebrated CEO, Southwest Airline's Herb Kelleher. To get close to his employees and customers, Kelleher would fly as an ordinary passenger or take on temporary assignments as a baggage handler or counter clerk. Najib does not have Kelleher's charm or sense of humor to carry that out. Air Asia's Tony Fernandez could, but not Najib.

Management by walkabout is a powerful and effective tool, but only when it is done right. As the management guru Edward Deming put it, "If you wait for people to come to you, you'll only get small problems. You must go and find them. The big problems are where people don't realize they have one in the first place."

Anything less, Najib's frequent forays out of his office would degenerate into *makan angin* or *jalan jalan*. All you get with *makan angin* is foul flatus. Worse, those visits would only disrupt the normal workings of the visited agencies. God knows, our leaders have engaged enough in those already.

May 3, 2009

Priority of Packaging Over Performance

Najib Razak's First One Hundred Days

I would have expected that the successor to the incompetent and do-nothing Prime Minister Abdullah Badawi has minimal difficulty shining as the bar had been lowered substantially. Despite that, Prime Minister Najib Razak has failed to impress us in his first 100 days. His priority is packaging over performance.

Najib may be more poised, his voice less grating, and he stays awake in meetings (Mahathir gave him top marks for that!), but in content and performance, he is of the same bottom-league *kayu belukar* (driftwood) quality as Abdullah, and far from the sturdy *meranti* (teak) quality we yearn for in our leaders. Abdullah lasted slightly over five years; it took Malaysians some time to see through his vacuity. Now sensitized, voters are less tolerant and even less forgiving of incompetence. Najib will have an even briefer tenure.

Najib's two signature and high-profile initiatives in his first 100 days were his 1Malaysia.com scheme and his micromanagement of Perak's legislative politics. The first illustrates his slick packaging; the second, the empty content and inept performance.

Najib's website is professionally designed and maintained. It makes full use of the new media including Facebook and Twitter. Unfortunately its contents do not reflect the man. When I surf the websites of Tun Mahathir, Lim Kit Siang, or Anwar Ibrahim I know that what is written reflects the person, right down to the tone and style of writing. I do not get that sense with 1Malaysia.com. It is written as if from a third person perspective instead of being personal, the very reason for having a social media presence.

Of course I do not expect Najib to write his own speeches; he has other important things to do like running the country. I do expect him however, to be on top of his speechwriters, and to do the final reading and make the necessary editorial changes so those speeches would truly represent and sound as if they emanated from him. He has to leave his imprint.

I also expect his speechwriters to be professional enough to study their subject well, right down to his favorite expressions and writing mannerisms, as well as style of speaking, so the final product would sound and look as if it had been from the man himself.

Not only is the style and tone of 1Malaysia.com divorced from Najib, so too is the content. When someone asked him what the "1Malaysia" concept meant, Najib was unable to articulate it coherently. He could have related his "1Malaysia" concept with his pursuit for a 'unity government,' for example.

If his "1Malaysia" website was meant to symbolize his "One Malaysia" vision, then it has failed miserably. Little wonder that his government had to launch a massive public relations exercise just to publicize his "1Malaysia" concept. Malaysians are still fuzzy about the content. I doubt very much that Najib himself understands what it means.

Far from being his guiding vision, Najib's "1Malaysia" is nothing more than a slick concoction of his highly-paid public relations personnel. It is just another slogan, the triumph of packaging over performance. Expect Najib's "1Malaysia" to have the same if not shorter shelf life than his predecessor's equally ballyhooed Islam Hadhari.

Perak's Mess

As for Najib's political and leadership skills, his handling of Perak's legislature politics is illustrative. There was no shortage of superlatives or praises effusive enough to describe his 'coup' in engineering the fall of the Pakatan government. Today, barely a few months later, Najib is desperate to distance himself from that still evolving mess. He is not in the least (or no longer) interested in trumpeting his earlier 'triumphant' role.

If all the Perak mess did was to soil Najib's already stained reputation, I could readily overlook his central role in it. Unfortunately we are not yet even near the end of the full ramifications of that crisis.

To date the Perak episode has exposed the ineptness of the state civil service and the Royal Malaysian Police, as well as ensnared the sultan. Commentators are now not in the least shy in criticizing the sultan, and often in very harsh and rude terms. They are throwing the sultan's own words when he was chief justice back at him. Sultans are not used to eating their words.

That was not all. The crisis also exposed what had been obvious to many and for so long, the thinness of talent in our political class. The sight of the Speaker of the state legislature being literally dragged out has now become and will forever remain the iconic image of the country's political leadership.

That case is still winding its way through the court system. Already it has exposed the glaring inadequacies and mediocre qualities of our judges. The exception was the initial trial judge, Justice Aziz Rahim, who had his written judgment delivered within days of his decision and whose legal arguments were the model of wisdom, clarity, and scholarship.

As for the Appeals Court judges who reversed Justice Aziz Rahim's decision, I would expect them to be a class above the trial judge. Instead their written judgments when finally released weeks later were not only tardy but did not address the pertinent issues raised by the trial judge. I would expect each of the three appellate judges to outdo each other in presenting a well reasoned and erudite judgment considering that this was not only a high profile case but one that would be cited frequently in future. It was also headed for the highest court. Obviously the appellate judges were not eager or perhaps embarrassed of their judicial logic and decision, as well as their writing skills.

Such are the caliber of our judges, Judge Aziz Rahim excepted. How on earth were they selected, let alone promoted? Their inadequacies would have remained hidden if not for the Perak political fiasco. At least on that count, we could thank Najib.

Elsewhere I wrote that Najib's predecessor Abdullah Badawi served a useful function as "practice prime minister." His sheer ineptness emboldened citizens to speak out and criticize him specifically and other leaders generally. Previously Malaysians, like most Asians, were a dutiful bunch, hesitant to criticize their leaders, mistaking that to be an expression of disloyalty. Abdullah Badawi, not intentionally of course, changed all that. He made Malaysians more assertive. At least on that point we could thank him.

Abdullah Badawi was our 'practice' prime minister, or as we would say in the kampong, a *main-main* (play-acting) one. He gave citizens ample opportunities to develop and acquire the courage to criticize leaders.

If Abdullah was *main main* prime minister; Najib serves a different role. He is our 'sacrificial zinc anode' prime minister. Boat owners are aware of the importance of the sacrificial anode. By installing that you preferentially divert the corroding effects of sea water to that anode, thus protecting the other elements on your boat, like its props. When the anode is corroded you would simply replace it. It is much easier and considerably cheaper than having to replace your eroded props.

Najib Razak is our metaphorical sacrificial zinc anode. He attracts all that is evil, brings out all that is corrupt, and exposes all the incompetence. Then when the nation has been cleansed, with all its evils, corrosions and incompetence accreted upon Najib, we can dispose of him.

So far Najib has served Malaysia well in this role. The critical decision with sacrificial anode is when to dispose of it. Keep it too long and it would spread the corrosion to other vital parts of the boat. The next general election is a good time to get rid of Najib Razak and the party he leads, time to dispose of Malaysia's sacrificial anode.

This anode metaphor for Najib is sad but appropriate. Like many, I would have preferred that he be the skipper of our ship of state. However, if you do not have what it takes to be that, and you do not even have the weight to be ballast, then I suppose being a sacrificial anode is still better than being dead weight.

July 19, 2009

Leaders To Bring Us Together

In having to appoint a Royal Commission of Inquiry to investigate the Malaysian Anti Corruption Commission (MACC) following the death of one of its witnesses, Prime Minister Najib clearly demonstrated his lack of leadership and inability to be in command of a rapidly evolving crisis. Events forced Najib's hand; he was reacting, not leading.

Najib is not a leader, at least not the type Malaysia desperately needs today. His meteoric rise in the party and government is less an expression of talent, more the gratitude his party has for his late father. For his part, Najib has not shown any indication that he had benefited from those splendid opportunities. On the contrary, like a spoiled child, those amenities merely indulged him. Granted, there are no 'training wheels' to prepare one to be prime minister, nonetheless any experience, profession or vocation, executed well, would prepare one for that office. Najib has excelled in none.

Najib's deputy Muhyiddin is in the same kampong (bush) league. Earlier, Muhyiddin dismissed calls for a royal commission, insisting that the police and the MACC are quite capable of undertaking the investigations. It reflected his low standing in the cabinet that many, including fellow UMNO minister Rais Yatim, pointedly pushed for the setting up of the commission.

Even the lowly UMNO Youth leader did not share Muhyiddin's faith in the police and MACC.

Consider a different scenario. If upon returning from his Middle East trip Najib had summoned his Home Minister Hishammuddin and the Director of MACC for an immediate briefing. They of course would not be able to give a coherent explanation. Whereupon Najib would announce that he was directing the MACC to put the involved officers on immediate administrative leave, pending a full independent investigation.

Had Najib done that, with his commanding baritone voice, he would have projected an image of a decisive leader in control of the situation. He would also put an immediate end to the current ugly spectacle of an unfortunate death degenerating into a polarizing political and increasingly racial issue.

Senior statesman Tengku Razaleigh noted that there have been too many custodial deaths, and Teoh Beng Hock's demise marks a watershed in the attitude of the public towards the government, setting a new low. This essence is missed by many in the government.

The ordering of a coroner's inquest or a Royal Commission should have been an executive decision; Najib does not need to involve his cabinet. The cabinet should be deliberating substantive issues, like how to make the economy competitive or reform the rotting education system.

Najib should have learned how his late father handled the national tragedy of the May 1969 race riot. Tun Razak stood in front of the cameras and in a solemn voice and with a serious demeanor announced the immediate imposition of martial law with a "shoot to kill" order for the police and military. He struck a reassuring and take-charge image, in stark contrast to the hapless and weeping then-Prime Minister Tengku Abdul Rahman.

The world may condemn Razak as a dictator or worse, but there was no disputing the fact that he established law and order quickly. To put things in perspective, the modern flare up of sectarian violence in Northern Ireland began at about the same time as the Malaysian 1969 riot. Today, to most Malaysians that nightmare is but a dim distant memory; meanwhile the folks in Northern Ireland are still busy settling their deadly scores.

The evolving public furor over Teoh's death shows every sign of continuing its destructive downward spiral, fed by racist opportunists of all flavors and colorations, with Najib on the sideline reacting instead of leading.

What stunned me were not the responses of the bigoted and uneducated; their chauvinistic views were expected and perhaps excusable because of their ignorance. It would be too much to expect them to have a perspective beyond their clan or kampong. To them this crisis is nothing more than yet another ethnic Chinese-Malaysian victimized by Malay officialdom, or the belligerent Chinese not missing an opportunity to mock Malay officials.

Instead what took me back were the responses of those 'educated' ministers and leaders. They just could not comprehend the public outrage over the MACC's interviewing a 'friendly' witness into the wee hours of the morning and who would later be found dead outside its premises. Perhaps those civil servants were trying to impress the public on how diligent and hard working they were in attending to their duties! If that was how

MACC's personnel treated their 'friendly and cooperative' witnesses, I shudder to think the reception a suspect would get.

Far from expressing condolences to the poor bereaved family, those ministers went on to impute evil motives on the victim's family and those who were outraged by the needless tragedy. How would these ministers feel if it was their son who had been victimized? Don't they have any empathy?

To their credit, Najib and his Women's Affairs Minister Shahrizat Jalil did convey their condolences to the family of the deceased. The two were the exceptions. Najib was even thoughtful enough to send his personal representative to the funeral. The vulgar behaviors of the others, especially Muhyiddin, were eagerly picked up by the toadying commentators and columnists in the mainstream media. They fueled the race fire.

In seeking answers and justice to this cruel death, we must refrain from injecting additional unnecessary and divisive elements. The case is complicated enough; there is no need to dump or impute extraneous factors. As *The Star* columnist and law professor Azmi Sharom rightly observed, people are angry over the needless death of a young *Malaysian*, not a young ethnic *Chinese*, and what they perceive as the abuse of power by MACC officers, not the abuse of power by *Malay* officers.

We need to mobilize the masses to this injustice. We are a democracy and public opinion matters. Thus far public outrage has caused the cabinet to set up the Royal Commission, but that is not enough. Without continued public pressure, the commission's findings would suffer the same fate as befell the Police Commission and the one investigating the so-called Lingam Tape. Nothing happens. We need continued public pressure so the coroner's inquest and the Royal Commission would be conducted openly and transparently, their findings readily available.

There is an art to mobilizing public opinion, and I am not attuned to its many subtleties. However, I do know that many share my disappointment that at one public rally over Teoh's death, most of the speakers were unable to convey their outrage in our national language. Many were young and presumably born and raised in Malaysia, yet they were unable, unwilling or uncomfortable to speak in our national language. That is definitely not the way to go about seeking broad public support to your cause.

I was similarly unimpressed with the rallying cry of HINDRAF (a Malaysian Indian NGO), *Makkal sakthi* (People Power). That would be an acceptable or even winning way to garner public support in Kerala, India, but if it is fellow Malaysians you wish to influence, then you had better articulate your arguments in the national language. HINDRAF would have been more persuasive had its slogan been in Malay – *Kuasa Rakyat* (People's Power).

Being a plural society Malaysia faces many challenging and continuing centrifugal forces threatening to rip it apart. Leaders must recognize this grim reality and then mobilize countervailing forces to bring Malaysians together. Malaysians need leaders who would view this diversity not as a liability but an asset, and a valuable one at that.

Unfortunately his much-touted slogan of "1Malaysia" notwithstanding, Najib Razak is not that kind of a leader. Neither is his deputy Muhyiddin Yassin. We need leaders the caliber of Tengku Razaleigh,

Anwar Ibrahim, and Zaid Ibrahim. The challenge for Malaysia is to make sure that they prevail.

July 26, 2009

Enough of Pledges, We Need Actions!

Prime Minister Najib Razak's pledge to improve six key areas (crime, corruption, education, infrastructure, poverty reduction, and public transportation) would have met widespread applause if only he had indicated just a wee bit more on how he would go about achieving those lofty goals. Malaysians are rightly fed up with highly optimistic targets and stirring slogans. What Malaysia desperately needs are leaders who could execute things and get us there.

Najib refers to those objectives as national "Key Results Areas" (KRAs). If he is not diligent and imaginative in the execution, Najib's KRA could very well end up as KeRA (monkey). *Kera* would then join up with Najib's earlier *glokal* (contraction of global and local) Malay to be the laughing stock of the nation.

The very manner in which Najib made the announcement does not give me much confidence. He made it at a huge gathering of civil servants and on a working day too. Thus during that entire morning, work at the various government offices was at a standstill.

More than likely the afternoon too was a washout, with those officers rehashing the morning's speech. With their superiors absent, the subordinates would even be more sluggish than usual. I pity members of the public who had urgent business with the government on that day.

Najib has acquired one of the many bad habits of his predecessor. Abdullah Badawi too used to convene his ministry officials for a monthly lecture *a la* school assembly. Just like a headmaster, Abdullah would stand on the podium sermonizing in his usual soporiferous monotone voice, putting everyone to sleep. That is, if he himself had not dozed off first. Of course work at his ministry would come to a screeching halt.

Chief Secretary Sidek Hassan has not thought of advising Najib to use other more effective and cheaper means to communicate, like newsletters or even taping the message onto a CD and then distributing it. Perhaps Sidek is in awe of Najib, imagining him to be the civil service's Steve Jobs. Apple's Jobs used to gather his employees in a huge hall at the launch of a new product or to make significant announcements.

If only Najib has a fraction of Job's charisma and executive ability, perhaps such large gatherings could be excused and defended as a way of rallying and inspiring the troops. Having seen the videotape of the assembly however, it was more a torture session for those civil servants to remain awake.

Najib deludes himself if he thinks that simply assigning a responsible minister would solve the problem of execution. None of the six ministers he has selected has excelled themselves or impressed me with their executive talent. Muhyiddin, for education, has not 'wowed' us, what with his flip flopping on the policy of teaching science and mathematics in English. As for Hishammuddin, responsible for crime reduction, his previous tenure in Education did not enthrall me.

Then there is Ong Tee Keat, responsible for infrastructure development. This poor soul has yet to explain the rapidly ballooning boondoggle that is the Port Klang Free Zone Development scandal.

I would have been more impressed had Najib, in assigning the areas of responsibility for his ministers, also indicated the price for nonperformance. Would Hishammuddin be relieved of his cabinet post should he fail to reduce the crime rate? Heads must role when there is a major lapse. That is the only way to make people accountable and take their responsibilities seriously. If there is no price to pay for failure, there is little incentive to perform, much less excel.

Take crime reduction; Najib is needlessly reinventing the wheel. All he has to do is revisit the recommendations of the Royal Commission on the Police of four years ago. Along the same vein, if during the tenure of the present Police Chief Musa Hassan the crime rates have soared, that is compelling enough reason not to renew his tenure.

My hunch is that Najib will renew Musa's contracts, thus making a mockery of the commitment to crime reduction. Najib would do more for crime reduction by firing the glaringly ineffective and incompetent Musa Hassan. Otherwise all those lofty goals would merely be *cakap kosong* (empty talk), KRA morphing into KeRA (monkey business).

Likewise his battle to curb corruption; Najib would do well to get rid of the present director of MACC, Ahmad Said Hamdan. His agency's record in the two latest high-profile cases is abysmal. Then there is the tragic death of one of its 'friendly' witnesses.

Simply renaming the old Anti Corruption Agency to the Malaysian Anti Corruption Commission would not combat corruption if you are still stuck with the same personnel, procedures, and mindset.

A Better Approach

A more effective approach would have been for Najib to gather his assigned ministers and the relevant senior officers to a private meeting where he would lay out his goals and inquire from them the steps and initiatives they would recommend in reaching those goals.

Those meetings should be working sessions, dispensing with time-wasting unnecessary protocols or preoccupation with seating arrangements. Everyone should be ready to literally roll up their sleeves, not fuss with the creases of their three-piece suit. There is much heavy lifting to be done, with ideas critically examined, resources wisely allocated, and markers put in place.

Such meetings would not only be cheap, they would also not disrupt the normal workings of the various departments, especially if they are held outside regular office hours. Those meetings would be the time to monitor progress, get feedback, and modify strategies.

Najib's meetings thus far have been heavy on press coverage and laudatory comments especially in the mainstream media. This is not the time for premature accolades; there will be plenty of time for that later once those objectives are achieved. Meanwhile we should all be critical lest these leaders get carried away with premature and unmerited applause.

Like his predecessor Abdullah, Najib is satisfied merely with making highly-publicized public pronouncements instead of attending to the necessary nitty-gritty of governance. It is attention to such practical and mundane details on which the success or failure of a policy depends.

Najib must act more as chief executive and less a sultan satisfied merely with issuing endless *titahs* (edicts). Malaysia has enough sultans already with the nine that it has; there is little need to add to the roster.

August 5, 2009

In the Spirit of Eid ul Fitri

I applaud Prime Minister Najib for releasing five more prisoners held under the unjust and abominable Internal Security Act (ISA). That he did it in the last Ashra (ten days) of Ramadan, and within days of Hari Raya, captures best the true spirit of Ramadan and the generosity of Eid ul Fitri.

Najib's generous gesture illustrates another important point. Leaders do not need to resort to catchy slogans or grandiose gestures in order to demonstrate the greatness of our faith. His releasing the prisoners (this latest group of five, plus the earlier 13 set free on his assuming office and the 16 a few weeks later) did more to enhance the image of Islam than all the pontifications of his predecessor and self-styled Imam of Islam Hadhari, Abdullah Badawi. Abdullah's frequent recitations of the ideals of Islam notwithstanding, he did not release a single prisoner during his tenure.

The only sour note to this latest action was the idiotic (what else is new?) comment by Home Minister Hishammuddin. He threatened "to fill Kamunting to the brim" if that was what it would take to protect the nation's security. Despite his long years in government he has learned nothing; he still has the same perverted priorities.

Hishammuddin and others of his persuasion must be reminded over and over, for they are prone to forget, that the greatest threat to our nation's security and indeed our well being remains our corrupt and ineffective institutions, including and especially the police and the anticorruption commission. Both agencies are under Hishammuddin's direct purview.

Two of the five just released prisoners had been detained for nearly eight years. That is a very long time to be deprived of one's freedom, and to be away from one's loved ones. It is well to remember that one of the purposes of Ramadan is to remind Muslims to feel for the pains of hunger of those less fortunate. In this regard, the wife of one of the men released, Mat Sah, had dutifully blogged (Merah Hitam: www.lailagmi.blogpsot.com) the sufferings she and her son Suhaib endured during the nearly eight years that the family was without a husband and a father.

I suggest that Hishammuddin and others who favor the ISA read her blog. If their conscience is not at all pricked by the running accounts of this young mother, then I suggest that they read Kassim Ahmad's *The Second University: Detention Under the ISA*, and Syed Hussin Ali's *Two Faces: Detention Without Trial*.

If Hishammuddin is still not persuaded as to the evil that is the ISA, then I respectfully suggest that he is not entitled to be the beholder of the title "Yang Berhormat," (The Honorable) let alone be a minister in charge of such an important portfolio.

For every individual the government sends to Kamunting without affording him or her due process means a failure of our security apparatus and other institutions. Had our institutions, especially our intelligence gathering and law enforcement agencies been effective, we should have been able to secure enough evidence to charge and convict these individuals if indeed they were subversive.

We were told that there were nine more still detained under the ISA. Until they too are released or charged in open court, their detention will remain a blemish on the nation's record. We should not remain quiet to their plight; the authorities are only too eager to read our silence as tacit approval. We should not rest or take comfort until Kamunting is emptied and the ISA repealed.

One of those still detained is a fugitive from Singapore, Mas Selamat. Hishammuddin should entertain an extradition application from that republic. If nothing else that would give us an opportunity to evaluate the conviction of Mas Selamat in Singapore.

If Hishammuddin feels strongly that the current detainees are a threat to Malaysia's security, then he should share the evidence and be prepared to charge them in court. Like his many predecessors, Hishammuddin has not demonstrated any credibility for citizens to believe his mere utterances.

Those citizens were deprived of their basic dignity and human rights by the decision of one man: the Home Minister. There is no provision for a judicial or other review. He is unchallenged. In our faith, only Allah is that.

That is an awesome responsibility to put on any human being. Only the reckless and conscienceless would shoulder that responsibility lightly or make flippant comments as wanting "to fill Kamunting to the brim." In the words of the Sudanese reformist Mahmoud Mohamad Taha (1909-85), "No person is perfect enough to be entrusted with the liberty and dignity of others." We need an effective system of checks and balances to minimize the risk of miscarriage of justice.

Tradition has it that once while Prophet Muhammad, s.a.w., was leading a prayer, there was some confusion over the verse he had recited. After the prayer he turned to his companion Umar and inquired, "Were you present with us [during the prayer]?" When Umar replied in the affirmative, the prophet then asked, "Why then did you not correct me?"

Muslims rightly regard Prophet Muhammad, s.a.w., as the embodiment of perfection. Our leaders and ministers are far from that. Thus we must not be fearful of or even hesitate in correcting our leaders when we think they have gone astray. The sooner we do this the less likely they would lead us further down the wrong path.

It is also incumbent upon leaders to straighten their subordinates who have strayed or demonstrated a tendency to do so. Najib should not hesitate to correct the waywardness of those under him, beginning with his cousin, Home Minister Hishammuddin.

In releasing this latest batch of ISA detainees, Najib Razak demonstrates best the spirit of generosity and forgiveness that is the essence of Ramadan and Eid ul Fitra.

September 9, 2009

Praising our Leaders Too Soon And Too High

Malaysians are generous to a fault. We are too charitable especially to our guests and those new to us, without pausing to consider the significant burden it imposes upon us and those we love. This is best captured in our saying, *Kera hutan di tetekan, anak di riba mati kehausan* (We breastfeed monkeys in the jungle while our infants die of thirst).

We treat our leaders as *kera hutan* (jungle monkeys), indulging them only too readily. We are overly charitable to and very forgiving of them, especially new leaders. I understand the rationale for such a sentiment; we desperately want our leaders to succeed. By praising them so highly and so early, we hope to inspire as well as encourage them to lead us to greater heights.

The adulation of followers can indeed be a tonic to leaders, invigorating them to redouble their efforts; likewise with prestigious awards and public recognition. The Nobel Committee in awarding its Peace Prize to President Obama so early in his tenure is clearly expressing the hope of many that he would indeed bring about a more peaceful world.

There is a dangerous flipside to that hope. Effusive praises, especially when clearly out of proportion or yet to be deserved, risk swelling these leaders' heads. Even if they do not have mega-maniacal tendencies to begin with, such incessant drumbeat of praises would inflate the ego of even the humblest of leaders. They would then think that they are divinely destined to lead us. From there it is but a few easy and enticing steps away from asserting that they are indeed God. Then no one could or would dare question them. There are many ready examples of such inept but egotistical leaders at home and abroad, now and in history. The ravages they inflict far outlive them.

Praising Najib Early and Excessively

Mohd. Najib Bin Abdul Razak has been Prime Minister for barely six months; he delivered his first presidential speech to his party only last week. As Prime Minister he had initiated only a few not-so-major policy shifts thus far, such as liberalizing a small sub-sector of the economy, the effectiveness of which has yet to be ascertained. Yet the high praises for him are already pouring in by the torrent.

In describing his performance at the recent UMNO General Assembly, one commentator in the mainstream media described it as "one of his best off-the-cuff speeches that many in UMNO had witnessed." She went on describing Najib as a "thinking president," gushingly concluding that the meeting he chaired "as one of those special moments in UMNO's history." Special moments! Wow!

Another concluded with undisguised "astonishment at the remarkable ability of the country's premier political party to renew, reform and reinvent itself after the severe setback it suffered in the 12th general election." All in the few months since Najib took over!

There was no shortage of superlatives to describe the new Najib, with terms like "transforming leader" and "thinking leader" liberally thrown in, based simply on that first address he gave at the UMNO Assembly.

Now that Najib has presented his first budget, dubbed "People first; Performance now!" expect even more extravagant praises. I do not however, share much of the artificially-generated enthusiasm, at least not yet.

It is a measure of our 'progress' that in discussing the economy in his budget speech Najib was giddy that it was contracting less severely now. I can see being exuberantly excited if it had actually expanded, however slim. On another item, he proudly announced the establishment of 30 "merit" scholarships for our students to attend top universities. I would have been more impressed if, after over 50 years of independence, those scholarships were for sending our students to top doctoral or MBA programs, not for undergraduate studies.

The Art of Making Dim Candles Appear Brighter

Such embarrassingly-embellished praises from established sycophants and would-be supplicants, as well as blatant favor seekers, are to be expected. After all, old habits are difficult to break even if you are committed to doing so. More problematic however, are the uncritical rave reviews from otherwise seasoned observers.

This is not a new phenomenon or unique to Najib. When Abdullah succeeded Mahathir, there were similar early outpourings of uncritical praises for Abdullah. One otherwise solid scholar, undoubtedly desperate to ingratiate himself to the new regime, unabashedly described Abdullah as a "social engineer par excellence."

Those commentators were not content with merely praising Abdullah. To make him look even better, they resorted to actively denigrating Mahathir. They must have felt that Abdullah's dim candle could only appear brighter by snuffing out Mahathir's.

When I took those commentators to task for their nauseating praises, they were furious, accusing me of being unnecessarily negative and not missing any opportunity to denigrate our leaders. How could I possibly know Abdullah with my being so far away and for so long, they sneered!

I wonder if those who were so enthusiastic about Abdullah earlier on now feel they bear some responsibility for his subsequent failure. Perhaps if they had been more restrained, Abdullah's ego would not have been so swollen. Who knows, his basic humility may have taken hold of him and he would have sought wider counsel. His tenure then might have lasted longer and would not have been the colossal waste of opportunities, for him and the nation.

At the UMNO General Assembly, Najib paid tribute to Abdullah for not criticizing Najib, a pointed reference to what Mahathir did to Abdullah. Both Najib and Abdullah are deeply mistaken in this. For had Mahathir not been relentless and even unmerciful in his criticisms of Abdullah, the latter would still remain as Prime Minister today, and we would all be enduring that terrible burden.

There is one positive aspect to the current orgy of praises for Najib; at least those commentators are not running down his immediate predecessor. I am uncertain whether that is necessarily a compliment to Abdullah.

Najib should welcome and actively encourage criticisms and not just from Abdullah or Mahathir but also others. That would be the best assurance that Najib would avoid grievous errors in his administration. Even a gifted and charismatic leader as Barack Obama, with an overwhelming mandate from the people, welcomes criticism. As he said in a White House Correspondents' Dinner, "I may not agree with everything you write or report. I may even complain …, but I do so with the knowledge that when you are at your best, then you help me be at my best."

Like others, I too want Najib Razak to succeed, less for his sake but more for Malaysia's. I fear that these uncalled-for and overly-generous praises so soon in his tenure might just go to his head, tempting him to rest on his laurels (slim as they are right now) instead of striving harder.

We must not treat our leaders like our pet monkeys; we must never indulge them. Instead we must subject them to the toughest scrutiny and not be afraid to criticize them, and do so early and fiercely. By all means, when Najib proves himself, then we can all be generous in our praises for him.

October 25, 2009

It Happened Under Your Watch, Najib!

"Don't point the fingers at UMNO or anyone else," so declared an angry Najib Razak in responding to a question on last Friday's bombing of a church. It was pathetic to see him react thus; a body language that bespoke of a sinister kid whose bag of malicious tricks had just exploded in his face.

Najib would like us to believe that those acts of arson were spontaneous. What a pathetic attempt at extricating himself from the ugly and dangerous mess he helped create! His performance was more to convince himself, for he could not possibly sway others.

Here he was after pouring gasoline feigning surprise when someone finally lit a match. It was Najib who only the day before the incident declared that "Muslim groups were free to protest and express their views about the 'Allah' issue." Just in case that message did not register, he added that the authorities would not stop groups from gathering at mosques and protesting there. Najib's cousin and Home Minister, Hishammuddin, echoed the same sentiment of implicitly encouraging the demonstrations.

Obviously many took them at their words. It is truly touching to see these two ministers belatedly becoming so protective of citizens' rights to protest! The pair obviously did not appreciate the subtle but enormous difference between having those rights and the wisdom to exercise them appropriately.

Najib and Hishammuddin must think that Malaysians are a dumb lot not to see through their charade. It was Hishammuddin who first unhinged that dangerous religious wrecking ball with his banning of the use of the word "Allah" by a Catholic Church publication.

Contrast the words and deeds of these two very public purveyors of the "1Malaysia" fantasy to that of the leaders of Pakatan opposition coalition. In a statement issued through one of its affiliates, The Justice Party, Anwar Ibrahim declared that "the wish of the non-Muslim community to use the term 'Allah' is a positive and welcomed development. We must not let that be an opportunity for those with malicious intent to seize the occasion to portray themselves as champions of Islam." Amen to that!

Anwar realized only too well the potential dangers of stoking the religious fire. To emphasize his point, Anwar called for restraint and urged his supporters not to participate in the planned Friday demonstrations. It was a particularly prescient call. Anwar must have read Najib,

Hishammuddin and all the other characters in UMNO well; he did not underestimate their mischievousness if not evil intent.

Anwar was not alone; leaders of PAS went out of their way not only to discourage the demonstrations but also to defend the rights of the Catholic publication to use the term "Allah."

I do not know whether Malaysians, specifically Malays, are becoming more sensible or the restraint urged on by Anwar and the others had an impact, for come Friday the demonstrations were definitely muted. The egging-on by UMNO leaders fell flat; instead the rotten eggs landed on their faces.

The exemplary stand of the opposition leaders was a stark contrast to the mischievous if not downright dangerous antics of UMNO. The contrast did not end there. Immediately following the tragic incident, Selangor Pakatan Mentri Besar Khalid Ibrahim visited the charred church. His was a much needed and comforting presence, as well as a deeply symbolic gesture. It was spontaneous, a splendid demonstration of common sense and deep concern for your fellow citizens, as well as of exemplary leadership.

Najib was content to condemn the hooliganism from afar, and in the process found himself in an uncomfortably defensive position. He did not visit the damaged church until the next day, but not before he had launched his party's "People's Champion" campaign in preparation for the next elections. That was Najib's priority.

The only UMNO leader who visited the damaged church was Khairy Jamaluddin. He conveyed genuine empathy; his condemnation and expression of sympathy were heartfelt, a welcomed change from the hollowness of Najib.

Khairy's presence made the absence of the other UMNO leaders that much more noticeable, and vulgar. These supposedly more seasoned UMNO leaders could learn a thing or two from Khairy on the importance of showing leadership in moments of crisis. You cannot teach that; either you have it or you don't. Obviously Najib does not have it.

Najib's bag of tricks was so crude that even foreign observers saw through it. "The real reason UMNO is politicizing the issue and pandering to its conservative base," wrote the *Wall Street Journal*, "may be to deflect attention from its own political vulnerabilities."

Najib had every reason to want to change the horrible headlines that were damaging his leadership, the latest being the jet engines stolen from a military base. The theft occurred during Najib's tenure as Defense Minister but was only recently made public.

That was not the only serious lapse of security during Najib's tenure as Defense Minister. There was the spectacular and potentially devastating collapse of the naval base in Pularek just before its official opening. Earlier, there was the lethal attack on the army base in Grik, Perak, by a band of sarong-clad Al Maunah gang members. This recent revelation of the stolen jet engines was merely part of Najib's trademark pattern of incompetent leadership. Thus far Najib is determined to repeat that same pattern of leadership as Prime Minister, except that he has now progressed beyond incompetence to being sinister.

It is downright malicious for Najib, Hishammuddin and others in UMNO to attempt at dividing Malaysians by needlessly treading on our religious sensitivities. Najib's "1Malaysia" campaign has barely begun and he has already made a mockery of the ideal.

Specifically, Najib's attempt to split Muslims in the opposition parties was brazen, crude and potentially destructive. There were initial intimations that his dirty scheming would work, what with the mainstream media continually harping on the supposed differences among the leaders of PAS and Keadilan over this issue. Najib and others must have been licking their chops, savoring the 'brilliance' of their strategy while remaining oblivious of the dangerous evil forces that they had unleashed.

Thankfully this time around Malaysians are far ahead of their leaders and did not fall for this ugly and dangerous ploy. I am heartened that even UMNO's own *New Straits Times* (NST) felt emboldened enough not to defend the administration on this matter.

In a thoughtful commentary, Rehman Rashid not-too-subtly reminded his readers of the terrible mess created by this manufactured crisis. Left unstated is the role of our leaders in leading us to be where we are today. Of course it would be too much to expect the mainstream media, specifically NST, to explore that. Under the circumstance, Rehman has gone as far as he could, and I applaud him for that.

In his piece Rehman wrote, "Debilitating dogmas need to be debunked, political parasites purged, and Little Napoleons stripped naked and hounded out of town." Strong words! At least he has demonstrated that sycophantic editors (or at least their toadying editorials) are out too!

I hope that the positive gestures by Khairy and refreshingly candid commentary by Rehman would move Najib, Hishammuddin and others in UMNO away from their dangerous games. If they do not, then it is time we take the match away from them before they burn down the country. It is also time we tell them in no uncertain terms that they are not only unfit to lead our great nation but they also pose an imminent danger to Malaysia.

The nation suffered terribly in 1969; that national tragedy was instrumental in elevating Tun Razak to the nation's top post. We should never risk our nation to another tragic episode under the inept and sinister leadership of his son. We must not let Najib and his UMNO cahoots continue with their bag of dirty tricks. The fire next time might not be so easily contained or doused. The conflagration then could rip us all apart. Let us not even contemplate giving them another chance. We have had enough!

January 10, 2010

Anwar and Najib – Up Close and Very Revealing

The side-by-side commentaries by Anwar Ibrahim and Najib Razak in the recent Asian edition of the *Wall Street Journal* illuminated a couple of salient points, in particular, the state of Malaysian journalism and the quality of our leadership.

Consider first Malaysian editors, specifically of the mainstream media. They missed the essential point that the best way to intelligently inform their readers is to present them with contrasting and opposing viewpoints, as illustrated by what *The Journal* did. Respect your readers' intelligence and treat them as adults.

Bernama mentioned the *Journal's* articles as a news item but referred only to Najib's piece. Obviously *Bernama* editors' instinct was to please Najib and protect his image. They see themselves less as professional journalists and more as propagandists for the state and Najib. Their reaction was predictable.

That the cue from *Bernama* was quickly picked up by the other mainstream editors too did not surprise me. They are after all from the same mold. What grabbed my attention however, was what *The Sun Daily* did. I remember that paper as one that had the courage right from the beginning to be a tad independent, and its journalists less willing to genuflect to the powerful; hence its success despite its recent entry into the business.

The Sun merely reprinted *Bernama's* piece, again with no mention of Anwar's contrasting viewpoint. *The Sun's* editors had access to both commentaries (they are available on-line) but chose to follow *Bernama's* lead instead of their own editorial judgment. That reflects the challenges in maintaining journalistic integrity in an oppressive environment.

Then there is MCA-owned *The Star*. It did what cowards typically do: avoid the issue entirely. I am uncertain whether that is better than blatantly kowtowing to the emperor, as *Bernama* did.

As for *The New Straits Times*, an UMNO newsletter masquerading as a daily, its behavior too was predictable. It did not directly report on the two commentaries, presumably deeming both not sufficiently newsworthy. That however, did not stop its editor Syed Nadzri from penning an editorial effusively praising Najib's literary contribution.

"In approach, tenor and presumably intention," Nadzri writes, "their articles went in practically opposite directions from the start–the prime minister taking a conciliatory, disarming style, as against the opposition leader's fault-finding digressions." What Nadzri calls 'fault-finding digression' is Anwar's trying to elucidate, understand and then educate us on the many daunting problems confronting the nation.

Towards the end even Nadzri's residuum of journalistic ethics pricked his conscience a bit, for he admitted that Najib's commentary was indeed a "rah rah piece," adding, "What else could anyone expect?" Such low expectations!

It would never occur to the likes of Nadzri to consider republishing both commentaries; they are of interest to all Malaysians. In short, emulate the *Journal*'s practice of having contributors with varying viewpoints. While the *Journal* is an avowedly conservative paper (its editorials leave little doubt about that), its Op-Ed pages routinely carry views from the left and right; likewise, its news coverage. The unabashedly liberal *The New York Times* counts among its regular commentators such conservatives as David Brooks. Unfortunately, the likes of Syed Nadzri are intellectually and professionally incapable of such a monumental shift in thinking.

In contrast to the mainstream media, the on-line portals *Malaysiakini* and *Malaysia-Today* chose a diametrically opposite tack. *Malaysia-Today* published both commentaries in full without any editorial comment. Its editors are confident of their readers' intelligence to draw their own conclusions. If those mainstream editors wonder why their readership dwindles while those of *Malaysiakini* and *Malaysia-Today* soar, the answer is right there.

Top Billing For Anwar

The Journal gave Anwar's commentary greater prominence; it appeared on top of the page. I agree with that editorial judgment. By whatever criterion–persuasiveness, substance, clarity of thought, and most importantly, readability–Anwar's piece clearly trumps Najib's. No wonder those mainstream editors dared not carry both side by side; it would embarrass their patron!

Anwar exhorts us to rise above our parochial interests and recalls the great moments in our Islamic history where tolerance and acceptance of divergent viewpoints were venerated. Najib excuses our prejudices and intolerances on the grounds that those have always been part of human nature. He condones if not encourages those extremists with their "passionate" views.

Najib claims to be "appalled by the irresponsible and dangerous finger-pointing of a few politicians who put personal political interests ... [and] try to score political points by hammering on sensitive issues." He forgot that it was his Home Minister who started the mess with his needless bureaucratic intervention of a long-established practice with respect to the use of the word "Allah." Talk about blatant pandering to the political base! Do not expect Najib to have second thoughts on that. Reflection, or for that matter taking responsibility, is not his strong suit.

He continues, "The values we hold dear–religious freedom, tolerance, peace and fairness–remain the bedrock of our nation." Too bad he does not take that to heart. While Anwar excoriates *Utusan Melayu*, an UMNO-owned Malay language daily, for inflaming religious sentiments among Malays, Najib remains eerily silent. Many perceive that as tacit endorsement and outright encouragement. One wonders just who is pandering to the Malay mob.

Anwar invokes our Koran and traditions to push us towards our better selves; Najib was only too ready to dismiss and excuse those "extremists." To Najib, the extremists, like the poor, will always be with us. There is not much that he could or would do.

The clarity of Anwar's message was elegantly encapsulated in his very first sentence, "Malaysia has once again resurfaced in international headlines for the wrong reasons." No one, not even Najib, could dispute that assertion. Anwar's thesis sentence was crisp, clear and stated simply. It may be embarrassing to have that ugly reality exposed, but it would be a serious abrogation of responsibility for a leader not to address it, as Najib awkwardly tried to avoid.

It was difficult to ascertain Najib's message; his essay was all over the place—mushy! This fits his leadership style: heavy on homilies, short on substance. He would prefer that our ugly problems be swept under the carpet, to save the nation's 'honor,' or at least his concept of it.

Through the *Journal*'s initiative we get to view these two leaders. In Anwar we have a leader in command of the situation, someone serious and fully cognizant of the dangers of fanning religious passions. He appeals to our better side to meet those challenges. In Najib we have an individual full of fluff, blissfully unaware of the fury he has unleashed, and totally incapable of handling the ensuing wreckage. He is, to borrow Nadzri's less-than-elegant phrase, a "rah rah" leader, reveling in his (Najib's) own Pollyannaish fantasy.

The *Journal* rendered a great public service to Malaysians in having these two commentaries freely available on-line. Its initiative also reveals the sad state of Malaysian journalism. I keep hoping that one day our media would learn something from the *Journal* and treat Malaysians as intelligent adults. I also keep hoping that one day we would have as prime minister someone who would treat us with respect and trust us with the truth. Malaysians deserve better than what we are being served now.

January 31, 2010

Najib's Ill-Disciplined Leadership

Prime Minister Najib continues his predecessor's practice of monthly departmental assemblies where he addresses his staff in the manner of a headmaster to his school children. His latest session on Monday, July 5th had him exhorting them to create "an ecosystem [to] recognize top performers."

You can tell much about a person by the way he behaves in familiar surroundings. Likewise, a leader reveals his true persona when he is in the comfortable presence of his followers. By that measure, Najib's performance at his monthly departmental gatherings exposes his ill-disciplined leadership.

His delivery was hardly smooth. There were awkward pauses, inarticulate bellowing of his voice, and irritating gesturing with his hands, all to feign emphasis and profundity. While the occasion was flashy, grand and elaborately planned, his speech betrayed his lack of preparation.

There he was in his dark suit, this time outside under the morning but still-blistering Malaysian sun, with his ministers and senior bureaucrats standing dutifully on stage in a neat straight row behind him. They too were similarly formally dressed in dark suits with flawlessly matched red ties and kerchiefs, seemingly in rapt attention. They looked more like pall bearers at a funeral, except for their red ties.

More typically these assemblies would be held in one of the maximally air-conditioned and minimally utilized auditoriums in Putrajaya. Then his ministers and senior bureaucrats would be seated comfortably in the front row. At least they would not be sweating in their thick suits, with their faces and foreheads glistening as they were that Monday morning.

It is hard to discern the purpose of this monthly ritual. I presume it is an opportunity for Najib to announce major policy initiatives, but there was nothing new or substantive that Monday. For the civil servants however, it was an opportunity to *ponteng*, to be away from their desks. They were like schoolchildren excited to be given a break from their classes. No wonder those civil servants were singing and waving flags! How juvenile!

Najib however, fancies himself not as a headmaster rather a Steve Jobs addressing a grand media gathering. Some fantasy! Najib forgets that when Jobs had his, it was to introduce a new product; an ingenious and effective marketing strategy to create excitement or "buzz."

Obviously Najib is unaware of the cost of his monthly assemblies. He thinks it is expense-free, as the government already owns the facility and those civil servants and ministers are not paid extra to be there. He could not be more wrong. Like his ministers and staff, Najib spends his entire career receiving a steady paycheck. He has never run a business and thus is blissfully unaware of what it would take to deliver regular paychecks. The concept of overhead or wasteful spending of time and resource is beyond his grasp.

With the assembly held in the morning, those civil servants are unlikely to spend the time interval before and after to do any meaningful work. If you think that they would rush back to their offices after the assembly, then you do not understand the mentality and culture of our civil service. The afternoon too would be wasted in rehashing the morning event.

Functionally, the whole day was a washout as far as effective work was concerned. Those bureaucrats were essentially *makan gaji buta* (lit. eating a blind salary; fig, not earning their keep) that day. So much for efficiency! I pity those who had any business to transact with the Prime Minister's office that day.

With all the talk of "transforming" the government, I would have thought that Najib could think of other cheaper and more effective ways of communicating with his staff.

Pidgin English and Bazaar Malay

The only thing prime ministerial about Najib during that assembly was his attire. As for his speech, he could not utter a complete sentence in either comprehensible English or proper Malay. He would begin in Malay and then without any hint switch into English, and then back to Malay, or endless combinations thereof. Listeners had to switch mental gears frequently and without warning. Najib's monotonous mumbling with his own peculiar brand of mangled "Manglish" made him sound like a third-rate Filipino politician.

Consider this: *"Sistem kita ini mesti kita lihat* (We must look at our system) the entire ecosystem *ini, mesti* recognize potential high performance, …." Another, *"Kalau kita* (If we) recognize potential high performance, … *kita* recognize *sumbangan yang luar biasa*, those who are prepared to go the extra mile, ..." Such boring and repetitious mumbo jumbo defies translation!

Najib set a bad example especially for our students. How could we criticize them when our Prime Minister could not even string together a complete sentence in either Malay or English? Najib's mangled syntax was incongruous in such a formal setting. This manner of speaking is disrespectful of his audience. Thank God he did not degenerate into his usual colloquialism as with "*Lu tolong gua, gua tolong lu*" (You scratch me, I scratch you!) mode as he did in the recent Sibu by-election.

Only Zee Avi with her sultry voice could make the mixing of Malay and English sound cute and captivating. Those less talented or with a grating voice should stick to one language only, and that includes Najib.

Najib's favorite buzzword at this last assembly was "ecosystem." He probably came across that in one of the "pop" business books or articles. I doubt very much whether he fully understands its meaning. An ecosystem is a dynamic functional unit where one participant influences and in turn being influenced by the other players. Altering one could have unpredictable consequences on others as well as the whole.

What Najib meant was culture or environment. Either word would have been more accurate and readily understood, but to Najib they were too ordinary and not as sexy as "ecosystem."

Another choice word of his is "transformation." In biology the term refers to the phenomenon where the genetic material is altered, and the organism consequently transformed. It means change at the core (nucleus), and from there to the rest of the cell and on to the next generation. The consequent change is thus permanent, profound, affects the whole system, and transmissible to the next generation. In sociology it means profound and irreversible change that begins with the leadership, and then spreads out.

To state it differently and more bluntly, it is Najib who has to change first before he could even dream of transforming Malaysia. For example, to streamline the government, Najib must begin with his own bloated department.

Another of Najib's favorite buzz word is "quantum," as in his declaration, "Civil servants would get bonuses, only the quantum is to be determined." Again, he must have looked that word up and found its meaning to be "quantity" or "amount." So he simply substituted the more sexy and scientific sounding "quantum."

"Quantum" as in quantum physics refers to the discrete energy levels associated with electron orbitals around the nucleus. Thus a quantum increase is a pre-defined or discrete and stepwise increase, and not just any amount. Non-scientists love these big words for their vicarious association with modern science without realizing that it only makes them sound stupid.

The Man and His Performance

My primary purpose here is not to critique Najib's vocabulary, syntax, or delivery, rather that those reflect the man and his leadership. His fondness for flashy and impressive-sounding words rather the more mundane but precise and readily understood is also reflected in his policies. His "1Malaysia" slogan is a ready example–high sounding and introduced with great fanfare. However when he had a chance to demonstrate its core meaning as with repudiating the racist theatrics of Perkasa and the likes of Ibrahim Ali, Najib backtracked. He was easily *gertak* (scared).

Najib's mangled syntax with its *rojak* (local delicacy of mixed vegetables) mingling of Malay and English words betrays his lack of mental discipline. Again this reflects his leadership. He announced with great flourish the "transforming" of his economic policy, with his NEM (New Economic Model) supplanting his father's New Economic Policy (NEP). At the first resistance to his NEM, Najib retreated.

Najib's gibberish sentences and garbled delivery also reflect his lack of preparation. Again, that is disturbing. The assembly was planned, not an off-the-cuff press conference. As such I would have expected him to be better prepared. That he was not showed the low regards he had for his audience.

My reaction to Najib's performance at these assemblies and elsewhere can best be summed up by singer-songwriter Zee Avi's lilting refrain in "*Kantoi*" (busted):

> *Sudah lah sayang, I don't believe you*
> *I've always known that your words were never true*
> *Why am I with you? I pun tak tahu*
> *No wonder lah my friends pun tak suka you!*

The exception is that I do not *sayang* Najib nor am I with him.

Come to think of it, Najib had been up to quite a bit of mischief in his career. However, his position effectively protected him from *kena kantoi* (being busted), at least thus far and in Malaysia. With the French authorities now stepping up their investigation on the scandal-ridden Scorpene submarine deal, this "protection" may soon break from overuse.

For Najib, getting rid of that monthly assembly ritual would be easy, but overcoming all those other deficiencies of his leadership would be far more challenging. Meanwhile we just have to endure his monthly and other spectacles, at least until he *kena kantoi*

July 18, 2009

A Whiff of His Father's Leadership

In announcing the repeal of the Internal Security Act and other repressive laws, Prime Minister Najib secures for himself an enshrined spot in Malaysian history.

Of the many thoughtful comments on Najib's historic announcement, the one that struck at the heart of the issue was that by former Mufti of Perlis, Dr. Asri Zainul Abidin. He declared, "The ISA is an un-Islamic law. It infringes [upon] individual rights and can be easily misused by leaders, so repealing it was a very Islamic move." Amen!

"Najib's announcement," Asri continued, "is more valuable than any bonus payment or salary increase because repealing the ISA means the restoration of human rights ... which is more valuable than money." That is putting things in their proper perspective.

I disagree however, with the Mufti's characterization of Najib's move as a "gift" to the people. When someone robs you of something and then returns it, that is no gift, merely restoring what is rightly yours. The ISA and other restrictive laws robbed us of our precious possession, our freedom. That is Allah's gift to us, as enshrined in the Koran. It is not for mere mortals, no matter how exalted their earthly positions, to tamper.

Nonetheless I do hear the Mufti. Good Muslims ought to be grateful for their blessings, however small. I want to be a good Muslim, and Najib's announcement is a huge blessing, so I am very grateful. *Alham dulillah!* Praise be to Allah!

Missing The Islamic Visuals

Najib and his policymakers must have deliberated for some time to arrive at that decision. Perhaps it was not a coincidence that only a week earlier Najib's younger brother, Nizar Razak, head of a Government-linked bank, intimated the need for Malaysia to change lest it risks a Middle East-type upheaval. Significantly, he made that remark at the Malaysia-China Trade Investment Conference, but more on China shortly.

Pursuing the religious theme, I was surprised that Najib and his advisors did not choose an occasion with some Islamic symbolism to make his momentous announcement.

Not that there was anything wrong with choosing Malaysia Day. However, we just completed Ramadan only a fortnight ago. Surely Najib had decided then. Imagine if he had announced it on Hari Raya, which also coincided (more or less) with Merdeka Day. What better way to demonstrate and acknowledge the special blessings of Ramadan and live its spirit, as well as fulfill the aspirations of merdeka—freedom! Ramadan is after all about remembrance and return—remembrance on the origin of Islam and return to its essence, in Eboo Patel's phrase.

When Islam was revealed, it emancipated the Arabs from their Age of *Jahiliyiah* (Ignorance); likewise, getting rid of the ISA would emancipate Malaysians, lifting us from our Age of Fear. As for the essence of Islam, our faith commands us to do good and forbid evil. Getting rid of ISA is getting rid of evil; it cannot be more Islamic than that!

Imagine the powerful symbolic impact globally had Najib made the announcement at the end of Ramadan, coming as it was only a few days before the tenth anniversary of the horrible 9-11, and with it the inevitable hysteria of Islamophobia. Imagine also the good that would do to the cause as well as image of Islam, one Muslim country bravely discarding its antiquated repressive laws, and doing so not in response to mass demonstrations or civil disobediences but as a normal turn of events. The contrast with America's renewal of its Patriot Act and the indefinite continuance of its Guantanamo detention camp could not be starker.

Speaking of image, had I been the administration's public relations consultant I would have arranged with the announcement a simultaneous release of some ISA prisoners. I would have alerted the news media so they could station their journalists and cameras at the gate of Kamunting prison.

Imagine the stunning and symbolic visuals! While Najib was making his historic announcement, the prisoners would emerge one by one into the arms of their eagerly-awaiting loved ones. If there were to be a mosque nearby, I would superimpose the call of Azzan to the visuals.

I would also have the producer use a split screen; on one side would be the Prime Minister making his solemn announcement; on the other, the prisoners with their families joyously celebrating their freedom, with the *takbir* (affirmation to the greatness of Allah) superimposed as the background soundtrack. I cannot imagine a more powerful symbolism. Those tapes would also be great campaign materials!

The Najib Administration forks out tons of money to foreign consultants in an effort to spruce up its image. Alas those "documentaries" that supposedly portrayed Malaysia in good light, as well as the many "interviews" Najib landed on the international media, all turned out to be unmitigated fiascos. Those "journalists" and "interviewers" were nothing more than hired hacks, and their "documentaries" unadulterated "infomercials."

Yet when a rare and splendid opportunity arose as with the recent release of the ISA prisoners, those highly-paid public relations pros missed it! That was not a surprise. After all they are all foreigners and non-Muslims to boot; they could not possibly pick up on the Islamic nuances I alluded to earlier. However, their fumbling on the international stage where they are supposedly the experts cannot be readily excused. There is no justification for their lack of professionalism, if not downright unethical behaviors there.

As can be seen, a good policy is the best PR. Notice the favorable comments locally as well as in respected foreign media to Najib's latest initiative, and it did not cost the government a ringgit to get them! Focus on crafting enlightened policies, and the favorable publicity would ensue. Even if you do not get any, a good policy is a reward in itself. Your people will be grateful for it.

A Whiff Of His Father

In committing to repeal the ISA, Najib did something no other prime ministers before him had dared even to contemplate. And he had some mighty impressive predecessors. In so doing, Najib also demonstrated a whiff of his late father's great leadership qualities.

The late Tun Razak did not hesitate to suspend parliament following the May 1969 race riots. Despite the howling protests at home and abroad, Razak was undeterred for he had a crucial job to do; restore peace and stability to a nation shocked by the horrors of that tragedy. And may Allah bless his soul, he accomplished his mission in short order.

To those who would belittle that achievement, let me remind them that the 1969 riot coincided with the flare-ups of sectarian violence in Northern Ireland. While Malaysians have been enjoying peace for the past four decades, those folks in Northern Ireland are still busy settling their deadly scores.

To this day Tun Razak remains unique in being the only leader in the world who seized power during a national emergency to pursue a much-needed critical goal, and then willingly gave that up once he completed his mission. No other leader could claim that. On the contrary, history is filled with leaders who had to be pushed or dragged out, or worse. Libya's Gaddafi and Syria's Assad are only the latest examples.

I am not concerned with how Najib arrived at his decision; I am focused only on the decision. There is no shortage of skeptics out there, and they are not without their reasons. After all, Najib's flip-flopping rivals that of his immediate predecessor.

Even if those skeptics were to be proven right later, there would be no turning back. Najib has clearly declared his *niat* (intention) to repeal the ISA. In Islam, *niat* is what counts. We declare our *niat* before we pray, fast, give *zakat*, or undertake the Hajj. If Najib fails to live up to his *niat*, then he has to answer not only to his Maker on the Day of Judgment but also more practically, to his political makers–the voters–right here on earth and now, as in the next election.

Najib's Nixon-in-China Moment

Najib's declaration last Wednesday reminded me of Nixon's pioneering 1972 trip to China. It took another seven years before America would send its first Ambassador to Beijing. Today, over 30 years later, we wondered why on earth it took America so long to recognize the obvious reality of this most populous nation. Regardless, America, China, and the world are now better for that initiative.

Nixon basked on the glory of his China trip and went on to win a landslide for his second term. Alas that triumph proved short-lived, for he was soon forced out of his presidency in shame on matters unrelated to his China move. Nonetheless his trailblazing China moment retained its luster in an otherwise blemished legacy.

If Najib's Malaysia Day *niat* proves to be just that and nothing more, well, like Nixon, at least he will have that as his legacy, and only that. However, if it proves to be *ikhlas* (sincere) and only his first step, with many more courageous moves ahead, then greatness awaits him; likewise for Malaysia.

September 18, 2011

What Will People Say?

When the late Tun Razak moved his family to Sri Taman, the Prime Minister's official residence at that time, his children pleaded with him to have a swimming pool installed. The Tun, acutely aware of the costs to the public, would have none of it. "What will people say?" he told his children.

Not that the Tun did not want to indulge his children or that he was being unduly stingy, rather he was conscious of the need to differentiate the personal from the official. Unlike many especially from the Third World, then as well as now, Tun Razak was the rare leader who did not consider the public purse to be his. Even when there were grey areas, as with the swimming pool, he would err on the side of not burdening the public with the cost.

It could be argued that since Sri Taman was government property, expenditures on improving it, as with building the pool, should be borne by the public. However, as the pool would benefit essentially only the prime minister's family and invited guests, he acted with an abundance of prudence and probity in refusing to have the pool installed.

There was another less obvious but more important reason for his not acceding to his children's wishes. Malaysia of the early 1970s was devoid of gleaming skyscrapers and towering condominiums. There were no modern suburbs with luxurious mansions sporting swimming pools in their backyards. Most Malays were still stuck in their kampongs, leading subsistence living and sleeping under a thatch roof. Tun Razak was sensitive to that social environment; he after all had served as Minister for Rural Development. To kampong folks, a backyard pool would have been opulence on an especially grand scale. This more than the cost was probably what prompted the late Tun not to have the pool.

"What will people say?" As Muslims we are reminded to have *taqwa* at all times, an awareness of the presence of Allah. He is "closer to you than your jugular vein," as the Koran puts it. If you have *taqwa*, being aware of Allah's presence all the time, that does tend to restrain you.

"What will people say?" could be viewed as a secular *taqwa*, an internal compass to keep us along the straight path, away from temptations and ill deeds. For a leader, that would be a path that would meet the approval if not praise from his followers. That expression reflects the power of the people or just peer pressure, the universal human need for social approval. Yes, leaders need this too.

There is a cautionary note however, especially for leaders. Pay too much attention to what people say and you reduce your leadership to a wet-finger-in-the-air mode. That is not a recipe for success, much less greatness. For others, as well as leaders, you risk being reduced to a pathetic fool, as per the fable of the old man, the boy, and the donkey. The donkey ended up being carried by the two.

Leaders who pay too much heed to what their followers say also risk pandering to their lowest common denominator, appealing to their baser and uglier instincts. That is the leadership of the Perkasa types [acronym for an extremist Malay nationalist group], obsessed with "them" taking over "our" *Tanah Melayu* (Malay Land), and of chauvinistic leaders forever paranoid over losing their culture and language. In America this is demonstrated by the ugly spectacles of the current candidates in the Republican Party primaries pandering to the extreme right wing nuts.

Backyard Pool, Luxury Condos, Half-Million Ringgit Engagement Party

Malaysian leaders today are a far cry from the caliber, competence, and integrity so publicly and unambiguously displayed by the late Tun Razak. Malaysians are being painfully reminded daily of these deficiencies, including and especially with his son, Najib Razak, the current Prime Minister.

It did not escape citizens' notice that when Tun Razak died, his estate, while not exactly destitute, was definitely not brimming with assets. The same could be said of his predecessor, Tunku Abdul Rahman, and successor, Hussein Onn. Today, our ex-Prime Ministers live in mega mansions and travel the world in private luxury jets. I do not know who foot their bills. At least American ex-presidents make a show of earning their wealth through their exorbitant speaking fees.

This brings me to Opposition MP Rafizi Ramli's latest revelation: Najib's recent half-a-million ringgit engagement party for his daughter allegedly paid for by the Prime Minister's Office, meaning the public. Rafizi had earlier brought us the National Feedlot Corporation's (NFC) "cow-gate" scandal.

Thus far Najib had issued only a general denial to Rafizi's serious allegation. Significantly, Najib did it not through a formal press conference but through his Twitter site. He has yet to address the specifics. Perhaps Najib is waiting to consult his high-priced public relations consultants on how best to spin this latest scandal.

Najib has to level with the people. A general denial would not do it; it insults the public's intelligence. As Rafizi has clearly stated, Najib has to address the eight points raised by the allegation. Even if the lavish engagement party were to be paid for personally, I shudder to think what the actual wedding would cost. Malaysia's self-styled "first couple" is competing with the Saudi royals with respect to gaudy extravagance and obscene opulence. The audacity and hypocrisy for Najib to then lecture the *rakyat* (citizens) on the need to save and be financially prudent!

As Rafizi rightly asserted, Najib has to show incontrovertible proof (as with copies of cancelled checks) that the funds did come out of his personal accounts. That alone would not be enough; he would have to explain how he accumulated such wealth to be able to afford such extravagance. As alluded to earlier, he certainly did not inherit much from his father, and Najib has been a government (or government-related, as during his tenure with Petronas) "salary man" all his life.

As for Rosmah, her father, like mine, was a Malay school teacher. And I knew exactly what my father's wealth was when he died, and he was a man not given to extravagance. Rosmah has to show that she had been a particularly successful entrepreneur to acquire such wealth. Anything less and the *rakyat* would have a right to assume that those riches had been illicitly acquired.

The sad part is that this obscene extravagance is but the latest show of unbridled rapacious greed in our leaders. Consider that dentist and former Selangor's Chief Minister Khir Toyo with his million-dollar mansion that he bragged to have paid for at half price through his "shrewd" bargaining. Then there was the sleepy head, Najib's immediate predecessor, with his equally opulent mansion in Perth, Australia, and another one given to him locally.

Diligent citizens like Rafizi Ramli could not have exposed these shenanigans without the help of honest fellow citizens, especially those on the "inside." The rash of such recent exposés signals a significant development. Malaysians are now no longer afraid of their leader or the state. When that happens, many wonderful things follow. Look at Egypt, Libya and Tunisia.

With such sordid examples at the very top, no wonder lowly ministers and others too are in on the act. At least Women's Minister Shahrizat had the decency to resign her cabinet post even though as she said, "I really have nothing to do with NFC except that I'm married to the chairman of NFC. But as a responsible member of the government, I feel the right thing for me to do is to step down." Yes, she did the right and honorable thing in resigning.

Will Najib do the same? As for the engagement party, it certainly cost much more than the proposed pool at Sri Taman. We will know what people say come the next election. More important however, is what would Tun Razak say if he were alive today? The unevenness of the tiles at Tun Razak's mausoleum at the National Mosque was probably the result of his rolling over in his grave.

March 11, 2012

Najib Razak as Property Developer and Investment Banker

With great fanfare, Prime Minister Najib recently announced a mega property development, The Tun Razak Exchange (TRX). The project would symbolize the nation's aspiration to be "the leading global centre for international finance, trade and services," to quote him.

Najib wants that to be his legacy. Even if successful (a very big if), it would simply be a physical monument, in the same manner that Petronas Towers is to his predecessor, Mahathir. The only thing Malaysian or Malay about that much-hyped edifice is the land on which it is sited. Everything else—from the design and soil studies to the engineering and construction—was done by foreigners. The only act done by a Malaysian (or Malay) was the ribbon cutting at the glittering opening ceremony.

The legacy of Tun Razak the father is his imaginative rural development schemes, like the massive FELDA program that benefited millions of poor landless rural dwellers. The beneficiaries with FELDA, let it be explicitly stated in case this fact is missed, are mostly if not exclusively Malays.

For Najib the son however, if TRX were to be successful, it would benefit leading global companies with their highly-skilled and generously-paid "knowledge workers" who most likely would be expatriates, or if Malaysians, only those highly educated and proficient in the language of international finance—English. Again, let it be said in case this fact too is missed, they will be mostly non-Malays.

What an irony for a former UMNO Youth leader who once threatened to "bathe the *keris* with Chinese blood!" Quite a transformation!

Veering off the race angle, it would take more than grandiose skyscrapers to be a leading financial center and attract global companies. I would have much greater confidence in TRX's success if the government were to simultaneously announce a comparable mega program to upgrade our universities (especially their economics and statistics departments as well as our business schools) so the nation would have the necessary brains to go with the brawns. Thus far only one of the nation's business schools (Universiti Pertanian Malaysia) has international accreditation.

This mega billion TRX, as with the recent Initial Public Offering of the massive FELDA Global Ventures (FGV), is orchestrated by the Prime Minister's Department. Najib Razak is now more property developer and investment banker when he should be the leader of all Malaysians and the nation's chief executive. There is no shortage of critical problems facing Malaysia. If he needs any reminding, there are our crippling corruption, rotten education system, and our deeply polarized citizenry. There are others.

Property development and investment banking are highly lucrative pursuits; I have no problem with either. If Najib wishes to pursue both or either, he should join his other brothers in the private sector and quit being Prime Minister. The awesome responsibilities of that high office are very different and much broader, not least of which is to help those who need it most, like those poor landless villagers, not global corporations or the highly educated. They can take care of themselves, thank you very much.

The Cart Before The Horse

On launching TRX Najib declared, "The Government will go out of its way to ensure that the exchange is a success and, as a first step, I can announce to you today that we will begin a comprehensive review of business regulation."

"Our logic behind this review is simple," he continued, "anything that contributes to future progress stays, anything that is outdated goes." Well and good! I wish he had done that first. That would also be less expensive. Businesses and investors are less attracted by fancy buildings, high rents, and generous incentives, more with ease of starting a venture, availability of talents, and most of all the prospects of healthy profits. Have them and businesses as well as investors from all over the world will pour in. *They* will then build their own mega headquarters.

The grueling work of modernizing the nation's business regulations and enhancing the investment climate, or modernizing our schools and universities to produce the necessary skilled personnel, is not as sexy or attracts media attention as much as unveiling glossy models of skyscrapers. In the long run however, the former would prove more effective and enduring.

Singapore did not become a major financial center because of its gleaming skyscrapers. Those were the *result* of the republic becoming a successful financial center.

I would have much greater confidence of TRX's success had Najib also announced securing a major anchor tenant or two (other than a GLC of course), even if only a letter of intent with oodles of wiggle clauses.

My worst fear is this. TRX may well prove successful, with all the major financial houses having their regional or even global headquarters there. However, the only Malays you would see at the upper and middle echelon would the "non-executive" chairmen, directors of "government liaisons," and public relations. There will be other Malays of course, as security guards. The highly-paid "knowledge workers" would be mostly non-Malays and non-Malaysians, thanks to our rotten national schools and public universities. Even the janitorial jobs would be taken by the Benglas! In short, not much of an improvement over the Petronas Towers project. That would be Najib's legacy as property developer.

Then consider Najib's other "achievements" as investment banker. His latest IPO, FGV, is by all measures wildly successful. It was the largest offering globally (in terms of valuation) after Facebook, and FGV's stocks soared after its initial offering!

For a dose of reality however, visit the typical FELDA plantation and settlement. The standard of living and lifestyle of those settlers have not improved since the days of Tun Razak. The roads on their settlements are still unpaved and homes still lack electricity and potable water. The palm nuts, the ultimate source of FGV riches, are still harvested in the same manual and inefficient and labor-intensive methods as they were half a century ago, with the nuts carried over the workers' shoulders. There are no trucks with hydraulic lifts to help the workers harvest the nuts, and no conveyor belts to load those nuts onto the trucks.

Equity markets and stock exchanges are alien to these settlers. Their more immediate problem is to feed and clothe their families. To them, TRX would prove to be nothing more than those expensive boondoggle tricks that Najib continues to perpetrate on his people, especially Malays. Yet we continue to be mesmerized by and pin our hopes on him and his grandiose projects. When will Malaysians, in particular Malays, wake up?

August 5, 2012

Longing For Enlightened Leaders

Before Malaysians grant Prime Minister Najib's request for a mandate in the upcoming election [May 5, 2013], his first as a leader, we should examine his performance during the past four years. It has been mediocre, satiated with slogans and drifting amidst an abundance of acronyms. If Malaysians are satisfied with KPI and PEMANDU, or One Malaysia This and Two Malaysia That, then expect more of the same, this time with ever incredulous inanity and flatulent fatuousness.

Najib has not demonstrated any ability or inclination to clean up his administrative house. An early indication of his second-term performance is this: Thus far no cabinet minister has voluntarily withdrawn from being an electoral candidate. As Najib will not drop them if they win, they will end up in his cabinet again. Nothing would have changed. A wisecrack definition of insanity is doing the same thing over and over and expecting a different result. That is true only if you let the same cast of incompetent characters carry out the task after they have clearly and repeatedly demonstrated their inability to do so. Pick others more competent and diligent, and the result may well surprise you, and it would be far from insanity.

The best and most helpful advice a science teacher could give a student who repeatedly fails to perform an experiment is to suggest that he pursues music instead, where "practice, practice, practice!" (doing the same thing over and over) may take him to Carnegie Hall. Likewise, the kindest gesture to Najib after he has clearly demonstrated his inability to lead would be for Malaysians to force him into another line of work, by not voting him and his party in.

After over half of century in power, what has UMNO, a party that claims to champion Malays, achieved? Malays today are even more morally corrupt, deeply polarized, and economically disadvantaged than ever before. Those are not my observations. I am merely summarizing what Mahathir, a man who led the country and UMNO for over two decades, said.

Take any social indicator–rate of incarceration, drug abuse, or families headed by single mothers–and the Malay community is over represented in all categories. Our educational and economic achievements are nothing to be proud of; in fact they are an embarrassment.

We confuse the glint of a pebble to be the glitter of a gemstone. UMNO Supreme Council members parade their 'doctorates' from degree mills as genuine intellectual achievements. The sorry part is that their colleagues believe them! Spouses and families of ministers brag that their luxurious condominiums are the fruits of their entrepreneurial flair where others see those as reflecting the corruption and cronyism of the system.

Current UMNO leaders are like that inept science student; it is time to force them to pursue other lines of work, anything other than leading us. Voters must be like the strict teacher; flunk the student who repeatedly fails to perform his assigned task. Letting him continue would not do that individual any service; it would only be detrimental to the rest of the class. Voters must flunk these corrupt and incompetent UMNO leaders by voting them out.

Not A Lost Cause

This does not mean that UMNO is a lost cause; nothing is. Even the most unseaworthy sloop could through imaginative and skilful craftsmanship (plus hard work) be brought up to Bristol condition. The operative phrase or caveat there is "imaginative and skilful craftsmanship." Is Najib imaginative and skilful?

I never underestimate the ability of an individual to learn or change. The diminutive, uninspiring and uncharismatic Deng Xiaoping was well in his 70s when he assumed power. He then took his giant nation in a radically different and far better direction.

Unlike Deng, Najib is far from being diminutive physically, but he exceeds Deng in being uninspiring and uncharismatic. Again unlike Deng whose path to power was littered with the carcasses of personal and political tragedies (his son was paralyzed by Red Guard goons and Deng was once paraded in a dunce cap on the streets of Beijing), Najib's ascend to the top was well paved–by others.

Deng was tempered by life's bitter lessons; Najib is the beneficiary of its many blessings. If Najib considers that a handicap and an excuse for his underperformance, then he should look up to another transformative leader of modern times, Franklin D. Roosevelt, for inspiration. Roosevelt, whose name means a field of roses in Dutch, was born into privilege. He uplifted the lives of the poor through his many New Deal initiatives. His progressive redistributionist policies earned him the sobriquet, "traitor to his class."

Najib's name is equally rosy; it means wise, intelligent, or high birth in Arabic. Like Roosevelt, Najib was also born into privilege though not on the same scale as FDR. Corruption and cronyism were not yet the norms when Najib's father Tun Razak was Prime Minister.

Like Deng, Najib too spent his formative years as a young man abroad, in Britain, to Deng's Europe. When Deng left, his father asked him what he hoped to learn. Deng replied, "To learn knowledge and the truth from the West in order to save China."

I do not know what conversation Najib had with his father before going abroad to school, but one thing I do know. Tun Razak sent *all* his children abroad to escape the very Malaysian system of education he was championing! Hypocrisy is a good word to describe such a stance. That is one trait Najib inherits from his father.

I risk flattering Najib by mentioning him in the same sentence with Deng and FDR. My doing so merely reflects a longing on my part for a leader who could inspire Malaysians to the degree Deng did to the Chinese and FDR to Americans.

Najib could initiate change now to give us a hint that he is indeed capable of being a "transformative leader" as he so frequently bragged, and not be content with merely mouthing slogans. He could announce his "shadow" cabinet now should Barisan be returned to power. Better yet, revamp his cabinet and pick his new team to go into the election so citizens could have a reason to vote *for* Barisan and not merely *against* the opposition.

Malaysians do not expect miracles or demand a super team, merely capable and honest ministers. It is not a tall order. Begin by getting rid of those stale politicians in his cabinet. If they haven't yet made their mark, they are unlikely to do so in the next few years.

Characters like Nazri, Rais and Hishammuddin are like durians that have remained unsold for far too long. They are *tak laku* (no longer salable); they are not even good for making *tompoyak* (durian paste). All they do is stink the place up and lower the value of what few remaining good durians Najib has. Nor are his junior ministers, the next tier of leaders, any better, as exemplified by the recent idiotic utterances of one Dr. Mashitah. She is supposedly better educated, sporting a doctorate of some sort.

There are others including Najib's deputy, Muhyiddin, and he has as much claim and legitimacy to the top post as Najib. It would make sense for the two to join forces and together pick the new dream team.

While Najib is at it, he should also pick a new Attorney General and Anti-Corruption Commission chief. If Najib were to name individuals with impeccable credentials and professionalism to those two offices, then those old *tak laku* durians he dropped from his cabinet would not dare create political trouble for him.

Najib's address to the UMNO General Assembly later this month will reveal whether he is content with another session of sloganeering or serious about transforming his party and country. The greater significance is this: by indulging in the former and naming the same old nincompoops to his cabinet and top positions, Najib soils the reputation of our community. It gives the impression that the Nazris, Raises, Mashitahs and Hishammuddins represent the best that Malays are capable of producing, and that we are bereft of talent. The shame reflects on all of us.

November 18, 2012

Najib's Farcical Presidential Speech

That Prime Minister Najib Razak is oratorically-challenged is obvious, and a severe understatement. The pathetic part is that Najib is determined to delude himself that he is otherwise. His presidential speech at the recently-concluded UMNO General Assembly was only the latest example.

He confuses ponderousness with deliberateness, equates yelling as emphasizing, and thinks that furrowing his forehead as being in profound thought. In the hands of a gifted actor, those could be great comedic acts. Alas, Najib is also far from being that either.

I learned early in my high school at Kuala Pilah that if you do not know what to do with your hands when delivering a speech, keep them in your pockets or behind your back. Do not gesticulate wildly like a traffic cop at a busy intersection as that would only distract the audience. Worse, you risked looking like a monkey on speed. Najib apparently did not learn that at his expensive British boarding school.

As an aside, from the personal hygiene perspective I hoped they sanitized the microphone thoroughly after he spoke. There was an awful amount of spit splattered on it during his delivery.

Najib should take comfort in the fact that there are many effective leaders who are neither charismatic nor great orators. Germany's Angela Merkel readily comes to mind. Najib should also be reminded that the converse is even truer. Leaders with great oratorical gifts and generously endowed charisma-wise can be among the most corrupt and inept. Sukarno mesmerized Indonesians with his mercurial personality and spellbound speeches, but that country remained a basket case economically and in many other ways during his presidency.

Had Najib delivered his address in his usual persona, without the put-on gravitas or pretensions of grandeur, he could have finished his nearly hour-long speech in half the time. Then he and his audience would not have missed their Maghrib prayers. Besides, there was nothing in Najib's speech that was so urgent or important to justify that. As self-professed champions and defenders of Islam, Najib and his fellow UMNO members do not need to be reminded of the importance of prayer. He and his fellow UMNO politicians might need it for the coming election!

Or perhaps those UMNO folks believed in the canard that their party is God's choice, and thus they were dispensed from having to pray.

With all the daunting challenges facing Malays, Najib could come up with only two piddling policy prescriptions. One was to increase Amanah Ikhtiar Malaysia's (AIM) loan amount to RM100K from RM50K; and two, reviewing the country's bankruptcy laws. This from the leader of a party that purports to champion the Malay cause!

In announcing the loan increase, Najib looked approvingly to Wanita (Women Wing) members, and they in turn responded in kind. Meaning, they were the intended beneficiaries. I have no problem giving those ladies who are hairdressers or trained pre-school teachers loans so they could start their own beauty salons or kindergartens, but simply by virtue of their being Wanita members would be folly. If all you have is some vague idea of starting a basket weaving enterprise, you do not need such outlandish loans.

AIM is Malaysia's government-sponsored version of "micro-credit." Muhammad Yunus, its pioneer, would be flabbergasted to know that a loan of RM100K is considered "micro." This is yet another example of Najib adopting an otherwise brilliant idea from elsewhere and then screwing it up in the implementation. AIM's generous program has degenerated into yet another massive and lucrative UMNO patronage machinery.

As for reviewing the bankruptcy laws, I would have been more reassured had Najib made it part of an overall scheme to encourage economic entrepreneurialism and business risk-taking especially among Malays. Alas, none of that! It was prompted simply to rescue the many UMNO leaders who are bankrupt purportedly from guaranteeing loans of their members in return for their political support. With the proposed changes, those local leaders would be spared from bankruptcy, and then they could be their party's next "winnable" candidates! Having not learned their lesson from their failed ventures, they would then mortgage the country's future.

What is obvious here is that Najib and the entire UMNO leadership are bereft of ideas. They are intellectually bankrupt. The brilliant political cartoonist Zunar captures well this degeneration of UMNO leaders with his latest cartoon, "Evolusi UMNO." The only remedy for the intellectual bankruptcy of our current leaders is to have an entirely new leadership.

Fully aware what Mahathir did to Abdullah Badawi, Najib heaped profuse praise on the still powerful Mahathir. It was "sucking up" performance par excellence! Najib singled out Mahathir's commitment of loyalty to leaders, which he (Mahathir) apparently forgot when Abdullah Badawi was in charge.

According to Najib, Mahathir had impressed upon UMNO members the importance of loyalty to leaders, presumably in contrast to fidelity to principle or organization. Najib readily or more accurately, desperately hung on to Mahathir's exhortation! These UMNO leaders are nothing but opportunistic characters, modern-day Hang Tuahs.

In his speech Najib was like a little kid desperate for approval and praise from grown-ups. Apart from gushingly citing Mahathir's approbation, Najib reminded his audience of IMF's Christine Legard's praise for Malaysia's "gravity-defying" economic performance. Najib needs be reminded that the IMF, World Bank, and other "respected" international bodies were running out of superlatives to describe the country's economic stewardship right up to the eve of the 1997 Asian economic contagion!

When he was not consumed with "sucking up" and seeking approval, Najib was obsessed with demonizing opposition leader Anwar Ibrahim. Najib feigned disgust at Anwar's alleged sodomy crime, for which he was jailed but subsequently acquitted on appeal.

Najib and others of his ilk conveniently forgot that whatever crime Anwar may have allegedly committed, no one was murdered. Yes, Anwar sustained a black eye, literally, but UMNO suffered worse metaphorically. Najib is forever linked with the gruesome murder of that beautiful young Mongolian lady, Altantuya. She and her unborn child were literally blown to pieces. Her savage killers were part of Najib's official bodyguard unit and the explosives used were available only through his Defense Ministry.

At that UMNO Assembly speech Najib smugly let on that he had other "secrets" on Anwar which he (Najib) would unhesitatingly reveal at the opportune time. Left unsaid are the many secrets involving Najib now swirling in cyberspace, apart from that model's death, that he has yet to answer.

It was hard to pick which part of Najib's speech was the most obscene or offensive as there were many vying for the top spot. His closing remarks must clearly rank high up there.

It is an accepted tradition in Islam that once you have uttered vile words or committed evil deeds, your *wuduk* (ablution) would be nullified. You would then have to re-cleanse yourself (take another *wuduk*) before reciting any *dua* (supplication) or verse from the Koran. The reason is clear and obvious: You cannot invoke Allah's name when your heart is filled with bile and hate. It makes a mockery of your good *niat* (intention).

In vilifying the opposition and uttering those ugly words, Najib had committed evil deeds. I could also add that he had demeaned himself, but then he could not get any lower.

Earlier, UMNO folks were appalled when PAS members led by their leader Nik Aziz had a special prayer calling for UMNO's downfall. Like many, I too was utterly repulsed by that vulgar gesture.

Yet there he was, Najib frothing at the mouth vilifying the opposition and attributing the most evil of motives to them, and then in an instant put on his cloak of piety to lead his followers in a recitation of *dua* calling for Allah's blessings! They in turn responded in kind with their collective exuberant "Amen!" and "Allahu Akhbar!" (God is great!) Only UMNO's *carma* (contraction for *cari makan*–lit. seeking food; fig. opportunistic) ulama would approve of that.

December 9, 2012

Najib's Leadership Deficiencies Undermine Malaysia's Future

Najib's glaring leadership deficiencies have now been exposed. Malaysia deserves better. His performance has not been up to par even when compared to his lackluster predecessor. If under Abdullah Badawi Malaysia had the modernity of Manhattan but the mentality of Mogadishu, under Najib, Malaysia risks degenerating, period.

Najib is not terribly bright or introspective. Like a little child, he always hungers for approval. He is also severely "charimastically-challenged." A leader could survive or even thrive despite having one or two of these flaws, but to be cursed with all three is fatal.

Najib has depended entirely on government paychecks throughout his career. No surprise then that his worldview is narrowly circumscribed. His solution to every problem is to distribute government checks, as exemplified by his many 1Malaysia handouts. His Majlis Ekonomi Bumiputra (Bumiputra Economic Council), was no exception; likewise its hefty price tag.

Not being introspective, Najib does not and never will recognize his shortcomings. Consequently unlike his immediate predecessor, Najib will never resign voluntarily; he would rather destroy his party and country first. If UMNO does not recognize this, then it too will go down with him; likewise the country.

A good leader, to paraphrase a hadith, is one who protects his followers from his hands and tongue. Najib does neither. Functionally, Najib slips his hands into the pockets of Malaysians as when he raises the price of petrol. He wants to do it again with his Goods and Services Tax

(GST). Meanwhile his smooth tongue bribes all with his ever-generous 1Malaysia gifts, using the rakyat's money of course.

While being smart is an obvious asset in a leader, not being one would not necessarily be a handicap. Reagan, one of the most successful American presidents of recent times, was far from being brainy. He however, knew his limitations and duly compensated for that; his cabinet was full of intellectual heavyweights and individuals of proven achievements. Incidentally my comparing him to Reagan, no matter how unfavorably, only feeds Najib's delusion of grandeur.

Najib thinks he is super smart; he frequently parrots the latest buzz words. It is not just any increase but a quantum leap; not just any strategy but a blue ocean one. Meanwhile the ship of state under his command is headed straight to the bottom. He does not appreciate his fundamental problem. You cannot scour the blue ocean on a leaky sampan with a crew familiar only with the *rakit* (bamboo raft), and hope to survive.

The embarrassing caliber of Najib's cabinet and advisors reflects his blissful ignorance of his deficiencies. He had over four years to scout for fresh talent, only to end up with the same mediocre core ministers he inherited from his equally dull predecessor. I cringe whenever I hear any pronouncements from his many "half-past six" (just beyond elementary school) ministers.

Even on the rare occasion when Najib picked a bright star like Idris Jala, the former chief executive of Shell, the sparkle is gone. It is hard to soar like an eagle when you are surrounded by turkeys. Idris is reduced to and consumed with his elegant Powerpoint presentations to any willing audience.

Tasked with "transforming" the government (note the bombastic buzz word!), Idris Jala either severely underestimated the enormity of the task or generously overestimated his talent in executing it. He forgot the evident reality that the government of Malaysia is not Shell with respect to size, scope of activities, availability of talent, or any other matrix. The bureaucratic inertia of the civil service pales the physical one of a loaded supertanker.

If Idris had appreciated the enormity of the challenge, or had a wee bit of humility, he would have focused on only one or two areas, and learned from the experience. Once successful, he would have minimal difficulty selling his ideas and initiatives. If Najib had been introspective, he would have assigned Idris a specific portfolio and then let him do his own "transforming." Idris would then be able to *show* instead of just merely *tell* us of his managerial capabilities.

Like a skillful carpenter, a good leader knows when and where to deploy his finest tools. Implicit in that observation is that a good leader must first recognize which tools are sharp and which ones are dull to be discarded. It is precisely this critical insight that Najib is severely lacking.

Najib second weakness, his hunger for approval, is equally crippling. He tried to ingratiate himself to extremist Malay nationalists by brandishing his *kris* (Malay ceremonial dagger) dipped in tomato sauce, but to no avail. During the last election he had his son utter a few words of Mandarin and gave generous on-the-spot grants to Chinese schools. Likewise, he visited Rome for an audience with the Pope. At home he garlanded himself in that outlandish floral arrangement while visiting Batu

Caves to ingratiate himself to Hindu voters. They however, readily saw through those silly overtures.

Like a spoiled brat who had grown accustomed to being indulged upon, Najib could not accept the harsh rebuke that was the last election. He reacted like the over-pampered kampong kid by sulking; hence his shameful silence during the many recent crises.

Lacking self-awareness, Najib has pretensions of great charisma. If contrast is the essence of art, then his on-stage performance with the South Korean Gangnam Group, Psy, during the last election campaign was truly, well, artistic. If that were his only gig, that would be harmless, though mildly funny even if it was at his expense.

A charismatic leader could at least attract talent to his cause despite lacking competence or not being generously-endowed intellectually. Najib does not attract the best. He confuses endless slogans for substantive efforts, frenetic activities as decisive actions, and sulking withdrawal as deep contemplation.

Take his endless sloganeering. First there was *glokal* Malay (contraction for global and *lokal*, Malay bastardization for local). Lacking traction, he shifted to "1Malaysia." Streams of slogans later, it is now "Endless Possibilities!" What's next? Najib is like the leader caricatured by Shahnon Ahmad's lead character in his novella, *Unggappan*.

The nation's current sorry trajectory cannot be altered without dispensing with the present leadership. The excuse that there is no one else capable may be solace to Najib but an insult to all Malaysians. Allah would not be so unkind and unjust as to deprive us of our share of leadership talent.

For Malaysia to get its rightful due, her citizens must first stop indulging the present incompetent leaders, beginning with Najib. Only then could Malaysians begin the diligent search for better leaders. Malaysia deserves better than to be saddled with Najib Razak.

September 22, 2013

Making Corruption History – *Cakap Kosong Je* 'Jib!

In San Francisco recently [September 2013], Prime Minister Najib confidently declared "to make corruption part of Malaysia's past, not its future." The man's delusion never ceases to amaze me. The reality is of course far different; corruption defines the Najib Administration.

If Najib is serious, he should begin by heeding Tengku Razaleigh's call for Najib to declare his assets, to set the example and to prove that his wealth is not ill-gotten. Otherwise it would be, to put it bluntly in the vernacular, "*Cakap kosong je* 'Jib!" (Empty talk only, Najib!)

Tengku Razaleigh's suggestion, if implemented, would do far more good than all of Najib's lofty declarations of "changing organizational as well as business cultures," or creating "a new governance and integrity minister," and "elevating the anti-corruption agency." Malaysians have heard all those *ad nauseum*, not only from Najib but also his predecessors.

If after doing what Tengku Razaleigh had suggested, Najib still aspires higher, then he could begin by getting rid of those tainted individuals in his administration. Beyond that if he is really committed to clean and effective governance, he should select only those with unquestioned integrity and solid accomplishments to be his new ministers and advisors. As Najib is slow to grasp concepts, let me elaborate on my three simple suggestions.

Consider asset declaration. Najib does not need yet another highly-paid consultant advising him how to do it. There are plenty of effective models out there, including one recommended by the OECD. The simplest is the one used by American officials including the president, cabinet secretaries, and Supreme Court judges. It covers their spouses and all dependent children.

Here is President Obama's, available publicly at: docstoc.com/docs/156786412/Obama-Financial-Disclosure. The simple eight-page report lists his assets and income, transactions during the year, gifts received (he had none), liabilities (his home mortgage), and contracts he is a party to (his old academic appointment). Simple yet effective! As the declaration is filed annually, citizens could tract any sudden ballooning of assets, income, or extra-generous gifts that could prompt further enquiry, as well as monitor contracts and activities that could pose potential conflict of interest.

Obama and his senior officials go further; they release their full income tax returns annually. If Najib were to do likewise, rumors of his wife buying million-ringgit rings and getting extravagant gifts would not have arisen, if indeed they were baseless.

If Najib's ministers were also to declare their assets, then we would not have the silly specter of a cabinet minister feigning ignorance of her husband's quarter-billion ringgit government-funded business, as Women

Minister Shahrizat tried to do recently. The pathetic part was that she truly believed that the public would buy her swiftly-concocted story.

Beyond publicly declaring his assets, if Najib aspires for a clean administration, then he should remove those tainted individuals. Since Najib is blind to reality, I will help him identify such *proven* shady characters.

The most glaring is Isa Samad, former Negri Sembilan Chief Minister. Dispensing with his lackluster tenure as the chief executive of that state, the man was found guilty of "money politics," UMNO's euphemism for plain ugly corruption. Meaning, he is corrupt even by UMNO's lax standards. I am assuming that his party has some!

In any system with even a semblance of integrity, slimy characters like Isa Samad would have been jailed. In China, they would be executed. Yet Najib appointed Isa to helm the billion- ringgit Felda Global Holdings, a government-linked company. One wonders why Najib is so enamored with this character. The more intriguing question is why the powerful hold Isa has on Najib?

Then there is Ali Rustam, also a former Chief Minister (of Malacca). Like Isa, Ali too was found guilty of money politics. At least voters in his state were wise enough to boot him out. Now Ali is eyeing for the UMNO Vice-Presidency, as is Isa. Watch it, Najib will also do an Isa on Ali, that is, appoint him to a senior lucrative position, making a mockery of Najib's ambition of making corruption history.

If after getting rid of the Isa Samads and Ali Rustams, Najib still harbors even higher aspirations, like wanting a crisp and efficient administration, then he could entice capable Malaysians to join his team.

I suggest co-opting Keadilan's Rafizi Ramli. This bright young man has done more than anyone else to heighten public consciousness of corruption at high places. He shamed the anti-corruption agency with his many exposés. Appointing Rafizi would go a long way towards a "unity" government. Only the likes of Shahrizat would not welcome his appointment. Rafizi's appointment would also lower the average age of Najib's cabinet and at the same time elevate its collective IQ!

At the other end of the experience spectrum is Tengku Razaleigh (TR). He is from Najib's own party too. If Najib is serious and committed to *memperkasakan ekonomi Melayu* (enhancing Malay economy), as he asserted recently, well, the Tengku has been there and done that, and remarkably well too! Malaysia's finances were robust during his tenure as Finance Minister. Look at Petronas and Pernas, companies that he helmed.

Yes, at one time he led the once-powerful Bank Bumiputra, now long gone. If TR's detractors want to taint him with that scandal, remember this. He is one of the few if not only public figure who successfully sued for libel the venerable *Financial Times* when it tried to implicate him in that scandal.

Co-opting TR would give the Najib Administration some adult supervision. Najib should seize the opportunity and take a sabbatical, just like what Lee Kuan Yew did. Take a temporary leave from UMNO and Malaysia; learn about the real world. Najib would learn that there is a vast other universe out there not dependent on public paychecks or political patronages.

At another speech during his recent San Francisco trip, Najib chided his critics especially those residing abroad who "criticize the country but they do not have any idea on how to contribute to the country."

Najib is not only slow in grasping concepts but he is also not a careful reader. We do not criticize Malaysia, only his inept leadership. Nonetheless since Najib has asked for specific ideas from those abroad, here is one.

Take an extended sabbatical. Let someone like TR take over. He is an excellent choice. His considerable experience aside, at his age he is not likely to stay long to contest the next election or in any way challenge Najib when he resumes his leadership three or four years hence in time for the next election. Meanwhile learn as much as possible about the bigger and considerably more wonderful world beyond UMNO. He would be a more effective leader for that experience, and Malaysia would be a much better country, both while he was gone and after his return.

September 29, 2013

Parliament Must Replace Najib with Tengku Razaleigh

Malaysia cannot afford Najib's continued inept leadership. As UMNO has failed to terminate his leadership at its last assembly, and the next election is too far away [no later than May 2018 by statute], it is now up to Parliament to do the necessary.

Najib, who is also Finance Minister, will table his budget on October 25, 2013. That would be the opportune time for Parliament to pass a no-confidence vote on his budget–and hence his leadership–thus forcing the son of Tun Razak (TR-1) to resign. MPs have a far greater duty beyond loyalty to their leader, and that is loyalty to their country.

Najib can spare himself this unprecedented disgrace and simultaneously relieve his fellow parliamentarians of this distasteful chore by ceding the Prime Ministership to Tengku Razaleigh (TR-2). By gracefully withdrawing now, Najib could return later to lead his party for the 14th national election in 2018, and would be a better leader for this voluntary hiatus.

Should Najib contemplate being stubborn, he should remind himself of similar parliamentary practices resulting in the ejection of his contemporaries. In August, British MPs denied Prime Minister Cameron's motion to intervene in Syria. This defying the leader is also not alien to UMNO. TR-1 did it to Tunku Abdul Rahman, albeit in a soft, subtle way. The wise and sensitive Tunku saw the signals and relented.

A parliamentary no-confidence vote would not affect Najib's UMNO presidency. The constitution does not mandate the leader of a ruling party should also be prime minister. That is only tradition, tenable only as long as he has Parliament's confidence.

As UMNO has the largest parliamentary representation, it is appropriate that one of its members should be prime minister. There is no better choice than TR-2. He is a glittering gem to the sparkle of pebbles that is the current UMNO leadership. He also has the exquisite synthesis of talent and experience.

Considering his age, rest assured that TR-2 would not be preoccupied with being reelected and the consequent pandering to various constituencies, Najib's destructive obsession. TR-2 would focus on running the country, specifically mending the economy. With no children, TR-2 would have no grandiose pretensions of starting a political dynasty, yet another preoccupation of current leaders.

Malaysians could be assured that TR-2, like TR-1, would pick only the competent and untainted to be his ministers and advisors. They would reflect the man; his team would be the antithesis of Najib's. TR-2 has no need for courtiers or cheerleaders.

Unlike Najib, TR-2's executive and leadership abilities have been tested inside and outside of government. Malaysians can be assured that there would be no freelancers or lone rangers in TR-2's team spouting out offensive racial taunts. Najib on the other hand could not restrain the extremist ulama on his payroll who think that the marriage of a Muslim to a non-Muslim is invalid!

Najib is not up to par even when compared to his lackluster predecessor, Abdullah Badawi. With Abdullah, Malaysians within and beyond his party clearly expressed their disapproval, some politely others less so. The man recognized this and wisely withdrew.

Dissatisfaction with Najib is palpable even or especially within his party. However, he is a stubborn mule, and with as much insight. He must be told in no uncertain terms by Parliament that his leadership is wanting. A dumb mule responds only to a big stick, anything less would not do it.

Relieved of running the country, Najib could focus on ridding UMNO of its fortune seekers. They mock the party's aspiration of *Agama, Bangsa, Negara* (Faith, Race, and Country). There is nothing Islamic or Malay about corruption, cheating and the plundering the nation's wealth. There is no reflected glory for Malays to see UMNO leaders grow glutton on hogging the public trough. Malaysia would be far better off without these scoundrels.

Leadership Crisis Akin to Post-May 1969

Parliament has the right–indeed obligation–to terminate Najib's tenure. Malaysia today has a critical leadership crisis comparable to the post-1969 race riot period. That too was triggered by an electoral setback suffered by the ruling coalition. Malaysia is fortunate so far to be spared the associated tragedies and destruction with this electoral defeat despite the incendiary taunting by many.

Malaysians cannot allow this dangerous situation to fester lest a mere spark would trigger an explosion. Already the current cesspool of racial poison would take generations to detoxify, assuming it stops right now. So far Najib has shown no inclination or competence to do so. Inter-racial as well as intra-racial–specifically intra-Malay–relationships are deteriorating rapidly.

As with a fish, this rot begins at the head. The solution must therefore begin with getting rid of Najib. Citizens today yearn for a more representative or "unity" government to de-escalate the dangerously heightened social and racial polarizations. The unprecedented failure of the ruling coalition to gain the majority popular vote in the last election adds to this demand. Granted, in our "first past the post" system, the number of seats won would not necessarily correlate with the popular votes, nonetheless the stunning size of the discrepancy triggered the angst.

Such a wide discrepancy could still be legitimate and accepted if the institutions and personnel conducting the elections were truly non-partisan and had unchallenged integrity. The Election Commission is far from either.

That 1969 tragedy led to the resignation of Prime Minister Tunku Abdul Rahman. His successor, TR-1, set up a unity government through enlarging the old Alliance coalition to the current expanded Barisan Nasional. A similar strategy would not be the best route today. Instead, the objective of a representative and reconciliative government would best be served by having the new prime minister invite a few talented opposition members into his administration. Consider that US President Obama, who has a stronger mandate than Najib, has the opposition Republican Chuck Hagel as Defense Secretary.

TR2 is TR-1's protégé. No one else, least of all Najib, could claim that. The late TR-1 was a sharp spotter of talent. He put TR-2 to set up and lead Pernas when he (TR-2) was only 32 years old, and four years later, Petronas. At Petronas, TR-2 took on the powerful global oil companies and pioneered the unique and highly profitable production-sharing contracts that later became the model for other state oil companies. Malaysia continues to reap the bounty from that brilliant and courageous initiative.

Unique among UMNO leaders, TR-2 has a cordial relationship with the opposition members; he has the credibility to execute a "unity government." TR-2 could spot talented MPs from the opposition to be in his cabinet in the manner of TR-1. Those ministers from the opposition would serve as individuals and not as representatives of their parties. They would continue to serve until such time they could no longer support the government's policy pertaining to their respective portfolios. The opposition is blessed with many bright members. It would be a great shame not to tap their talent.

Such an initiative would also break the current incestuous coupling of party positions with governmental appointments, and go a long way towards "cleansing" UMNO of its "fortune seekers." Decoupling would also relieve ministers of their party's chores. The duties of a minister are onerous enough. American cabinet secretaries for example, are freed of these extraneous burdens. Consider this UMNO election season. For months now, those UMNO ministers and government appointees have abandoned their official duties as they are now busy campaigning.

UMNO is the single greatest contributor to public corruption because of the close nexus between party and government. Decoupling would sever this sinister link. As an added and substantial side benefit, those party positions now held by ministers would become vacant, thus allowing greater upward mobility for the members. At another level, those senior party leaders no longer in government would provide a much-needed system of checks and balances on their party's governmental appointees. Currently there are no such checks and balances within the party.

TR-1's unity government was instrumental in restoring normalcy post-1969. Today we need Parliament to strip TR-1's son, Najib, of his leadership to pave way for TR-2 to lead a new, invigorated unity government. We may contemplate the irony, but the action is an absolute necessity.

Najib Razak could spare his fellow parliamentarians this distasteful chore by resigning and paving the way for TR-2. Such an action would portray Najib as someone who put the nation ahead of himself, the very definition of a patriot. It would also be a great tribute to the memory of his father, Tun Razak.

October 13, 2013

Sudah lah 'Jib! You Haven't Got It!

Sudah lah (You are a goner) 'Jib! You do not have what it takes to lead modern Malaysia.

Humiliated by the recent national election (March 2013) and overwhelmed by mounting problems, Najib resorts to the typical tricks of Third World leaders. He travels abroad frequently to distract himself and Malaysians, and when at home he bribes his way through problems.

Barisan's loss in the popular votes during the last election was only the latest expression of this lack of confidence in Najib's leadership. He has been coasting on the memory of his illustrious father, the late Tun Razak. Malaysians have been too generous in giving Najib a pass for so long.

This cannot go on; the nation can ill afford it. There will be a splendid opportunity for the nation to be rid of his leadership without having to wait till the next national election [not due till June 2018], and that will be the upcoming parliamentary budget debate. All that is needed is for a handful of Barisan MPs (12 to be exact) to see through this character so he can be ejected from the Prime Minister's seat. He does not belong there.

Peripatetic Wanderer

Back to Najib's Third World leadership tricks, his most recent–and most expensive–was his junket through San Francisco on his way to New York, literally around the world. Rest assured there will be many more such trips in his ultra-luxurious, custom-fitted Airbus jet, burning the rakyat's precious ringgit.

The only saving grace this time was his uncharacteristic prudence financially in landing his jet at Oakland Airport instead of at exorbitantly expensive San Francisco's. Najib however, more than gobbled up whatever savings from that move by staying at the Fairmont Hotel in a suite that would have pleased King Saud.

In the 1960s, traveling extensively abroad was also the favorite refuge for Indonesia's Sukarno. It was left to his ministers back home to tell the *rakyat* to eat rats and thereby simultaneously solve two problems–widespread starvation and rat infestation.

More recently there was the Tunisian leader Zine el Abidene, now languishing in the Saudi desert with only his ill-gotten wealth to sustain him. He faces a death sentence at home, and an Interpol arrest warrant. As for his wildly extravagant and obscenely ostentatious wife, a former hairdresser, she has long ago abandoned him. She too is on Interpol's list for money laundering. Take a glimpse of her during her heyday; she has the uncanny resemblance of someone familiar to Malaysians, and not just in facial features and generous frame.

Sukarnos's fate in contrast was less severe. At least he died and was buried in his native land. Something for Najib to ponder!

Malaysia is far from being Sukarno's Indonesia. That however, is setting a very low bar. It tells us how far we have fallen that the two leaders are now often mentioned in the same sentence. While Malaysia is also infested with rats, Malaysians are not starving. However, the rats we have are even more rapacious, continually raiding the people's Treasury. The biggest rat of all is Najib.

Bribing His Way Through Problems

With his unrestrained access to the Treasury, Najib's mode of problem solving is to bribe his way. He bribed Malaysians with his multitude of expensive 1Malaysia giveaways. Just before the election his largesse became more targeted, as with his instant generous grants to Chinese schools and special allocations to East Malaysia. Those bore his trademark *lu tolong gua, gua tolong lu* (You scratch my back and I'll scratch yours) ethics.

Like bribees everywhere, the Chinese eagerly took the money and ran. Come election time they saw through what was going on and dumped Najib. Najib the briber was reduced to lamenting the Chinese tsunami. They abandoned him in droves. Najib mistook the Chinese to be like UMNO Malays, readily bought with only a few million devalued ringgit. In the end it was Najib who was left scratching himself.

East Malaysians were sufficiently grateful for the bribe to vote for Najib, only to be rewarded post-election with a court order banning them from using the word "Allah!" I hope that their Barisan representatives in parliament will now stage their own mini tsunami and flush Najib away.

Malays too are complaining. Again Najib resorted to his favorite trick of bribing, a few billion here and there under the bombastic package of *Memperkasakan Ekonomi Bumiputra* (MEB–Strengthening Bumiputra

Economy). Malays this time have shrewdly anted-up their price, learning from the Chinese. Malays this time are less than enthusiastic with the only few billion thrown their way. Even though in devalued ringgit, it is real money.

I thought that the whole purpose of the New Economic Policy and its various iterations during the last four decades had been to enhance the economic status of Malays. Obviously had the NEP been successful, we would have little need for this MEB.

Unfortunately for Najib, even the dumbest ass learns eventually. Malays have smartened up and realized that this MEB will just be another massive and lucrative bribery scheme for UMNO cronies. Their beneficiaries may be Malays, the pseudo as well as wannabe, but they do not represent our values.

Indications are, MEB notwithstanding, this time Malays are no longer *mudah lupa* (easily forgetting). Like the Chinese, Malays (at least the lucky ones) are becoming shrewder and will readily take the money and then run. Rest assured that come the next election, there will also be a Malay tsunami.

Or perhaps sooner! The recent UMNO election produced more malcontent losers who will be skipped by the gravy train. They will be grouchy enough to take their frustrations out on Najib.

Commentators of various persuasions have already pronounced Mahathir a loser in this UMNO election. One sure way to make a grouchy loser more so, and thus likely to strike back, would be for the winners to gloat. Abdullah Badawi gloated after his spectacular 2004 national victory, and lived to suffer the ignominious consequence.

Back to Najib the briber, he is finally learning a painful lesson. That is, bribees, be they national or party voters, continue to demand an escalating price tag, especially with soft and lucrative targets. Najib is one such target.

What is obscenely despicable with Najib is that he is using *our* money to bribe *us*, after he takes his usual generous cut, of course! At least when a Malaysian bribes a cop, he is using his own hard-earned cash, not anyone else's.

It is not just Malaysians that Najib is bribing. He thinks the rest of the world too is easily bribable. Soon after becoming Prime Minister, Najib was all over the global media giving high-profile interviews. Alas those "interviews" were nothing more than "infomercials," paid crass commercials masquerading as legitimate news items.

Far from being embarrassed, Najib still revels in the "glory." That was his mode of operation. Malaysians too were embarrassed, as were such media giants as CNN and BBC once they realized they had been duped. The "journalist" involved was duly fired, *after* earning his millions from Najib. Back in Malaysia, the consultants who thought of the idiotic scheme were rewarded with even more lucrative public relations contracts. For them, it was truly "endless possibilities" as well as endless profits with their desperate-for-praise client Najib.

On his recent trip to America, Najib was back in his old form. He addressed the Commonwealth Club of San Francisco and Harvard Club of New York, among others. Bribing is illegal in America, except where it is nicely wrapped as 'lobbying' or 'consulting' fees.

All this bribe money has to come from somewhere. Even the Saudi Treasury is finite. Watch this upcoming budget; Najib will once again squeeze the *rakyat*, this time with his Goods and Services Tax (GST) together with his scheme for "rationalizing" subsidies. He will again bribe his way by offering in return, a puny reduction in the income tax rates.

GST is the most regressive tax, meaning it imposes a disproportionately heavy burden on those least able to afford it. What Najib gives away in *sens* (pennies) as with his income tax reduction, he will haul back hundred-fold more through this GST.

I hope that Malaysian parliamentarians especially in Barisan will finally see through this man's façade and terminate his tenure once and for all. Muslims have just celebrated the *Eid Qurbani* (Celebration of Sacrifice). It is time to *qurban* (sacrifice) Najib for the good of Malaysia.

Nothing happens unless Allah wills it, so says our Koran. Muslims conveniently forget that our Koran then goes on to state that nothing happens until the people makes it so. If Najib does not see the light, then those parliamentarians should shine it to his face.

October 10, 2013

Sudah lah 'Jib! You Are Just Another Pak Lah!

Sudah lah 'Jib! You are just another Pak Lah (Abdullah Badawi)! Malaysia cannot afford two consecutive incompetent leaders as it enters the 21st Century. The precious and critical first decade is already wasted.

Najib's latest "Pak Lah moment" came when his Chief of Police, Khalid Abu Bakar, threatened to arrest Mariam Mokhtar for sedition over her article, "One Ideology, Two Reactions," posted on *Freemalaysiatoday.com* on November 29, 2013. Mariam dared to highlight the favorable treatment Aishah Wahab (the woman held as a slave by her Marxist master in London) received from the Najib Administration versus the visceral contempt it heaped upon Chin Peng, leader of the defunct Malayan Communist Party.

Mariam had written that the Najib Administration's generous gesture to Aishah was to exploit the favorable publicity surrounding that slavery case.

"She had better watch out," the Chief warned, "or we will go after her!" The "her" is of course Mariam.

Jantan kampong betul! (A real village bull!), as we say in the village when referring to such petty bullies. The Chief of Police should display his manhood where it would really count, as with confronting the Singaporeans spying on Malaysia, those intruders at Lahad Datu, or the alleged treachery with the loss of Pulau Batu Puteh. Those are the real threats to the nation's security and stability, not the eloquent writing of a young woman.

Clearly Najib and his officials are threatened by Mariam's ideas. Najib is stuck in the time warp of the old feudal ways, unable to grasp the new reality of a porous digital age. He and Khalid should be complimenting Mariam for her ability to write well in English, as well as her courage to express her views.

If Najib and Khalid had a better grasp of English, they would have discovered that Mariam's earlier essay in *Malaysiakini.com*, "Three Slaves and the Rakyat," on the same case carried more punch. In that piece she noted that while the three London women were imprisoned for three decades, Malaysians have been "metaphorically imprisoned for the most part of 56 years," and just like those three women, Malaysians had been shackled by "invisible handcuffs."

"It is doubtful," Mariam continues, "if many Malaysians realize the similarities between themselves and those three women." That's powerful stuff, but Najib and Khalid missed Mariam's well-chosen metaphor and imagery!

Congratulations Mariam! Your voice is being heard at the highest level, and widely too as judged by the outpouring of comments both articles elicited. Keep writing! I hope the police chief and Najib's other top officials would continue widening their reading repertoire beyond the UMNO newsletters, *The New Straits Times* and *Utusan Melayu*.

Mariam is not the first writer the authorities had tried to intimidate. She does not need to be reminded of the horrible experiences of Kassim Ahmad, Syed Hussein, and Raja Petra, among others.

I offer Mariam my best wishes for her continued success in writing so she could knock some sense into these characters. Additionally I can pass on the advice from that great Indonesian writer, the late Ananta Pramoedya Toer, a man who had endured much from his government.

"*Orang boleh pandai setinggi langit,*" Pramoedya wrote in *Rumah Kaca* (*The Glasshouse*), "*tapi selama ia tidak menulis, ia akan hilang di dalam masyarakat dan dari sejarah.*" (Your intellect may soar to the sky but if you do not write, you will be lost from society and to history.)

Rest assured that when the collective "invisible handcuff" gets unshackled, as ultimately it will, Malaysians owe a huge debt of gratitude to brave individuals like Mariam Mokhtar. As for that police chief, only his family would remember him, or if remembered by others, he would prefer not to be. Look at his many 'illustrious' predecessors; one jailed for punching Anwar Ibrahim, another a defendant in a multimillion-dollar lawsuit, and a third rewarded by being chairman of a casino. That last character had gambled right!

Najib's Ultimate Pak Lah Moment

Back to Najib's other Pak Lah moments, the supposedly pious and humble Pak Lah squandered millions of taxpayers' funds to renovate Sri Perdana before he deemed it livable. This from a man who only a decade earlier did not even own a house! Najib however, bested Pak Lah on this front. Najib burned over two million ringgit *a year* just on electricity bills. When citizens complained, he haughtily defended his wasteful ways by suggesting that his official guests should not have to dine by candle light! He must have the whole United Nations delegates as his guests, and every day too!

More likely, Najib must have really turned on high the air conditioner and then had the fireplace roaring to simulate the English ambience of his student days so he could cuddle up to Rosmah.

Najib should remember the advice he received from his prime minister-father when he (Najib) and his brothers were clamoring for a swimming pool at the old Sri Perdana. "What will people say," Najib quoted his old man as saying in turning down their request.

Then there is the ultra-luxury, custom-fitted Airbus jet. Even Queen Elizabeth and Prime Minister Cameron do not have one. Abdullah Badawi was severely criticized for his excessive use of that expensive toy. At least his wife (the first and second) did not get to use it in her personal capacity. Today we have Mrs. Najib (the second) jaunting off in it on her own, oblivious of the cost to the taxpayers. I do not know who is more reprehensible; Najib requesting the approval from his cabinet for his wife's use of the jet or the cabinet approving it. This at a time when he warned that the country is on the brink of bankruptcy!

Abdullah Badawi burdened Malaysia for over five years; the nation is still paying for his many follies and general incompetence. Many claim that Najib is worse than Pak Lah; that is being petty. When you score is already a miserable F, it does not really matter whether it is F-minus.

Expect at this week's [December 2, 2013] UMNO General Assembly for Najib to execute yet another Pak Lah moment–reading his "own" pompous self-congratulatory *pantun* (poem). Expect the delegates to swoon but not to even mention let alone review this critical issue of his glaring incompetence and profligate ways.

It behooves Malaysians to ensure that this burden of Najib's inept leadership comes to an end soon. Malaysians must force Najib to perform his ultimate Pak Lah moment–resign–and do so now!

December 1, 2013

Najib Desperate To Be Relevant

Last Saturday, September 6, 2014, marked a milestone of sorts for Prime Minister Najib Razak. On that day he exceeded the tenure of his predecessor, Abdullah Badawi. Abdullah served for five years, five months, and three days, the extra day thrown in with the 2008 leap year. Najib had his too in 2012. The traditional time lines for a new leader are the first hundred and first thousand days. For Najib that was July 12, 2009 and December 18, 2011.

The "First 100 Days" is President Roosevelt's (FDR) phrase. To him that was the best or most opportune period for a new leader to reshape the course of a nation. Did he ever! The "First One Thousand Days" also referred to FDR, the title of a book by his senior aide. The expression now is associated more with Kennedy's Camelot days in the White House. In my profession, thousand days refer to the period before a child's second birthday when good health and nutrition, as well as parental involvement and a stimulating home environment, are critical.

Najib had little to show by all three timelines. Today he struggles and is in fact desperate to be relevant. He is less being criticized, more ignored; a much worse fate for a leader.

Najib's One Hundred Days

In a television interview on his hundredth day in office, Najib pleaded for his administration to be assessed after a full term, not a hundred days. Fair enough, after all he is no FDR. The end of Najib's first term came and went with the May 2013 election that saw his coalition's worst performance, surpassing the humiliation suffered by his predecessor. Abdullah took responsibility for his debacle and resigned, albeit after much prodding. Najib continued on.

When he assumed office I predicted that with Malaysians now sensitized to and less forgiving of incompetence having been through with Abdullah, Najib would have an even briefer tenure. Alas, I was wrong; I overestimated Najib's sense of honor or responsibility. He has neither. So unlike Abdullah, voters would have to kick him out, and do so in no uncertain terms. A point to remember come the next election.

Najib announced his brave economic liberalization moves soon after taking office. At the first resistance however, he did not just flip flop like Abdullah but reversed course. He assured his UMNO Putras that their favorite rent-seeking activities would not be curtailed but in fact enhanced. Over five years and an election later, Najib is still busy buying favors.

Then there was the Commission of Inquiry he was forced to set up to investigate Teoh Beng Hock's death. Teoh was a "friendly" witness who died after being interviewed by the anti-corruption agency in the early hours of the morning. Later, a few days before Najib's hundredth-day anniversary, there was a massive but peaceful BERSIH 2.0 rally which he had earlier declared illegal. That notwithstanding, there were its leaders—a beaming Ambiga Sreenivasan and Poet Laureate Samad Said—getting an audience with the King. Apparently His Majesty too ignored Najib, and so soon into his tenure!

If Abdullah was a *main-main* (play-acting) or "practice" Prime Minister, then Najib is the sacrificial zinc anode one. He attracts the corruption, ugliness, and extremism of his supporters. Then when weighted down with the accumulated accretions, voters would toss him out, sparing the nation. Najib however collects those corrosions way too fast; Malaysians must consider chucking him sooner. I had suggested doing that during the last parliamentary budget debate on October 2013. There will be another opportunity next month.

Najib's One Thousand Days

Najib's thousandth day in office went unheralded. Not even he took notice, and for good reason. He had nothing to show for it. In a speech Najib was forced to defend his 1Malaysia.

"It is a philosophy, not a mere slogan," he insisted. Poor fellow, when you have to defend or clarify what you mean three years on, it could not have had much of an impact.

By his thousandth-day Najib had forgotten or ignored his earlier "courageous" move to liberalize the economy. He was back to his bribing ways, offering RM400 million to the mostly Malay bus companies' owners. Despite many more and ever generous giveaways to buy his way into the election, Najib fared worse than Abdullah.

Najib Outlasting Abdullah

A few days before Najib exceeded Abdullah's tenure, Teoh's death haunted Najib again. To recap, a lower court had earlier declared an open verdict, meaning, no one was at fault, incredulous though that may seem. The family appealed, and a few days ago in a landmark and unanimous decision, the Appeals Court set aside that verdict.

The court went beyond and declared that his death was caused or accelerated by unlawful acts by individuals unknown, *inclusive* (my emphasis) of MACC's officials. Justice Mohamad Ariff asserted that the interests of the family and the public required the case to be further investigated. Justice Ariff is indeed *Yang Arif*, the honorific exclusive for judges. It means wise and knowledgeable.

That is a rare public rebuke from an increasingly assertive and independent judiciary; a good omen for Malaysia but a bad one for Najib.

That was not the only past to haunt Najib. His earlier commitment to do away with the sedition and internal security acts was exposed for the fraud that it was when he charged his prominent critics, including law professor Azmi Sharom, for sedition.

The Economist was wrong when it concluded that those charges hurt Najib's image as a reformer. The man was never one. That tag merely reflects smart packaging, like his earlier string of high-profile international "interviews" later exposed to be unabashed infomercials. Even CNN and the venerable BBC were snared.

Najib's memory must be faulty as he is oblivious of these inconsistencies. This May he vowed "no bailouts" for beleaguered Malaysia Airlines. Today he declared the over six billion-ringgit infusion as "investment" and equating it to a patriotic duty!

Kata di kota, goes an old Malay wisdom; with Najib, *kata di lupa*. Our word (*kata*) must be as dependable as a fort (*kota*); otherwise forget (*lupa*) it.

Malaysians cannot forget Najib as his image appears everywhere, rivaling the gaudiness and ubiquity of North Korea's "Dear Beloved Leader." Malaysians can however ignore him, and they are doing just that.

Former Law Minister Zaid Ibrahim sums up Najib best. Referring to Najib's questioning the opposition's "loyalty" to the Sultan of Selangor, Zaid wrote two days after Najib exceeded Abdullah's tenure in office, "This cheap political trick … should not come from a Prime Minister. … Instead of telling the people … the complexities of democracy and how constitutional monarch and political leaders should conduct themselves, the PM took the lazy route of inflaming the feelings of the Malays …. For a man who talks about the great transformation for the country, this is irresponsible conduct and most disappointing."

Malaysians cannot ignore an irresponsible leader. That would be height of irresponsibility.

September 8, 2014

Part III

The Labu and Labi Team of
Najib and Muhyiddin

On Malay Heroes and Traitors

It is despicable that Deputy Prime Minister (DPM) Muhyiddin would see fit to label the leader of the loyal opposition Anwar Ibrahim a traitor. I expect such infantile name calling and boorish behavior from the likes of UMNO Youth leaders and mainstream media editors, not from a DPM.

Muhyiddin has yet to learn that as DPM he is leader of all Malaysians, not just of UMNO and Barisan supporters. In mentality and behavior he remains a parochial UMNO politician, not a national leader. He has yet to make the necessary transition to being the occupant of the second highest office in the land, and literally a heartbeat away from being Prime Minister.

Muhyiddin is now clearly way over his head. He personifies the classic Peter Principle, of someone finally rising to his level of incompetence. Not that he was particularly capable in his previous role as Agriculture Minister.

Muhyiddin as DPM does not necessarily alarm me except that our recent history has shown that even incompetent DPMs do ascend to the top post. Were Muhyiddin to succeed likewise, it would be a horrifying prospect for Malaysia. As he has demonstrated, this character simply does not have what it takes to lead our great nation.

In calling Anwar a traitor to Malays, and ipso facto to Malaysia, Muhyiddin is treating the millions of Anwar supporters, Malays and non-Malays alike, also as traitors. In so doing Muhyiddin exacerbates the already deepening and increasingly dangerous polarization of Malaysians, especially Malays. This is no way to further the aspirations of 1Malaysia.

Muhyiddin is not ready for prime time, and he has not shown that he will ever be. With the economy tanking and the escalating health threat from the H1N1 influenza, I would have thought he would have his hands full helping Prime Minister Najib. More specifically, as Education Minister he has enough on his plate with our pathetic national schools. If he has been diligent in attending to his official duties he would have little time to indulge in such infantile behaviors.

As DPM and also the minister in charge of education, Muhyiddin has all the opportunities to rise to the occasion and prove himself a hero. Instead, unable or incompetent to deal with the myriad pressing problems of our schools, he resorts to ugly name calling.

If Muhyiddin truly believe that Anwar is a traitor, and thus a threat to the nation, then he (Muhyiddin) should act on his conviction. There are enough statutes on the books to deal with traitors. That Muhyiddin is satisfied only with name calling shows the true character of the man and the silliness of his charge.

Part of A Greater Problem

Alas Muhyiddin is only part of a much greater problem, the pathetic lack of talent in UMNO, and thus the government. The party's top leaders are knaves, not heroes.

As non-Malays still see UMNO as representing Malays, many would not unreasonably conclude that the Malay race itself lacks talent, and that we are essentially a community of dumbbells. Consequently no amount of special privileges, enhanced opportunities, and molly coddling would or could change that reality. That is the scary and destructive part. It also hurts—deeply.

One cannot fault those non-Malays for their erroneous conclusion. After all, hardly a day goes by without them (and us) hearing something silly coming from these senior UMNO leaders. A few days ago there was Information Minister Rais Yatim wanting to censor the Internet. Then there was his predecessor Zainuddin Maidin foaming at the mouth eager to demonstrate his utter stupidity in front of a worldwide Al-Jazeera audience by complaining about those 'traitorous' HINDRAF demonstrators and defending the abusive behavior of the police. I yearn to hear something sensible emanating from these "half-past six" leaders.

In my earlier book *The Malay Dilemma Revisited* (1999), I suggested that then Prime Minister Mahathir revamp UMNO's entire top leadership by totally bypassing the next (now the current) generation of leaders as represented by the likes of Muhyiddin Yassin, Rais Yatim, and Zainuddin Maidin.

Mahathir then was (and perhaps still is) the only UMNO leader capable of undertaking such a massive transformation of his party. Had he done that, he would have spared the nation the agony of half a decade of wasted opportunities under the inept leadership of Abdullah Badawi, Mahathir's chosen successor.

Worse, the nightmare continues, to haunt not only Mahathir but more significantly, Malaysia. For succeeding Abdullah was the equally inept though more polished Najib. Compounding that, we now have the specter of a moronic Muhyiddin taking over after Najib.

Mahathir is today reduced to a cranky, pathetic old man continually bitching on the sideline on the fate of his party and country. And if I may add, ineffectually too! His recent passionate calls for not abandoning the teaching of science and mathematics in English were ignored by Muhyiddin and the cabinet. Mahathir's success in bringing down Abdullah was an aberration, contributed greatly by Abdullah's own spectacular ineptness.

With Najib and Muhyiddin however, we have a pair of rapacious politicians not at all shy in abusing the powers of the state to silence their critics. The only difference between the two is that Najib is more polished and thus presents a seemingly more sophisticated image, while Muhyiddin's brute utterances only reinforce his thuggish looks.

With Muhyiddin set to succeed Najib, and tired characters like Rais Yatim, Hishammuddin and Nazri Aziz ensconced in the cabinet, the future for Malaysia is bleak.

UMNO is incapable of self-renewal. The party's upcoming October General Assembly purportedly to revamp its constitution will not alter anything. Increasing the number of delegates to select the top leaders, one of the proposed changes, will only result in more sharing of the loot. As they all have the same insatiable appetite for avarice, 'money politics,' UMNO's notorious euphemism for corruption, would only expand.

There is no reason for Malaysians to remain fatalistic and accept such a fate. Malaysia is a democracy; Malaysians have the power to change their government and thus alter the fate of the nation. So come the next election throw these bums out, the whole lot of them.

Once these characters are out of power, watch them resort to ugly name calling. At least then those tirades would be directed at their fellow UMNO leaders. They deserve that, and each other. That is the fate of knaves.

August 16, 2009

The Dysfunctional Najib/Muhyiddin 'Team'

The dynamics between Prime Minister Najib Razak and his deputy Muhyiddin Yassin is one of destructive rivalry. They compete rather than complement each other. They give every indication to be the least productive and most dysfunctional 'team,' if I can stretch that term. Their relationship has awful *feng shui* and exudes bad karma. They are politics' Labu and Labi team.

Labu and Labi are the bumbling hired hands in P. Ramlee's comedy movie of the same name who spent their time fantasizing about their employer's daughter while neglecting their assigned chores.

Alas, leading the nation is anything but a comedic act; it is an awesome responsibility. Najib and Muhyiddin treat their positions as they would a trophy wife; with Najib content with displaying it while Muhyiddin barely conceals his own desires.

Najib has nothing substantive to show after a year in office. It is emblematic of his inept leadership that when the recently-acquired new Scorpene submarine could finally dive, it made the headlines! Incidentally, that sub was bought during Najib's tenure as Defense Minister.

Abdullah Badawi significantly lowered the bar for citizens' expectations of our leaders. Soon we would be excited if Najib were just to show up! Consider that former Prime Minister Mahathir had praised Najib merely for not dozing off at meetings! As for Najib's much ballyhooed 1Malaysia, a check on its website today showed that it is still inviting readers to register to join him for tea on March 13th, a good two weeks ago! Well at least that is better than the fate of his deputy's blog.

On major issues, from the teaching of science and mathematics in English to the controversy over the "Allah" terminology, the two leaders are not even on the same page. They are complete opposites. Often that is the catalyst for a dynamic and creative relationship. That however, is true only with highly-accomplished and self-confident personalities. Najib and Muhyiddin are far from being either.

I will compare the current duo of Najib and Muhyiddin to their predecessors, and then suggest a course of action Najib should take to salvage his tattering leadership. I will focus on three preceding pairs: the best and ideal team of Tun Razak and Dr. Ismail; the longest and most enduring partnership of Tuanku Abdul Rahman and Tun Razak; and the destructive and dysfunctional combination of Mahathir and Anwar. These three examples (two positive and one negative) provide many relevant lessons for Najib and Muhyiddin.

Unaltered, the present course will lead to a breakup of the two and with destructive consequences to them, their party, and the country. The scale would be many times worse than the Mahathir-Anwar explosion of 1998. That crippled the party and deeply divided the country, but only temporarily. In that ruinous split there was a definite victor, the mercurial Mahathir, which made the conflict mercifully not protracted.

If Najib and Muhyiddin were to split, it would come at a time when their party is at its weakest and most vulnerable; likewise the nation. As neither Najib nor Muhyiddin is strong enough or commands sufficient respect and support within the party and country, their split could consume both of them, as well as fatally cripple UMNO.

As for Malaysia, it has come a long way since the traumatic events of 1998 and could thus take the Najib-Muhyiddin breakup in stride. Indeed I would argue that the split would be good for the nation.

Nothing however, is preordained; prophecies need not be self fulfilling. Even bad karma and ill *feng shui* can be ameliorated. Najib's future is in his own hands and in the fateful decisions he makes, not with the alignment of the stars or the tea-leaf reading of some village soothsayers.

Earlier Teams

The first and longest pair was that of Tunku Abdul Rahman and Tun Razak. It spanned over 15 years and was the most successful the country has ever seen, or likely to see again. Even when the duo broke up following the 1969 race riots, it was done discretely and with minimal public repercussions. The pair remained unique in that they maintained their respect for each other long after one exited the stage. They never uttered an unkind word for the other, at least not publicly. It was a class act right to the end.

Compare that to the nasty things the Tunku and Hussein Onn heaped upon Mahathir when he was Prime Minister, or the scorn and contempt Mahathir poured on his chosen successor, Abdullah.

At the other extreme, we had the initially very promising and dynamic but later proved to be highly destructive and dysfunctional pairing of Mahathir and Anwar. The nation is still paying the price for that ugly split. The pair was like an unstable radioisotope with a long half-life; when it split it continued spewing its toxic radiation, defying all attempts at containment.

The team of Tun Razak and Dr. Ismail that succeeded the Rahman-Razak duo was easily the best and ideal. Perhaps the brevity of their tenure spared them the inevitable tensions and rivalries. Malaysians today look forlornly to that team, especially considering what is being served to us today.

The Razak-Ismail team was not the briefest; that distinction (if it can be called that) belongs to the immediately succeeding team of Razak and Hussein Onn. That was also the most forgettable pairing. The Razak and Hussein duo demonstrates that it takes both sides to make a great or at least workable team. It is not enough to have only one member shine; a laggard partner would bring the pair down. This observation would be validated many times later, as with the Mahathir-Musa Hitam and Mahathir-Ghaffar Baba pairings.

When both members are lightweights, then we would have a laughing stock of a team, a political Labu and Labi. At worse it would be a disaster, for them as well as the country. We had that with the Abdullah and Najib; we are now re-living it with Najib and Muhyiddin.

The Best Team

The Razak-Ismail duo lasted just a month shy of three years, prematurely cut short by the sudden but not unexpected death of Tun Ismail. At first glance they had all the ingredients for a divisive and acrimonious relationship. One was a lawyer the other, a physician; two professionals not known to get along well with each other. Members of the two professions view society differently; likewise their approaches to problem solving. Lawyers cross examine their witnesses; doctors get a history from their patients. Lawyers assume their clients would lie; physicians implicitly trust theirs. Attorneys' clients may think it is in their interest to lie; patients however risk their lives if they were to mislead their physicians.

What made the Razak-Ismail team work well was that both were true professionals as well as consummate politicians in the best traditional mold. It was this combination that made their partnership blossom. As professionals they were able to separate their personal feelings to address the problems at hand; as accomplished politicians they were skillful in the art of compromise in the fine tradition of politics. They were able to sink whatever personal, political and professional differences and ambitions they harbored in order to best serve their client: the nation.

They also shared many similarities. Under different circumstances or with other personalities, those similarities could well be sources of unending conflicts. Consider their age; only seven years separating them, with Razak the younger. Politicians are inherently ambitious and competitive; they all aspire to be the number one. The number two could hardly wait for number one to exit, making for an often stormy relationship towards the end, as demonstrated by the Tony Blair and Gordon Brown show. Being comparable in age would only aggravate that aspect of the rivalry.

Surprisingly, we did not see that with Razak and Ismail. While Ismail was as ambitious as the rest, he was the original and genuine citizen-legislator. Meaning, someone who takes time off from his regular vocation to serve his nation, and then after giving his best, leave. Ismail was a rare breed, especially when compared to the specimens we have today who make politics their permanent careers. Najib's cabinet, like Abdullah's and Mahathir's before that, is infested with tired old career politicians who have no life outside of politics. They hang on long past their shelf-life.

Both Razak and Ismail were also aristocrats, Razak from Pahang and Ismail, Johor. They both attended English schools and the best institutions; Razak read law at Lincoln's Inn and Ismail, medicine at Melbourne. *Jagoh kampong* (village champions) they were not. They were not insular and both had competed successfully against the world.

Those similarities may have contributed to their cordial and workable relationship, but those were not the main factors. Instead what made them "click" was their deep commitment to public service. They were true patriots. It was this that made them overcome whatever personal and professional differences they may have had between them.

And differences there were! In personality, the two could not be more dissimilar. Ismail was the gregarious type; he knew how to enjoy life. As a medical student he idled his time on the cabaret floor on the evening before his crucial anatomy oral examination during his brief year at the University of Malaya.

Razak was the studious one; he was a legend at Malay College. He completed his law studies well before his scholarship ended. At social gatherings I could not imagine Tun Razak backslapping his guests or joining them in uproarious laughter, as Dr. Ismail would.

Being from the predominantly Malay state of Pahang, Razak's political philosophy was more towards Malay nationalism. Ismail hailed from the more urban and cosmopolitan Johor; that shaped his worldview.

Yet those differences complemented them rather than being sources of rivalry, a reflection of their great sense of self-confidence. Ismail did not need to aspire for the top post in order to show his stuff, while Razak was not in the least threatened by having someone of the caliber of Ismail as a deputy. Malaysians were blessed to have a pair of such high caliber helming the nation. It is sad that their success did not inspire the present generation of leaders to emulate if not better that team of Razak and Ismail.

The Longest and Most Enduring

If as Prime Minister Tun Razak did not feel threatened by having a highly capable deputy in the person of Dr. Ismail, the Tun also did not feel that being a deputy to the Tunku would hamper his ability to contribute towards the nation. He also did not view being in the number two slot for an inordinately long time as a reflection of his ability. Only when the Tunku's leadership was wanting in the aftermath of the 1969 race riots did Razak assert himself.

Razak could have headed UMNO and thus be the country's first prime minister if he had wanted to; the opportunity was there. When UMNO's first president, the towering Datuk Onn, left the party sulking in 1951, many wanted Razak to take over. He was not yet 30 at the time, and already they recognized his exceptional leadership and executive talent.

Razak politely declined the honor, not out of a sense of false modesty or lack of confidence, rather his astute reading of the Malay psyche and culture. He rightly believed that his community would more readily accept as leader someone older and thus perceived to be more experienced. In Malay culture, age equals wisdom; hence his declining the honor. Instead,

Razak was instrumental in persuading the initially reluctant Tunku to head UMNO.

At another level, UMNO's stated mission then was merdeka. Razak was shrewd enough to recognize that the party would need someone whom the British would find comfortable to negotiate. The affable and anglophile Cambridge-bred Tunku fitted the bill. That was a particularly prescient call on Razak's part, reflecting his wisdom and foresight despite his youth.

Razak's wisdom in turning to Tunku was manifested in other ways. It turned out that the major obstacle in the negotiations leading to merdeka was not with the British but the Malay sultans. The British knew that colonialism was no longer chic or compatible with the values of a civilized society. They were ready and eager to let go of their colonies. The sultans however, were an unanticipated issue. Their concerns about their status in an independent Malaysia made them recalcitrant. They were not without reasons; they saw only too clearly the fate of the Sultan of Jogjakarta in neighboring Indonesia, as well as the multitude of Maharajas in India.

With Tunku, a member of the Kedah royal family, leading the negotiations, the sultans felt reassured. Had it been the commoner Razak, the negotiations would definitely have been tougher.

Many ascribe the enduring partnership of Rahman and Razak to their presumed traditional Malay father-son relationship, with the loyal son always deferring to the father. Nothing could be further from the truth. I had never seen any public display of filial genuflecting by Razak to the Tunku, no low bowing or kissing of the hand. When the Tunku was swamped in the aftermath of the May 1969 riot, Razak was not at all bashful in taking over. That was certainly not the response of a supposedly obedient son or a display of undivided filial devotion.

Instead their relationship was akin to that of a non-executive chairman of the board and the chief executive president. While Tunku was prime minister, it was Razak who actually ran the country. All the major initiatives, from overhauling of the education system to the massive rural development, originated from and executed by Razak.

A comparable dynamics would be between the ambassador and his deputy *chef de mission* (DCM) in the old Soviet embassies. The real power and authority resided with the DCM, not the titular number one, the ambassador. He was merely the figure head, the sultan as it were. In that way, he (very rarely she) could indulge himself at diplomatic functions like getting drunk without compromising embassy secrets. Similarly if the ambassador were to be blackmailed, he could be readily expended.

I always thought that to be an ingenious scheme! It was certainly successful with the Soviets; it was no less so with Tunku and Tun Razak.

The Ugly and Dysfunctional Mahathir-Anwar Pair

As leader, Mahathir was essentially a one-man team, a loner. He exhibited the typical alpha-male monkey mode. An alpha monkey could tolerate other males in the colony only if they were to submit to him, or be seen doing so. Any hint of a non-deferring behavior or "dissing" would be dealt with quickly until the challenger is either driven out or fatally finished off. Such leaders have little use for a deputy, partner, or a team. Instead he needs a sidekick, in the manner of a Jim McMahon to Johnny Carson; someone to make the leader look good and be the butt of his jokes.

Consider Mahathir's relationship with his first deputy, Musa Hitam. It went well so long as Musa deferred to Mahathir, that is, by being submissive. In the beginning Musa did exactly that. When he began to assert himself or received more attention, it was the beginning of the end for Musa.

The same dynamics governed Mahathir's relationship with his third deputy, Anwar Ibrahim. Like Musa, Anwar was only too willing to be Mahathir's sidekick and to humor him–initially. And why not; Anwar was handsomely rewarded, as seen by his rapid ascent in the party and government. Mahathir never viewed Anwar as a threat seeing that he was very much younger and thus could patiently bide his time. That scenario would have successfully played out to the end had Anwar not succumbed to the goading of his many impatient and greedy supporters.

A blatant display of Mahathir's alpha male traits was during the aftermath of the contentious UMNO leadership convention of 1987 which saw Tengku Razaleigh nearly toppling Mahathir. Following that, Mahathir had to do what every alpha monkey male would, that is, get rid of its challenger.

It did not surprise me that the deputies Mahathir was most comfortable with were Ghaffar Baba and Abdullah Badawi. Both played the role of the sidekick only too well, especially Abdullah Badawi. Unfortunately they, specifically Abdullah, only *played* the role, as Mahathir found out too late and much to his regret.

Ghaffar Baba also played the second-fiddle role exceptionally well, leading many to underestimate him. His inability to speak English reinforced that public perception of his shortcomings, and many doubted his intellect.

Nothing could be further from the truth. He had a formidable intellect; however being a kampong boy with only a Malay education and no family connections, his highest reach was the Sultan Idris Training College for Malay school teachers.

Not only was Ghaffar well endowed with innate intelligence, he was also "street smart," but he skillfully hid both under his characteristic and very Malay humility. Make no mistake, the late Ghaffar Baba could read the Malay psyche very well, a skill that Mahathir exploited. In that respect he contributed much to the partnership with Mahathir. Ghaffar was no mere sidekick, as many viewed him.

With his vast understanding of the nuances of Malay culture and psychology, Ghaffar could have successfully fended off Anwar's challenge, but Ghaffar knew that his party was in desperate need of new blood. At the same time he did not wish to see the party that he loved so dearly be fractured by intense rivalry at the top. It was those noble considerations that made him give way to Anwar, and not, as many believed, his fear of defeat. Ghaffar exhibited class as well as courage in bowing out early in that tussle with Anwar; he put his party's interest ahead of his own. That is a rarity among today's politicians.

As for Abdullah, when a previously non-alpha male monkey takes over, it first instinct is to kill all the babies of the previous alpha male in an attempt to eliminate his predecessor's genes in the colony. This was what Abdullah did by attempting to 'kill' Mahathir's many 'babies'—his pet mega projects.

Abdullah's mistake was not realizing that Mahathir had not been 'killed' or banished from the colony. That alpha monkey was still in the same jungle, imperiously perched high up the Petronas Twin Towers. He was still very much alive and influential. Abdullah never knew what hit him when Mahathir unleashed his fury.

Because he ran a one-man show, Mahathir's legacy would be at considerable risk once he is gone. We saw that already when Abdullah took over, only that he was so clumsy and inept. Had Mahathir cultivated younger leaders *a la* Tun Razak to Tunku, or even a not-so-young but a capable one *a la* Razak to Dr. Ismail, Mahathir would have greatly enhanced the caliber of his leadership as well ensure that his legacy would endure.

I predict that once Mahathir is gone, his long tenure would merit only an asterisk in modern Malaysian history, as Mao Zedong is to China today. Mao ruled for over a quarter of a century. He had the greatest (though not necessarily positive) impact on China and the Chinese. Yet today, if one were to ask the throngs of shoppers at Beijing's many modern shopping malls who Mao was, the likely response would be, "Mao, who?" Not too long ago they even threw his wife into jail. Some legacy!

Sizing Up Najib and Muhyiddin

Najib is an aristocrat, the son of a former prime minister. He comes from a modern nuclear family: father, mother and five brothers, Najib being the oldest. He had a privileged upbringing, including boarding school and university in England. Najib and his brothers had plenty of parental love, what with their stay-at-home traditional mother. Even though the late Tun was a busy man, rest assured that with only five sons he would remember and celebrate their birthdays.

Muhyiddin is one of over four *dozen* children of a village alim with multiple wives. It would be unlikely for his father to even remember

Muhyiddin's name, much less his birthday. In dynamics, young Muhyiddin had essentially a fatherless childhood. He attended the local village school and later a small town high school before proceeding to the local university.

The wives they have chosen too are very different. Najib's current wife, his second, is the poster girl for extravagance and vulgarity, a Malaysian Imelda Marcos, except that Imelda had a weakness only for shoes. Muhyiddin's wife is the typical kampong girl; she views her job as being to be by his side; to be seen but never heard.

It is easy to imagine Rosmah being actively engaged in her husband's business. I cannot even contemplate Muhyiddin seriously engaging his wife in serious matters. He is the typical alpha kampong male; he knows what is best and his word rules.

Their seven-year age difference means that Muhyiddin could not possibly succeed Najib in the usual transition process. Muhyiddin is the older, so by the time Najib retires, Muhyiddin would be too old to take over. The only conceivable way for him to get the top slot would be if Najib's tenure were to be prematurely cut short, by unexpected death or sordid scandals. Both are not remote possibilities. Najib's father died in his early 50s from leukemia, and that malady remains lethal even today. As a timely reminder, many a Third World leader has succumbed to fatal "accidents."

Scandals would be the more likely career killer for Najib. He certainly has some nasty ones hanging over him, from the brutal murder of the Mongolian model to his admitted conversations with Anwar Ibrahim's alleged sodomy victim. Then there are the steady streams of squalid incompetence during his tenure as Defense Minister, from stolen jet engines to newly-acquired submarines that could not dive.

It does not escape everyone's notice that far from defending Najib, Muhyiddin seems to relish his superior's travails. Worse, he does not even bother to hide his delight.

In UMNO politics, followers could sniff right away rivalries at the top. They would then quickly realign their positions and shift their loyalties in the hope of latching onto the winning team. The game would quickly degenerate into a sport of running down the opposing camps, with temporary alliances forged, broken, and then re-constituted to meet the quickly evolving dynamics. Thus expect even more ugly revelations from all sides.

This is already happening. Many were shocked at the utter corruption and rottenness of the party and its leaders. While such exposés would be bad for the party, they would be good for the country, especially considering that the next general election will only be a few years away.

Many predict the inevitable collapse of UMNO under Najib, a fulfillment of the so-called RAHMAN prophecy, the "N" of the acronym representing Najib. I argue otherwise. There is no alignment of the stars that would preordain such an outcome. Rather what we have here reflects nothing more than Najib's lack of leadership and the dearth of talent within UMNO. Had Mahathir chosen Najib instead of Abdullah as his (Mahathir's) successor, Najib's and thus UMNO's political demise would have come sooner.

Were that to happen, my only regret would be to see the inglorious end to what was once an illustrious Malay institution–UMNO. Tun Razak was one of the key personalities instrumental in setting it up. It took only a generation to destroy what he had worked hard to create and build. What a supreme irony if his son were to be the one responsible for UMNO's demise.

Salvaging Najib

Najib's predecessors offer many lessons if he chooses to learn. The first necessary exercise would be for him to determine which leader he identifies with or resembles most.

One thing is certain: Najib is not his father's son; biologically yes, but not politically or intellectually. Najib also does not have his father's personality or trait, in particular the Tun's acute sense of probity and prudence. In persona, Najib lacks his father's great presence; the late Tun Razak commanded instant respect. No one would dare crack a joke in his presence, not out of fear but awe and respect. With Najib, he would probably join in with his own ribald riposte to an off-color joke by his colleagues or juniors.

In physique, Najib should have a commanding presence; after all he is tall and broad-shouldered to his father's perpetual stooped posture. Alas a favorable body-build would take you only so far.

The late Tun would never let his wife loose on extravagant shopping sprees. Then there was his famous riposte to his children when they clamored for a swimming pool. "What would people say?" Najib never learned that important lesson from his father.

Mahathir may have been Najib's political 'father' but he does not have Mahathir's vision, charisma, or determination. There is not much that Najib could learn from the mercurial Mahathir, no matter how hard the latter tries to influence Najib.

Najib resembles the Tunku the most; smart enough to be accepted into a provincial British university but not brilliant enough to have a transformational vision for his country. Najib's attempt at having one–his now crumbling 1Malaysia–is an embarrassment more than an inspiration.

Like Tunku, Najib has a fondness for the good life. I would not however, recommend that Najib pattern himself after the Tunku in this regard, like resorting to regular nightcaps. The cultural environment today is far less forgiving; it would be political suicide were Najib to indulge in such worldly pleasures. Pleasures of the flesh are more tolerable to today's crowd than pleasures of the palate, and Najib has exploited that to the hilt.

Very unlike the Tunku however, Najib is burdened by an overbearing spouse. With Tunku, Malaysians had a soft spot for his wife, the late Sharifah Rodziah. There was a good reason for that; she was humble, modest, and stayed in the background. She was the very antithesis of Rosmah, Najib's present wife.

Najib could usefully emulate Tunku in one respect, in having an able, young and brilliant deputy, that is, have his own Tun Razak. That someone should be like the late Tun, smart, competent, diligent, and not corrupt. That person should also be satisfied if not actually enjoy wielding power in the background while letting the number one hog the limelight and credit. Needless to say, Muhyiddin has none of those admirable qualities.

Tunku was only 52 when he became the country's first leader, only a few years younger than Najib when he became prime minister. Tunku's deputy, Najib's father, was only 33. Like Tunku, Najib should groom someone young, a generation younger, to be his deputy. He needs to cast his net far and wide, and outside the party, to find fresh talent to entice into

UMNO. In his quest for his own Tun Razak, Najib must be willing to gamble and consider those who are not initially sympathetic or even hostile to UMNO. Who knows, by co-opting them into government they might just become UMNO members. The late Ghazali Shafie was not an UMNO member when Tun Razak brought him into his cabinet.

Najib should consider including in his team such individuals as Khairy Jamaluddin, even though I risk puffing up his already inflated ego. Khairy is not even half as smart as the late Tun, but then that is all UMNO has to offer these days. By specifically bringing in Khairy, Najib would be declaring that he is out of Mahathir's shadow, or at least could not care less what he thinks. That would be quite a statement!

The danger is that unlike the late Tun, Khairy, apart from being not as smart, is not content remaining in the background; he likes to hog the headlines. Khairy is also "damaged goods" because of his earlier overbearing ways while the under "protection" of his Prime Minister father-in-law, Abdullah Badawi. However, if a severely discredited politician like Nixon could be rehabilitated, so could Khairy.

As the search for his own Tun Razak would be slow and difficult, Najib needs to do something quick in the interim. First, he would have to dump Muhyiddin; he would of course still retain his UMNO's deputy presidency as he was elected to that position. To make that move palatable as well as lessen the repercussion, Najib would have to appoint someone with gravitas to replace Muhyiddin, someone who would command instant respect and credibility not only among Malaysians but also the world.

Fortunately UMNO has such a person in Tengku Razaleigh. Muhyiddin would not dare squeak if he were to be replaced by someone of undisputed integrity, competence, and stature as Razaleigh.

Earlier during Abdullah's tenure as prime minister I suggested that he pick Razaleigh as deputy prime minister, but for a whole set of different reasons. Had Abdullah done that, his fate as well as Malaysia's would be far different today.

If Najib were to be bold enough to dump his current deputy, he would accomplish many objectives simultaneously. One, he would certainly make all Malaysians take note. For another, he would reassert his leadership of the party. After all there is nothing in the party's constitution to stipulate that the deputy leader should also be deputy prime minister. That is only tradition. By boldly breaking the party's hallowed practice, Najib is signaling his commitment to a new path, for his party as well as country.

Muhyiddin cannot be unceremoniously dumped; that would trigger a severe backlash and precipitate a leadership crisis. We are an Asian culture where 'saving face' is supreme. Thus instead of dumping Muhyiddin, Najib would have to sell the exercise as a 'promotion' for Muhyiddin–to undertake the more important and immediate task of 'revitalizing' UMNO. After all he already heads the management committee to reform the party; that crucial job has yet to be completed. To further soften the impact, Najib would have to compensate the loss of Muhyiddin's ministerial income by offering him a lucrative chairmanship of one of the GLC's, like the Iskandar Development Project.

Najib should not be satisfied only with 'promoting' Muhyiddin; he should simultaneously radically revamp his cabinet by reducing the bloat and getting rid of the dead woods. I would begin with such old tired characters as Nazri, Rais, and Hishammuddin. Replace them with fresh young candidates.

All those ministers are tainted. If they were to create problems or in any way try to undermine his leadership, Najib could always unleash the MACC upon them. That ought to shut them up. We saw how quietly even the boisterous Rafidah Aziz went when Abdullah fired her. And he was a meek leader!

As deputy, Tengku Razaleigh would pose no political threat to Najib. Razaleigh would be focused on serving the nation; he is too senior to be involved in mere politicking or conniving to topple Najib. Together with Razaleigh, Najib could aggressively recruit fresh bright young talent into public service and revamp UMNO.

There is only a limited time window for Najib to act. If he were to delay revamping his cabinet till just before the election, that would be dismissed as political gimmickry. Then there is the UMNO leadership convention; if Najib were to delay making these changes, those dropped UMNO ministers would retain their clout and could be re-elected. By removing them now, their influence would have waned come the party's election.

These radical changes may be unpalatable to Najib and he may shy away from undertaking them, but then he has to ponder the consequences of his staying the course. At a minimum he risks becoming another Abdullah Badawi, except more pathetic. At worse, the battle between Najib and Muhyiddin would consume more than just the two. It would also take down UMNO, the RAHMAN prophecy coming true.

It is not enough for Najib to endlessly declare that he is "ready to make the difficult changes that Malaysia needs." He needs to demonstrate that through his deeds, or as my old kampong folks would say, "*Bikin saja, jangan cakap!*" (Just do it, dispense with the hollering).

Najib and Muhyiddin may have bad karma and ill *feng shui*, but as practitioners of those ancient occult arts will tell you, those can be mitigated though appropriate actions. Najib's destiny lies in his own hands, on whether he is willing and capable of undertaking these much-needed radical changes.

If he does not, then it is time for voters to take actions. In P. Ramlee's movie, Labu and Labi's strict taskmaster Haji Bakhil would punish the pair by making them perform *ketok-ketampi*, a Malay version of humiliating pushups, every time they goof off. It is time for voters to make our political Labu and Labi team of Najib and Muhyiddin perform their *ketok-ketampi* by booting them out at the next election.

April 18, 2010

Part IV

The Dinosaur That Is UMNO

Lessons From The American Election

The 2008 American election campaign is now in full swing although citizens will not cast their votes until November. In fact this presidential campaign cycle started right after the last general election over three years ago. America seems to be in a perpetual campaign mode, with precious little time left for these elected public officials to perform the duties for which they were being elected.

I much prefer the Malaysian election cycle, modeled after the British, where the ruling party could call an election any time before its five-year mandate is over. Yes, it gives an unfair tactical advantage to the incumbent, but it spares the country from degenerating into perpetual campaign mode.

Malaysia does have a predictable election cycle comparable to the Americans, in its party elections–specifically UMNO. Since its leaders would also lead the nation, those party elections are hotly contested. While Malaysia may be spared perpetual campaigning, UMNO and its leaders are not. Therein lies the problem. UMNO leaders are less interested in leading the country and attending to its myriad problems but more in ensuring their survival in the party's hierarchy.

During the last cycle of UMNO elections, a number of ministers were chastened to learn that their positions as party leaders were threatened and with that their chance of being appointed to plump governmental, especially cabinet, positions. Hence the disgusting sights of ministers like Hishammuddin (in charge of education) slavishly pandering to party members instead of paying attention to the deteriorating schools.

Decoupling Party From Governmental Positions

In my book *Towards A Competitive Malaysia* [2006], I suggest that one way of overcoming this blight is by decoupling party positions from governmental appointments. Apart from widening the talent pool, such a system would also diffuse power and create some semblance of a system of checks and balances, which is severely lacking at present.

Currently, a Menteri Besar (Chief Minister), for example, is not only the state's chief executive but also the party's head, chief executive of the state's myriad development corporations, and chairman of the municipal council of the state capital.

Even an ordinary Member of Parliament and state legislature is burdened by these multiple added responsibilities. A fast rising star in UMNO confided to me that she could not do justice to her official as well as political duties, what having to attend the numerous weddings and funerals of her constituents as well as constantly humoring petty party bosses and members. Imagine the extraneous burden on a minister!

This is where the American system is superior. Cabinet secretaries (ministers) and other senior political appointees can concentrate fully on their executive duties and not have to worry whether some political punks back in their home town would be scheming to usurp their party positions, and thereby rob them of their cabinet posts.

An American president is not restricted to his elected party members in choosing his cabinet. He has a wide and deep talent pool to tap, including beyond his party. In contrast, an UMNO prime minister restricts himself only to his party, and then only to top leaders. Consequently young party members are diverted from fully developing their individual talent that could benefit their party and country but to clawing their way up the party hierarchy. The skills they learn and habits they acquire along the way are mainly of the unsavory variety, like brandishing their *kerises* (ceremonial daggers) and other race-taunting antics. They have to pander to the extremist elements of their party, and when they reach the top, they are reduced to being political animals of the worst type. They cannot kick the old bad habits.

Consequently while America counts seasoned executives, accomplished professionals, and smart scholars as cabinet secretaries, Malaysian ministers are for the most part scheming and opportunistic politicians.

Malaysia would do well to adopt some of the elements of the American practices, in particular the decoupling of cabinet and other senior appointments from party positions. That would diffuse power and provide for greater accountability. At present ministers are also powerful party figures. That is too much concentration of power. The most important reason for decoupling is that the skills needed to win elections are not necessarily those needed to run an agency or department. In fact they are the very opposite; successful politicians are poor executives.

Unfair Criticism of the Malaysian Model

An oft-stated and unfair criticism of the Malaysian electoral system is that it "disenfranchises" urban dwellers in favor of rural ones. The "one man one vote" mantra should be viewed as a statement of an ideal and not be taken literally. With greater urbanization, an urban constituency of 100,000 would cover only a few square miles and be readily served by one individual, while a similar-sized rural constituency would cover hundreds of square miles, taxing the physical ability of its lone political representative.

In America, the bastion of democracy, this "one-man-one-vote" rule applies at best only to the House of Representatives (Lower House). California with the largest population has the largest contingent of representatives to that body. With the Senate however, while California has a population 70 times larger than Wyoming, both have the same number of senators–two. Similarly, Alaska with a land mass 700 times that of Rhode Island and where you would need days if not weeks to go from one end to the other, yet the two states have the same number of senators. Meanwhile the District of Columbia with a population larger than Wyoming does not even have any Senate representation.

Viewed from another angle, the Malaysian Senate, while not an elected body, is far more representative of Malaysian society than the US Senate is of American, where the ideal of "one-man-one-vote" perversely makes its senate less representative of the people.

Having elected representatives is not enough; the electoral process must also be fair and accessible. America has little to offer Malaysia in this regard. Public debacles such as Florida's "hanging chads," obstacles to voter registrations, the stranglehold of the two-party system, the staggered primaries, and the endless campaigns run by professionals have turned the public off politics. The decline in voter participation reflects this, as well as the perennially low opinion the public has of Congress.

The Malaysian Elections Commission is determined to best its American counterpart by not being voter friendly, and prides itself in doing so.

Fortunately in America, once in a while there comes a candidate who is so inspiring, who makes ordinary citizens believe again in themselves, and who appeals to their better side such that voters are galvanized once again to take part in the electoral process. We had that in 1960 with Jack Kennedy, in the 1980s with Ronald Reagan, and today with Barack Obama.

I long for the day when the Malaysian political system would produce its own Kennedy, Reagan, or Obama. With the present entrenched power of political parties, this is not likely to happen anytime soon.

January 27, 2008

UMNO's Ultras Defanged

One least noted but most consequential impact of this last general election [March 21, 2004] is that those rabidly racist UMNO ultras have been effectively defanged. Malaysians can now be assured that the next UMNO General Assembly will not see the likes of Hishammuddin Hussein or Khairy Jamaluddin putting on their ugly race-taunting, kris-wielding stunts.

These hitherto UMNO young bulls have been, as we say here on the ranch, "cut off." Yes, castrated! They are now reduced to being steers destined for the slaughterhouse; they are not worthy to propagate the herd.

Khairy Jamaluddin in particular had a near-death political experience in Rembau, his father's village and a previously safe UMNO seat. Unknown PKR's candidate Badrul Hisham Shaharin, or Che'gu Bard, a product of the local kampong school and the nearby Raja Melewar Teachers' College, proved a formidable opponent for Khairy, the self-puffed ego and product of Oxford University via Singapore's World United College.

Khairy is smart enough to realize that had it not been for the timely "rescue" in the form of postal votes, together with the earlier last minute cancellation by the Elections Commission on the use of indelible ink that would have prevented fraudulent voting, Chegu Bard would have humbled Khairy. How else to explain an initial hundred-vote victory for Chegu Bard would turn out to be a massive 5,000-vote victory for Khairy on "recount"?

Even UMNO morons are teachable. That is not a surprise, for the ability to learn is an attribute of all living things. The only variable is the slope of the learning curve. UMNO operatives may have learned their lesson with this election, but it is already too late. The implosion of UMNO has begun.

That said, there are still some slow learners within UMNO where this lesson has yet to sink in. Take Abdullah Badawi; he still claims that he had a thunderous victory with this last [2008] election and vows to carry on with business as usual. Fortunately for Abdullah, his ministers and UMNO Supreme Council members are all *lembik* (soft or slow). To them, their naked emperor is still immaculately attired in fine embroidery. There is no *jantan* (male) left in UMNO to disabuse Abdullah of his delusion. That is, until now.

Enter Mukhriz Mahathir

Enter Mukhriz Mahathir, yes the scion of *that* Mahathir. Abdullah had earlier selected Mukhriz to contest the "iffy" seat of Jerlun instead of the "safe" one of Langkawi. Much to the surprise of his detractors, in particular the hierarchy of UMNO Youth, Mukhriz won handily, with no need of a recount!

In a letter to Prime Minister Abdullah immediately following the election, with convenient copies to top UMNO leaders who were too chicken to convey the blunt message directly to Abdullah, Mukhriz called for Abdullah to resign for the greater honor of the party and "*bangsa, agama dan negara*" (race, religion, and nation).

I do not know whether this was on his initiative or his father speaking through him. Regardless, that message needed to be sent.

Much to my surprise (and also to Mukhriz, I presume), the mainstream media carried his letter. Perhaps those editors have also learned their lesson with this election. At any rate, it would not have mattered as that letter is widely circulated on the Internet and foreign press.

Many would think that Mukhriz is a chip off the old block, recalling that nearly forty years ago his father, then a defeated candidate in the parliamentary election, also sent a comparable letter to Prime Minister Tunku Abdul Rahman asking him to resign following the 1969 election mess and the ensuing horrendous race riot.

Nothing could be further from the truth. Unlike Mahathir's letter which was written in traditional Malay filled with self-degrading terms like *patek* and *hamba* (slaves), and was excessively deferential as a peasant would in addressing his lord and master, Mukhriz's was direct and with the minimal of formality. It was to be sure polite, but there was no mistaking his blunt message.

One would think that Mukhriz would shy away from such a bold move. For one, he is a relative newcomer to politics. Mahathir had expressly forbidden his children to be active in politics while he was in power, a lesson he unfortunately did not impress upon his successor. Mukhriz should therefore be a "good" and "obedient" Malay; meaning, he should "know his place."

For another, Mukhriz should at least be *terhutang budi* (indebted) to Abdullah for having selected him to contest this election. Clearly this young man saw his duties not in terms of personal loyalty or gratitude to a leader. Instead he saw his loyalty extended beyond—to his party and country.

Obviously Mukhriz is not your grandfather's Malay. He is a true modern-day Hang Jebat, loyal to institutions and principles, not personalities and titles. He is a worthy and necessary adversary to the hordes of latter-day Hang Tuahs who surround Abdullah these days.

As an added measure, Mukhriz let it be known in his letter that he was prepared to face the consequences of his action, as if daring Abdullah to "Go ahead! Make my day!" Mukhriz was challenging Abdullah *mano a mano*, man to man, a gauntlet that could only have been thrown down by an assured and confident *jantan*.

Abdullah's reaction? He deferred to UMNO Youth leaders to "take the necessary action," being that Mukhriz is an UMNO Youth member. *Lembik* leader! As for UMNO Youth's leader, task-baring, nose-flaring, and kris-wielding Hishammuddin, his muted response was simply to assure the public that Mukhriz was speaking in his personal capacity.

Earlier on party veteran Tengku Razaleigh also called on Abdullah to "take full responsibility" for the rout. Razaleigh was too genteel and indirect such that Abdullah missed the *sendir* (subtlety). Razaleigh should have been more direct like Mahathir; he too called on Abdullah to quit. Rest assured that there will be many more and louder such calls coming soon.

I do not see Abdullah giving up voluntarily much less gracefully. He has to be literally dragged out and figuratively hit on the head with a two-by-four.

In Mukhriz UMNO finally has its true "young Mahathir." All along we had been duped by that other pretender, that Kurang 'Jar (K'J) character who had been publicly fancying himself as one.

We all know the tragic fate of Hang Jebat in that great fable of our hallowed literature. Before today's Hang Tuahs in UMNO gloat however, they should remember the fate that befell the more important Malacca sultanate.

March 23, 2008

Sarong Index of Political Corruption

The eminent economist Ungku Aziz, whose insight on rural poverty remains unmatched, once proposed the "sarong index" as a measure of rural Malay poverty. You count the number of sarongs in a household and divide that by the number of dwellers (excepting infants, who presumably would still be in their diapers).

The lower that number the greater is the poverty, with an index of less than one (more people than sarong) signifying extreme poverty. Perhaps that explains why the poor have large families; they are, in the language of my old kampong, sharing the same sarong too often!

With politicians now routinely giving out sarong *pelakat* to Malay voters during election campaigns, I suggest a new "sarong index," this time as a measure of political corruption. Divide the number of sarongs distributed by the number of Malay voters. (Non-Malays do not fancy sarongs; they prefer cash.) The higher the number, the more corrupt the politician, and the more competitive the constituency or position sought.

My index is superior in that it simultaneously measures two variables: the degree of political corruption, and how keenly a position is being contested. Like Ungku Aziz's old index, mine too could be refined by, for example, noting the material of the sarong. If it is only the cotton Madras variety, you could conclude that the corruption is low, or that the election is only for a lowly branch position and not an important national one.

I imagine Abdullah Badawi's team is now aggressively handing out the more expensive and finely-embroidered Kelantan sutra in anticipation of defending the party's presidency in the upcoming UMNO elections.

Bless those folks of Permatang Pauh, for they (at least the Malay voters) will now be inundated with gifts of sarongs given out by generous UMNO operatives intent on denting Anwar Ibrahim's assured victory in the upcoming by-election.

It may be argued that my index is so, well, 1960s or kampong-like. In these days you would need an extended stay at a plush hotel in the capital city or even an overseas trip to carry any weight. Rest assured that my sarong index would still apply in those circumstances, albeit with some modifications.

For in addition to the number of sarongs and type of material, the manner by which the sarong is presented would also matter. For the ordinary villager, simply leaving the sarong in its original clear plastic wrapping would be acceptable and enough. For more important or exceptionally influential clients, that would not suffice. Not only would you need a better material like the sarong *sutra*, but you would also need to wrap it around something attractive, like a voluptuous body *a la* the Mongolian model, with the carrier included as part of the gift! And if your target has shall we say a more *avant garde* taste, you would have to wrap the sarong around a Saiful!

A note of caution for those ill informed on matters of chemistry: biological stains on fabric, unwashed, last a long time, as President Clinton so woefully found out.

In traditional Malay culture, the gift of a sarong is the most personal and thoughtful, bestowed only on special occasions. For a youngster, it would be the traditional gift at the time of circumcision and on *khatam*, the completion of reciting the Koran, both seminal events in the life of a young Malay boy. The sarong is also a wonderful wedding gift.

The sarong has both religious and traditional significance. The more embroidered and expensive *sutra* is worn at weddings and to adorn the *pelamin* (wedding dais). The simple cotton sarong is for daily prayers. Imagine wearing the sarong given to you (with the intent to corrupt) for your prayers!

The gift is also very personal, literally next to your skin. When donning the sarong one would immediately be reminded of the generosity of the giver as well as the unique occasion on which it was given. I still have the *samping sutras* given to me by my friends and family decades ago. On the special occasions like Hari Raya and wedding receptions when I would don them, it would inevitably rekindle favorite memories of those dear friends and family members, as well as the warm occasions when I received those gifts. Such is the meaning of the gift of a sarong.

I also treasure the sarongs given to me by my grateful patients, not so much for the gift as for the emotions and sense of gratitude expressed with the giving. On those occasions I would feel a certain kinship with the village *dukuns* (medicine man), for whom the gift of a sarong from their cliental is the tradition.

It saddens me that such a pristine part of our culture is today debased. Far from being the symbol of affection and generosity as I know it, the sarong is now part of and the emblem of corruption.

Earlier we saw the obscenity of our very symbol of honor and nobility, the *keris*, being publicly degraded by those who would claim to be our future leaders and defenders of our culture. What saddened me were not the thuggish behaviors of these young pseudo leaders rather that they were wildly cheered on by their followers. Such perverted values!

Alas the sarong, like our beloved *keris*, is now a metaphor for the erosion of our traditional values and the desecration of our culture. There is no index to measure that.

August 10, 2008

Looking For UMNO's Next Ex-Leader

At a recent gregarious social gathering, a colleague whose luck in personal relationships could best be described as challenged was teased on whether she was scouting for her next ex-husband. With the current frenzied UMNO divisional nominating meetings, I am tempted to ask a similar question of its members. Are they too looking for their next ex-leader?

If there is any lesson UMNO members should have learned is that the way they pick their leaders needs to be revamped. By now they should have realized the devastating consequences of the "no contest rule" for the two top positions and the onerous nomination quota system, as well as the equally atrocious track record of letting a leader (no matter how seemingly wise and brilliant at the time) anoint his or her successor.

There are indications that this reality is now gradually sinking in, at least on the brave and perceptive few. Thus far that is all there is, only a realization, and nothing more. Shahrir Samad, a cabinet minister and UMNO Supreme Council member, called for "a generational change" in his party's leadership. He viewed UMNO as becoming overly bureaucratic, with heavy emphasis on seniority and hierarchy. At age 58, Shahrir considered himself too late and too old to go for a top post.

Whether that statement reflects reality or merely his undisguised expression of lack of confidence on the current generation of leaders is for Shahrir to clarify. Both Najib and Muhyiddin, candidates for the number one and two slots respectively, are of the same vintage as Shahrir.

If Shahrir was expressing his low opinion of current UMNO leaders, then he is on to something. There are no *jantans* (males) among them. In the current leadership fiasco they have chosen to remain quiet and dutiful until it becomes quite obvious that their leader has become the butt of jokes. Only then do they dare speak up.

Of course there are exceptions but few, and Shahrir is not among them. The caliber of present UMNO leaders, in the cabinet as well as the party's Supreme Council, is such that were they to see their leader stark naked, they would more likely compliment him for his nice tan instead of throwing a sarong at the hapless man and save everyone the embarrassment!

Among the few and ready exceptions are Tengku Razaleigh and Zaid Ibrahim. Razaleigh saw through Abdullah's vacuity early on and challenged him for the leadership. Only the onerous burden of the quota on nominations prevented Razaleigh from contesting; the same hurdle that may confront him now. As for Zaid Ibrahim, he remains the only Malaysian minister to have resigned over a matter of principle. [Correction: Decades earlier Foreign Minister Dr. Ismail also resigned over policy differences.]

There have been many ministerial resignations in the past, as Abdullah's dutiful spinmeisters in *The New Straits Times* pointed out in an attempt to soften the impact of Zaid's action. What those media supplicants pointedly failed to differentiate is that all those earlier resignations were essentially forced upon them or from out of shame.

Incidentally neither Razaleigh nor Zaid is on UMNO's Supreme Council. That speaks volume as to the caliber of individuals attracted to and voted into the party's top leadership.

The current frenzy of divisional nominating activities is likened by that keen observer of UMNO politics, Kadir Jasin, to the behavior of passengers stranded on the freeway by their broken-down bus. In their desperation, they are less interested in the comfort, safety or reliability of their replacement vehicle, only with reaching their destination, and on time. They reason that once they get there they could then leisurely shop for a better and more comfortable substitute for the return trip. It would never cross their mind that in their haste and less-than-prudent choice now, they could end up in a ditch or worse before reaching their destination.

Soon after Abdullah assumed power and was searching for a deputy, I suggested that he pick Tengku Razaleigh. As both are at about the same age it would be unlikely for the Tengku to pose as a potential succession threat. They would also complement each other in skills and temperament. Together they could then revamp UMNO so as to attract fresh young talent and then completely bypass the current crop of ineffective and parochial leaders as represented by Najib, Hishammuddin and Muhyiddin.

Had Abdullah done that his fate today, as well as that of Malaysia, would be far different. It is still not too late for him to recoup. As President he could summon a special General Assembly of UMNO specifically to dismantle the nomination quota. In so doing Abdullah would effectively undo one of Mahathir's less-than-laudatory legacies.

Abdullah would effectively make the current nominating exercise mute, and simultaneously open up the party elections. That could prove beneficial especially if his son-in-law were to be unsuccessful in securing his quota of nominations, which now appears increasingly possible. Abdullah would also then have the great pleasure of watching Najib Razak desperately scrambling to fend off a strong challenge from Tengku Razaleigh. There is little love lost between Najib and Abdullah, and that single maneuver would be the perfect finale from Abdullah to Najib: don't get mad, get even!

Muhyiddin the Meek

Recently Muhyiddin had been incessantly clamoring for change in UMNO's top leadership. Much earlier, as head of the party's committee tasked with changing its rules, he was forceful in advocating removing the current nomination quota system. On meeting a not-unexpected resistance from Abdullah, Muhyiddin meekly yielded.

Muhyiddin is rooting for Najib to replace Abdullah. With Najib slated to win *sans* competition, Muhyiddin has chosen to remain uncharacteristically passive. He even urged all divisions to unanimously nominate Najib as party president, and only Najib, as a "show of party unity." Quite a remarkable and considerable shift in position, and a very quick one at that! Muhyiddin is banking on riding Najib's coattails to the top, and doing so unopposed! As an aside, someone should now ask him what he thinks of the nomination quota system that he was so against earlier.

With that tantalizing prospect, Muhyiddin is now pathetically reduced to mouthing sycophantic praises for Najib, claiming, "I have no doubt that I will work very well with Najib ...." As a preview of the kind of leader he would be, Muhyiddin reassured everyone that he "would not dictate policies." Rather as Deputy President, his is "to support and follow whatever directions and visions the president has spelled out." In short he sees himself as a glorified office boy in the highest office of the land!

Muhyiddin does not see a higher responsibility to the party or country; his loyalty is strictly to the president, a latter-day Hang Tuah. Thankfully thus far he has refrained from dipping his *keris* with ketchup in defense of Najib.

Muhyiddin was the chief executive (Mentri Besar) of Johore state for a decade before Mahathir "promoted" him to the federal level. In the UMNO scheme of things, a *mentri besar* is a major "warlord," certainly more so than a minister, especially for a state like Johore. Back then he grabbed headlines in a regional publication over his tussle with a foreign developer with substantial holdings in his state. I believe firmly in the ability of individuals to change, for the better as well for the worse. My retelling this old story is merely to temper the fast growing enthusiasm for him shown by local commentators.

Najib Not "*More Bettah!*"

Assured of being unopposed for the top slot, Najib wisely chose not to be a part of this emerging attempt at setting up a mutual admiration society with Muhyiddin, declaring that he (Najib) "has not decided if Muhyiddin would be his running mate." That is quite a rebuff! Najib went further and remarked "the more the merrier" when others like the double Muhammad Taib declared their intention to seek the number two position to compete directly with Muhyiddin.

However, when Perlis UMNO Youth leader Ismail Hashim had the temerity to consider competing directly with Najib, he (Najib) abruptly changed tune, expressing doubt whether Ismail could even muster the necessary nominations. Najib would like to have the top prize handed to him on a silver platter, as has been the pattern throughout his political career. To ensure that, Najib expressed his definite lack of enthusiasm for dismantling the current nomination quota rule even though his mentor and champion Mahathir has called for it. Najib did not rule out doing so eventually, once he is gone!

With all his sordid baggage, Najib is understandably scared stiff in getting not only a formidable competitor in Tengku Razaleigh but also insignificant ones like Ismail Hashim. Najib is scared that Ismail would provide an avenue for protest votes.

Do not expect a change in UMNO's leadership come the party's election in March 2009, merely a change of faces. The insular attitude and feudal mindset behind those faces remain the same; likewise the corruption and incompetence, to the detriment of the party and nation.

Meanwhile enjoy the spectacle of UMNO members frantically searching for their next ex-leader. Try not to let your concerns about the future of Malaysia detract you from enjoying the spectacle!

November 3, 2008

UMNO Crippled By Institutional Inertia

Notwithstanding the high hopes and exhilarated expectations of many, especially UMNO members, the upcoming UMNO leadership elections [now deferred to March 2009] will not bring any changes to the party. There will only be the changes of faces, nothing more. The party is crippled by institutional inertia; it is incapable of self-renewal, of making the desperately needed reforms to meet the changed environment.

All institutions suffer from some degree of inertia; that is how they maintain stability and continuity. The law of inertia, otherwise known as Newton's First Law of Motion ("A body in motion tends to remain in motion, a body at rest tends to remain at rest."), is not the curiosity of physics, it is also applicable to social systems.

The reason is obvious. Those currently benefiting from the status quo would vigorously resist attempts at change. The promised gains from any change will remain just that, a promise, and only a potential until that change is successfully accomplished. Meanwhile the loss is being felt right away whether the change is successful or not.

For another, the beneficiaries of the current system, while may be small in number, clearly see their self-interest linked with maintaining the status quo. They will be vigorous beyond their small numbers to resist change. Meanwhile the likely beneficiaries, though they may be more numerous and even be in the majority, are diffused. They have yet to be convinced that they would benefit from the change. Even if that could be shown, they first would have to be convinced that the change would be feasible. Otherwise they would not risk investing their stake (personal and otherwise) to bring about the needed change. Such asymmetric dynamics will remain so until the later stages when the whole system would break down (or threaten to) and everyone would be the loser. This is the perennial dilemma plaguing those charged with formulating public policies and who advocate change.

To its members, UMNO is not yet at that final stage; it will be inevitable come the next general election, if not sooner. It lost significant power in this last election but the magnitude of that loss has not registered on the members and leaders because they still maintain a simple majority at the federal despite major losses at the state level. To UMNO members and leaders alike, this last election was an aberration, not a portentous defeat or the harbinger of future collapse; hence the lack of a sense of urgency.

Re-Branding Instead of Re-Engineering

At the last UMNO Supreme Council (the party's governing and policymaking body) meeting, the leaders were preoccupied with "re-branding" the party. The assumption is that there is nothing wrong with the organization, only it is being wrongly perceived by voters. Hence the preoccupation is not with reforming the organization, rather with public relations exercises.

The millions spent by the party's Youth and Puteri wings to set up cyber-troopers and UMNO-friendly websites reflects this mindset. When that did not work, party operatives did not re-examine their assumptions. Instead they assumed that they were right all along and re-directed their efforts towards intimidating and censoring individuals, organizations, publications, and websites deemed hostile to UMNO in the hope of neutralizing if not eliminating them. The jailing under the ISA of *Malaysia-Today*'s Raja Petra is part of this nefarious grand scheme.

This search for a convenient scapegoat, somebody or anybody to take the blame for the party's recent electoral debacle has also turned inwards. To me the surprise was how quickly the blame landed squarely on its leader Abdullah Badawi. After all, this was the leader who right after the last election claimed that he still had a "victory." Even more remarkable, his assertion was supported by everyone in the party, barring a few brave dissenting souls like Tengku Razaleigh.

Abdullah is without a doubt an inept, incompetent and far-from-incorrupt leader. His earlier "Mr. Clean" moniker is now a cruel joke.

Though necessary, getting rid of Abdullah will not solve UMNO's problems.

The party has yet to address the fundamental issue of how such a clearly untalented individual could have risen to the pinnacle of leadership. The party has failed to even acknowledge that let alone begin to solve it.

UMNO's biggest structural impediment to reform is its inability to attract talent. This is due to three major factors. First is the concentration of power within the party, made worse by the coupling of party with governmental positions. State party leaders are also divisional heads, Supreme Council members, and heads of the party's many wings. In addition they may also be in the cabinet or holding senior governmental positions. Such a concentration of power not only breeds corruption in the party as well as in the government but it also inhibits the nurturing of fresh leadership talents.

Dismantling the system so party leaders are not allowed to hold more than one position would immediately open up many leadership slots and channels, and a chance to preview new talents. A leader cannot be a division head, wing chief, and a Supreme Council member all at the same time, except in an ex-officio capacity. Nor should party leaders (except for the president) be appointed ministers. Decoupling party and governmental positions would make these leaders more effective. It would also provide some rudiments of checks and balances, at least within the party. Besides, it is tough enough being a Youth leader without at the same time leading the Ministry of Education. You cannot do justice to either.

The second impediment is that the current election system heavily favors incumbents. The glacial change in UMNO's leadership matches only that of the old Soviet Politburo! Mahathir introduced this nomination barrier following his close leadership battle with Tengku Razaleigh back in 1987. It was meant to minimize divisive party politics, but the long-term price was high. Even Mahathir is now calling for dismantling it! If the American political parties had UMNO's nomination system, the Democrats would not have discovered Barack Obama to be its presidential nominee.

The third deficiency is that there are no recruitments into UMNO at the senior levels. Its leaders all have to trek the ladder from the very bottom; consequently they are very insular and susceptible to dangerous "group think." By the time they reach the top they are old and sclerotic. Many young and highly qualified potential candidates are too busy developing their careers to be bothered with party politics at the ground floor. Consequently UMNO is left with the less talented, those who could advance only by using the party.

The party has a provision for the president to "helicopter in" high profile candidates into its Supreme Council; he could appoint an additional 10 (now increased to 15) to the 25 already elected. The late Tun Razak effectively exercised this option to bring in fresh talent into the party and his administration.

Looking at the next generation of UMNO leaders currently in its Youth and Puteri ("princess") wings gives me little reason to be optimistic. Many are bright and talented, infused with a generous dose of idealism– initially. They professed their commitment to changing UMNO, but after being in the party, instead of changing the party they were changed by it. These young leaders are even more chauvinistic and corrupt; they are hopelessly trapped in a warped time frame. They too are fond of the current system; thus guaranteeing that UMNO will never grow.

The one bright spot is that at least UMNO Youth members collectively have yet to acquire the sheep-like mentality of their elders. These youths have shown wisdom in nominating at least three candidates to lead their wing. The members have not succumbed to the misplaced faith of their elders; they still believe in competition. Give them time, however.

Money politics, corruption at all levels, and continued factionalisms with various "warlords" exerting their controls are all signs of an organization unable to correct itself and incapable of self renewal.

The current leadership of UMNO is in no hurry to change the rules as they are clearly benefiting from the system. Besides, their mindset is already fixed; there is nothing wrong with UMNO, the fault lies with "them," those outside the party. Consequently, expect the momentum towards UMNO's implosion to accelerate.

November 23, 2008

Sharp Slap to UMNO's Leadership

The humiliation suffered by UMNO in the January 17, 2009 by-election in Kuala Trengganu, a seat previously held by one of its deputy ministers, is further proof that the party's thumping in the March 2008 General Elections was the beginning of the end. Getting rid of its leader Abdullah Badawi will not alter UMNO's fate; a future with Najib Razak will be no solution either.

The party is no longer salvageable; UMNO is beyond redemption. Its leaders and members are incapable of appreciating and thus adapting to the profound changes now gripping the nation. As Tengku Razaleigh aptly put it when commenting on the results, "We are in uncharted waters with no one at the wheel."

There are of course exceptions to the current lack of talent in UMNO's leadership, but they are rare. Zaid Ibrahim had some sensible ideas on reforming the judiciary for example, but look at what they did to him! Tengku Razaleigh's speech at the recent ASLI economic conference was simply brilliant; he rightly pinpointed the major problems facing our nation and offered sensible strategies to approaching them. His was an insight and articulation that Malaysians should expect of our leaders. There again however, he was essentially ignored by UMNO's leadership hierarchy.

In this by-election UMNO resorted to its old corrupt ways that had served it well in the past. There were the sudden announcements of disbursements of public funds to key constituent groups as well as the usual co-opting of government agencies to do Barisan's bidding. If those tricks were not enough, there was the literal stuffing of envelopes with cold cash for voters and reporters covering the campaigns.

Judgement on Najib's Leadership

The victory by PAS candidate Wahid Endut is even more impressive considering that the soon-to-be (come March) Prime Minister Najib Razak literally made his temporary home in Kuala Trengganu during the entire 11 days of campaigning, returning only briefly to the capital to take part in the *Tahlil* prayers on the anniversary of his father's death.

Those voters viewed the upcoming transfer of power from Abdullah to Najib less a promise of better things and more a threat of the same tired corrupt and corrosive ways of the past. The political status quo would only further divide instead of bringing Malaysians together, and they were rightly fed up.

Win or lose, this election would not alter the political reality; Barisan would still maintain its majority in Parliament. In perception however, this loss only reinforces my earlier "beginning of the end" and "beyond redemption" assessment of UMNO. Undoubtedly these were the reasons that compelled Najib to expend his political capital and risk his reputation by actively campaigning.

Ignored by voters, Najib tried to rationalize the outcome by dismissing it as a "minor setback" with "no impact on the national political landscape." He was reduced to declaring that Barisan was "still relevant." Pathetic!

I would have expected that as Finance Minister, Najib would be busy in Putrajaya dealing with the rapidly evolving global financial crisis now threatening our nation. Instead there he was in Kuala Trengganu acting like Santa Claus, distributing candies to voters. They gleefully took the gifts, but being adults (and Muslims, at least most of them) they did not believe in Santa Claus, or Najib Razak.

These past few weeks reflected Najib Razak's leadership priorities and sensibilities. Kuala Trengganu voters were rightly not impressed. Neither am I.

Greasing UMNO's Slide

Come this March, Najib Razak will be the party's (and thus country's) leader. He will have as his deputies Ali Rustam, Muhyiddin Yassin, and the Double Muhammad Taib, individuals with tainted pasts and less-than-impressive resumes. Sobering thought!

Barring divine or other interventions, this will also be the team that will lead UMNO and Barisan Nasional into the next General Election scheduled no later than March 2013. UMNO has its leadership convention every three years; theoretically it could change its leadership before the next general election. However, the party has a tradition of "no contest" for its top two positions and a past pattern whereby leaders would conveniently postpone the leadership convention till after the general elections in the name of "party unity."

That would be great news for Anwar Ibrahim-led Pakatan Rakyat, further enhancing its prospects of assuming power. This may occur even sooner if Barisan Members of Parliament, sensing the political change, were to abandon their parties. The shift could also come earlier if, as expected, Sarawak were to call an earlier election. Then there is the volatile political situation in Sabah.

The objective of any political party is in assuming power. Anything less and you will be relegated to the status of a perpetual fringe party. While that may satisfy the purists in your party, you risk being permanently dismissed by voters. The country's political graveyard is littered by the ghosts of such parties.

Then there is the crucial difference of being voted into office because of the positive choice of voters versus their rejecting your opponent. Anwar Ibrahim and his fellow leaders in Pakatan Rakyat are fully aware of this. It is not enough for Malaysians to be fed up with Barisan Nasional, they must be sold on the promise and potential of a Pakatan Rakyat administration.

As leader of the party that is the centre of the political, racial and other spectra of the Pakatan Rakyat coalition, Anwar has adroitly handled the many competing interests within his coalition by focussing on their commonalities and less on their differences. Differences there are, many and consequential; they could potentially fracture the coalition. If that were to happen, it would crush the hopes of Malaysians long yearning for change.

Besides, there are enough commonalities of purpose among the component parties of Pakatan Rakyat, from eradicating corruption and strengthening our institutions to reducing poverty and fostering economic development, among others. Ameliorate them, and you would have the cheers and votes of those currently advocating for an Islamic State, "Malaysia for Malaysians," or *Ketuanan Melayu*.

Tackling each of these problems (and all must be addressed at once) would challenge the ingenuity of even the most enlightened and committed leaders. There is no need to harp on their differences. All these could be done without getting entangled with such highly divisive and emotional issues as *hudud* or special privileges. Besides, those slogans as "Islamic State," "Ketuanan Melayu" and "Malaysia for Malaysians" have now become meaningless, having been corrupted to being code words for those with more sinister motives.

The corruption and incompetence of the Barisan coalition should motivate Pakatan leaders to focus on solving the glaring and pressing problems of our nation. That would be the sure way to power, quite apart from greasing the downward slide of UMNO and its Barisan Nasional coalition.

January 18, 2009

UMNO's Incompetent Disciplinary Committee

Now that the UMNO election is done with, the raging controversies over the party's Disciplinary Committee's decisions will soon be forgotten, until the next election. It is a sad commentary that the party's attempt at eradicating corruption succeeded in only creating more problems and aggravating existing ones. It reflects poorly on members of the Disciplinary Committee, made up supposedly of the party's distinguished elder statesmen. Its chairman was a former foreign minister. They were given a major task and they bungled it.

Their botched performance reflects a more general theme: the dearth of talent and competence within the party's upper reaches. That, together with pervasive corruption within the party, is what ails UMNO.

The internal affairs of UMNO would not ordinarily interest me except that the party still represents a major (though fast diminishing) segment of the Malay community, and UMNO leaders are also the leaders of the country. Until this reality is altered by voters, what happens in UMNO should concern all Malaysians.

Root Cause Analysis

That UMNO is rotten to the core is acknowledged by all, including its leaders. Unfortunately that is the extent of their insight. I have yet to hear any reflection on the part of the party's leaders, from Prime Minister Abdullah down to the lowest *cawangan* (branch) head, of how or why the party had degenerated to such a sorry state.

To date they have been content dealing merely with the symptoms of corruption. Like other human vices, corruption is infinite in its variations. Thus dealing with any one manifestation forces corruption to morph into other more sophisticated forms that would be even more destructive and difficult to detect or eradicate.

The Disciplinary Committee has been at it now for years, mechanically investigating the cases reported to it. The committee has yet to reflect on how to avoid or prevent the problem in the first place.

The committee members are like *amahs* (household maids) preoccupied with wiping the wet floor but never figuring what caused the problem. Had they looked up they would have noticed that the problem could have been more effectively dealt with by first fixing the leaking faucet. In fact these UMNO operatives are worse than amahs. A maid may not know anything about sealing the leak but at least she has the common sense to call for a plumber.

The committee dealt with hundreds if not thousands of alleged cases of money politics and other breaches of party ethics. Yet it has not issued any report to share its insight with the rest of party, like how to prevent money politics in the first place.

Even if that was not part of their mandate, I would have thought that they would have been unrestrained in wanting to share their accumulated wisdom. They must have learned something, unless of course they were content with merely being amahs busily and robotically mopping the soiled floor but never noticing the leaking faucet.

There are two ways for the committee to discover the metaphorical leaking faucet. One is through a careful systemic analysis to determine patterns and elicit commonalities. The other is to do a "root cause analysis" and "follow the money," especially with the more egregious abuses, as when top personalities were implicated or large sums of money were involved. Examples would be the current case with Ali Rustam and the earlier one involving former Federal Minister Isa Samad.

There are definitely patterns to be discovered. One, money politics plagues UMNO only during party elections, with the worst offenders being those pursuing top positions. Ali Rustam was after the Deputy President position; Isa Samad, the Vice-President.

The other is that most of the offences were committed in the pursuit of securing the party's nominations. So why not dispense entirely with the current quota system of nominations? Let those who wish to be a candidate, do so without having the division nominate him or her. Do away with the current "tradition" of no-contest rule for the top positions. With those barriers removed, there would no longer be the need to bribe anyone just to get your name on the ballot. Such a reform would also open up the process and attract talented candidates. Under its present rule UMNO will never see its Barrack Obama emerge.

With many more candidates contesting, members would get a better and wider choice. The election process would of course need to be changed to accommodate the anticipated bigger slate. Thus should any one candidate fail to secure a majority vote, there would be run-off elections with the bottom candidate eliminated at each round until one candidate secures a majority vote. Failure to have run-off elections would generate divisiveness and rancor, as seen with the recently-concluded UMNO Youth election where its leaders failed to gain the confidence of the majority of its members.

A "root cause analysis" would reveal that money politics involves the trading of cash for votes (or promised thereof). Tengku Razaleigh made an eminently sensible suggestion of not only removing the nomination quotas but also having the entire membership vote for the national party leadership instead of at present, leaving it to the delegates. It is near impossible to bribe three million UMNO members; it is much easier to tamper with only 2,500 delegates.

UMNO could hire the Elections Commission to conduct such party elections. That would be considerably cheaper than the costs of the current "money politics." It would also be fairer and cleaner.

If incoming UMNO President Najib is aware of this problem, he did not spell out in his recent speech how far he was willing to open up UMNO's election process.

Another productive pursuit would be to "follow the money." Where do these guys get their cash? After all it was not too long ago that they (or their parents) were stuck in the poverty of the kampong. Many are also former civil servants; we all know how much they earn, at least their legitimate income.

The other major source of money politics and outright corruption is in securing juicy government contracts. Again here, having open tenders would ameliorate if not eliminate this scourge. The problem would also be reduced were the government to curtail its involvement in business. Fewer contracts to dole out, fewer opportunities for corruption!

The Disciplinary Committee missed out on these sensible recommendations because its members were too busy mopping the floor. They had no time, or more likely no intellectual capacity, to think and reflect on these matters. Or perhaps they were thinking of their job security! As long as that leaking faucet is not fixed, the floor will always need to be continually mopped!

A Superior Solution

No wonder those committee members find their task onerous and unappreciated, or in the words of its chairman, "Damn if we do and damn if we don't!" They have no clear idea of going about their work. My kampong folks have an apt phrase to describe those who bungle their work. "*Tak tau buek kojo!*" (Don't know what they are doing!)

The Committee did not spell out its rules of evidence and the level of burden of proof required. Did it use the threshold of "beyond reasonable doubt" as with criminal prosecution, or merely the "preponderance of evidence" as with civil cases?

The Committee could streamline as well as enhance the quality of its work if it were to classify the cases it received into three categories. First would be those that were obviously without merit. The second would be the egregious abuses with more than just a hint of criminality. The third would the large number of in-between cases.

The Committee should deal only with this third group. It should quickly dispose of the first group, while those with shades of criminality should be referred to the Anti Corruption Agency (ACA). The Committee should have nothing more to do beyond forwarding all the evidences to the Agency, which is equipped with the necessary investigative and prosecutorial tools.

It boggles my mind that to date the Committee has yet to make a single referral to the criminal justice system. I would have expected where the Committee imposed such severe penalties, as with Isa Samad and Ali Rustam, it must have found compelling evidence that ordinary citizens would classify as being criminal. Yet even in both cases there was no referral to the ACA.

Corruption is a criminal act regardless where it is perpetrated. It does not magically become sanitized to "money politics" or "breach of party ethics" just because it is committed within the confines of UMNO.

The chair and vice-chair of the Disciplinary Committee are both lawyers; they were or perhaps still are members of the Bar. As officers of the court they are duty bound to report to the appropriate authorities if they suspect that a crime has been perpetrated. Failure to do so would be a serious breach of their professional ethics that would merit disbarment, at least in America.

Perversely, the best commentary on the Disciplinary Committee's work was the response from Isa Samad to a television interviewer who inquired as to the extent of money politics in UMNO today. He replied, with a straight face, it must no longer be a problem since he was the only one the committee found guilty a few years ago!

Isa summed it well! Unfortunately it is unlikely that UMNO leaders or members of its Disciplinary Committee would grasp the subtle sarcasm of Isa Samad's sharp but accurate observation.

April 2, 2009

Same Old UMNO, Same Old Ethics

Biar mati anak, jangan mati adat! (Sacrifice your child if need be, but never your tradition!) Growing up in Negri Sembilan, that wisdom of my culture was continually drummed into me. To those outside the clan, that adage may seem extreme, an ugly manifestation of unyielding and irrational conservatism.

With my children now grown up, I recognize the verity of that village wisdom. Yes, it was hammered into me on the importance of our cultural tradition of fealty towards elders (our parents in particular), but there was also the equally important reciprocal tradition for the elders (who are presumably wiser) to be more patient and forgiving of the young.

It is this fidelity to *adat* that made my parents not put a guilt trip on me when I chose a path that was not what they had expected. Cognizant of this *adat* too is what made me not stand in the way of my children when they too decided to venture on a journey beyond what was familiar to me.

My old Negri saying could be more accurately and less graphically re-stated as: *Jaga adat, jaga anak!* (Save our tradition, and save our children!)

Such an intricate system of social norms however, would easily be shattered if any of its component parts were to be compromised or exploited.

Consider our esteemed cultural trait of respect and loyalty to leaders and kings, and the associated severe penalty for *derhaka* (treachery). In tandem with that however, is the reciprocal tradition encapsulated in the saying: *Raja adil raja di sembah; Raja zalim raja di sanggah* (Venerate the just king; defy the tyrant).

Yes, my culture demands that I revere and be loyal to my leaders and elders, but they must also be fully aware of the traditional countervailing restraints not to abuse that reverence I have of them.

Consider the nomination of Isa Samad to be UMNO's standard bearer in the upcoming Bagan Pinang, Port Dickson, by-election. He was a Mentri Besar for 22 years and a Federal minister for a few years after that. He epitomizes the "local boy done good" and his fellow villagers in Port Dickson have every right to be proud of him. To them, no honor however exalted would be adequate for their local hero; they would wish upon him even more.

Thus it should not surprise us or Isa Samad that they would want him, and no one else, to have the singular honor to represent them in the state legislature. The surprise is that many are surprised by this expected and proper gesture of generosity on the part of Isa's people towards him.

As per our *adat* however, it is not for the people to deny Isa Samad this honor; that would leave a bitter taste in their collective mouth as well as an affront to their cultural sensitivities. Rather it is for Isa Samad to have the wisdom and magnanimity to decline that honor. If he were to do that at the first round, again as per custom, they would once more beg him to reconsider, and again Isa Samad should decline.

The social norms demand that these back and forth offers and declines would go on for at least three rounds, all to demonstrate (or at least make a show of) the "genuineness" of the gesture. Anything less and it would be interpreted as perfunctory.

It is through such displays of finesse and subtleties that our culture and traditions have stood the test of time and smoothed our social order. Alas today our traditional values and generosities have been abused not by outsiders but by our own people. It is our own leaders and kin who betray us and our values, as so crudely and ruthlessly demonstrated by Isa Samad.

Nonetheless true to our tradition of "*Raja adil raja di sembah; Raja zalim raja di sanggah*," we should not hesitate, and do so in no uncertain terms, to *sanggah* (defy) these leaders should they betray our trust in them.

UMNO's Wet-Finger-In-the-Air Leadership

When UMNO chose a disbarred lawyer to contest the recent by-election in Penang, I commented that the next time around expect the party to scrounge even lower in search of even slimier characters to represent the party. I ventured that it would be difficult to find someone more unworthy than a disbarred lawyer, but trust those UMNO folks, they did find someone. I did not expect to be proven right, and so soon.

In Isa Samad UMNO has someone who had been expelled from the party for "money politics," the euphemism for corruption. Knowing UMNO's shady ethics, to be expelled for that must take some doing.

In justifying his party's pick, UMNO's Deputy President Muhyiddin Yassin declared, "We have decided that this is what the people want." He was jubilant when making that declaration. Surrounded as he was by senior leaders of Barisan and fellow ministers, and judging by their beaming smiles and other body language, they too shared his enthusiasm for the candidate.

Just in case we might miss the point, Muhyiddin went on to reassure everyone that the choice was made "after much thought and scrutiny." Meaning, it was deliberate.

Even ignoring Isa Samad's blatant bribing of UMNO delegates and then bragging about it (the reason for his expulsion), the more fundamental issue is this. The man has nothing more to offer the state after serving as Mentri Besar for over 24 years. If he had any talent or innovative ideas, that should have been obvious during all those years.

At this stage of their careers, leaders like Isa Samad should be seeking out and mentoring the next generation of leaders, not desperately hogging the stage and their followers' fast dwindling reservoir of respect and gratitude.

Only last week Muhyiddin was at pains to point out that he was intent on seeking fresh talent, especially after the Bagan Pinang branch folks brazenly declared that Isa was their only choice. In succumbing to local pressure, Muhyiddin's leadership is nothing more than a wet-finger-in-the-air variety. That is fine in leading a herd of *kerbau* (water buffaloes) but not a nation aspiring for Vision 2020.

There is nothing wrong with a leader sticking his wet finger in the air to check the prevailing wind if that would lead him to trim his sails and steer his ship of state better, while keeping his eye on the compass. Indeed that is the hallmark of a skilled skipper. However, if you keep changing course and be oblivious of the compass, you will never reach your destination.

The earlier rhetoric about UMNO having "to change or be changed" is now proven to be nothing more than just "cock talk," to put it in the vernacular. Muhyiddin is also Deputy Prime Minister, a heartbeat away from the nation's top job. This preview of his leadership, as in his selecting Isa Samad to be UMNO's standard bearer in the by-election, does not reassure me.

In picking Isa, Muhyiddin obviously had to compromise his principles and abandon his commitment to reforming the party. He should be reminded of the old Xeno mathematical paradox: You will never reach your destination if you are satisfied at reaching only the halfway mark at every try.

Once you start compromising your principle at the first obstacle, then it gets easier the next time. Soon you would have no scruples compromising all your principles. By that time you would not only be willing to dispense with your *adat* but you also would be willing to part with your first-born son.

Your corruption then would have been complete, with nothing worthy left to defend or honor. Then it would be: *Mati adat dan mati anak* (Death to your culture, and death to your children).

October 4, 2009

The New God of UMNO

In his celebrated novel *Ranjau Sepanjang Jalan* (*RSJ* – Spikes Along The Way), Shahnon Ahmad chronicles the seemingly endless traps of poverty endured by a kampong family. Or in his elegant words, "*bencana-bencana yang tidak bisa langsai selagi jantung berdegup [dan] nadi berdenyut ...* " (never ending cycle of calamities endured as long as your heart beats and pulse throbs). Shahnon asserts that the pain could only be felt by those willing to reflect on and empathize with the struggles of our *pak-pak tani* (peasant farmers).

This thought haunts me as I reflect on the hoopla surrounding the recent UMNO General Assembly. The soaring rhetoric of 1Malaysia and of reform is a universe away from the world inhabited by Shahnon's main character, Lahuma. The irony strikes hard as the Lahumas are the very people UMNO professes to champion.

The biting irony does not end there. Many of the Assembly participants, including the high-flying ones, are only a generation or two away from the deprivations so painfully detailed in *RSJ*. Those agonizing memories must have been seared into them by their parents and grandparents. That should motivate them to do something to alleviate the debilitating poverty still experienced by so many today.

Yet I did not sense even an inkling of that sentiment at this grand gathering of self-declared "defenders of the Malays." Even more bizarre is that these UMNO delegates still have many friends and relatives who continue to suffer the pain of peasant life. And let's face it, stripped of their political patronages many of the currently high-living delegates would quickly be reduced to a Lahuma existence overnight.

I doubt that many of the delegates have heard of Shahnon Ahmad, let alone read any of his novels. Hence they would not know what I am writing about. I once tried to buy his books at one of KL's major bookstores, only to be greeted by the sales clerk's response of, "*Shahnon siapa?*" (Who?) A stinging indictment of our education system!

Thus a brief summary of *RSJ* is warranted before proceeding. The book describes the endless cascading calamities of droughts, floods, and infestations suffered by one poor farmer (Lahuma). His tragedy (but not the book) ends with his unnecessary death from an untreated trifling sliver injury. His demise compounds the anguish of his wife, who goes berserk and ends up being locked up in a cage by her fellow villagers.

The pathos of Shahnon's depiction of the tyranny of poverty is a universal theme. We see this in John Steinbeck's *The Grapes of Wrath*, the travails of a sharecropper's family who left drought-stricken Oklahoma in pursuit of their golden California dreams during the Depression, and Pearl S. Buck's *The Good Earth*, also about a peasant family, this time in pre-revolution China. Today, the descendents of Steinbeck's Tom Joad are busy running their thriving agro-businesses in Salinas Valley, while the grandchildren of Buck's Wang Lung are actively trading US Treasury papers.

In contrast, Lahuma's *cicit* (great grandchildren) are still scraping a harsh existence in their disintegrating kampong; his fears of their being reduced to begging painfully prescient. Over half a century of unchallenged UMNO leadership, Malays are reduced to begging: begging for handouts from their government, begging for economic scraps from non-Malays, and begging for respect from others.

UMNO leaders may have been to Oxford and resided in sophisticated capitals of the world, alas scratch their hide and the 'kampongness' oozes out of their pores. They are still trapped by the same cultural genes of Lahuma. Where he is crippled by religious fatalism–*"Mati hidup dan susah senang dipegang oleh Tuhan"* (Life and death, hardship and ease, are in Allah's hands)–UMNO members are ensnared by the political variety. They believe their fate is in the hands of the party; it is their savior, their new god–*UMNO dulu, kini, dan selama nya*! (UMNO, then, now, and forever!)

To UMNO folks, the party has replaced Allah as the source of bounty and benevolence, as well as the punisher and decider of their fate. Corrupt leaders are forgiven not by Allah but by the party. The benevolence does not end there. Isa Samad had his political corruption sentence reduced, and then he was rewarded to be the party's election candidate. Khairy Jamaluddin had his "money politics" conviction essentially pardoned, and then was blessed by being made head of UMNO Youth!

With such compelling examples, no wonder UMNO members turn to their new god with the gusto of a fresh convert. Just as Lahuma would never question Allah's design, UMNO members too would not dare question their new god and risk his wrath.

There was one thankful departure with this recent Assembly. Gone were the obligatory race-taunting theatrics, shrill calls for defending the 'honor' of the Malays, and other ugly chauvinistic displays. Time will tell whether this shift represented a change of heart or tactic.

My take is that it is more the latter. For one, UMNO leaders have not been known to utter anything sensible. When they to do, one wonders whether it comes from within or merely the parroting of poll-tested printouts from their public relations operatives. For another, there is a huge gulf between what those leaders preach and practice.

UMNO's latest obsession is combating corruption and rejuvenating the party. At least that is the impression their leaders give. Yet when given an opportunity to demonstrate its resolve, as with the recent by-election in Penang, the party chose a tired and tainted character in the person of a disbarred lawyer to be its standard bearer. I would have thought that it would pick someone who best exemplified the "new, rejuvenated" UMNO.

In judging UMNO leaders, there was only one who understood the plight of our Lahumas. Because he understood them, Tun Razak was able to craft imaginative and effective policies such as his massive rural development schemes, in particular FELDA.

The Tun's massive expansion of educational opportunities (*Gerakan Lampu Suloh*–Operation Torch) brought light to the families of the Lahumas, enabling them to escape the trap of poverty. His expansion of health facilities in rural areas (*Klinik Desa*) ensured that they would not die unnecessarily from simple treatable diseases.

Tun Razak did not belittle or poke fun at the cultural beliefs or biological heritage of those villagers. While they fervently believed that their fate was in Allah's hands, Tun Razak demonstrated there was much that his government could do to persuade if not prod Allah to alter their destiny. He was persuaded more by another Koranic verse: Allah would not change the condition of a people unless they first make an effort at it. As leader, Tun Razak felt a great obligation to help his people change their conditions by bringing education, health care, and development to the villages.

He could not care less about Malay leadership, *Ketuanan Melayu*, *Glokal* Malay, or any other cutesy slogans. Take care of those three basics (health, education, and economic development), and the rest will take care of themselves. There are no shortcuts; stunts or showy development projects cannot replace the real need for improving our schools and healthcare, or bringing development to rural areas.

Now that the delegates are back home to savor the memories of their brief moments in the limelight, I am left wondering what specifically did they do that would directly impact the lives of our villagers. None! The Pak Lahumas would continue enduring their dreary life, one that has remained unchanged for the past half a century under UMNO rule, save for Tun Razak's brief tenure. If UMNO gets its way, that life will remain the same for the next few generations.

Pondering the fate and empathizing with the plight of our *Pak-Pak Tani* are furthest away from the thoughts of these UMNO leaders. They will however, make a brief and perfunctory show of both come election time, when our Lahumas can expect gifts of *sarong pelakat*, in return for their votes.

October 18, 2009

UMNO's Opportunistic Ulama

Like his predecessors Abdullah Badawi and Mahathir Mohamad, Prime Minister Najib Razak endlessly proclaims Malaysia to be an Islamic state.

Now with 40 young ulama joining the party, Najib must feel that his assertion to be the truth. He could not be more wrong.

Yes, ulama play a central role in an Islamic state. In his book, *The Fall and Rise of the Islamic State*, Noah Feldman attributed the longevity and eminence of earlier Islamic states to the critical role of ulama and scholars.

The Islamic governing principle is simple. Rulers are to govern according to God's law, as stated in the Koran and elaborated in the hadith (sayings and practices of Prophet Muhammad, s.a.w.). The central tenet is, "Command good and forbid evil!" As long as the ruler fulfils this obligation, his power and authority are legitimate and deemed divinely-sanctioned.

It was a tribute to their political skills and intellectual prowess that those early scholars were able to formulate from the Koran and hadith a set of laws–the Shari'a–that today still governs the everyday lives of Muslims, even those not living in Islamic states. At its time the Shari'a represented a quantum leap in the recognition of basic human dignity and rights. As Feldman noted, "For most of its history, Islamic law offered the most liberal and humane legal principles available anywhere in the world."

The central precept of the Shari'a is that all, rulers and the ruled alike, are governed by it. No one, not even the sultan, is exempted. That is the rule of law at its core.

The ulama's other major contribution was that they exerted the necessary checks and balances on the powers of the rulers. It was the scholars, not the rulers, who determined what was "good" or "evil." A ruler had to abide by the decisions of the ulama, for not doing so would mean deviating from God's law, a sure route towards de-legitimatizing the ruler's authority.

These two central elements (fidelity to the rule of law and institutionalized checks and balances on the powers of the rulers by the ulama) accounted for the remarkable success and endurance of early Islamic states.

The absence of both is what dooms many so-called Islamic states today, or indeed any state. Show me a backward society, and I will show one that has no respect for the rule of law and without an institutionalized system of checks and balances. This is true not only in the Islamic World but also elsewhere. Sadly, Malaysia is fast headed there.

To many Muslims the most "Islamic" state today is Iran. There the clergy class has assumed absolute power; there are no checks and balances. Criticizing the mullahs is viewed as criticizing Islam; they thus effectively put themselves above the law. Those who view Iran as the model Islamic state obviously missed the essence and beauty of Islamic principles of governance.

UMNO's Opportunistic Ulama

As for the 40 ulama joining UMNO recently, the charitable part of me would like to believe that this was a noble move on their part, an attempt at emulating their illustrious ancient predecessors. That is, they saw the excesses of UMNO and felt compelled to step in to save a venerable institution by providing much-needed checks and balances.

Alas that was not the reason, at least not the one stated by their representative, Fadlan Othman, a junior academic at a local university. His primary reason for joining was to "proselytize from within, for the benefit of UMNO members whom I feel are ripe to have their knowledge, religiosity and spirituality uplifted."

Well, at least he read UMNO members well. I would have been satisfied if he had a more modest goal, like making UMNO and its members more honest and less corrupt.

I am heartened that the announcement of the ulama joining UMNO coincided with the party's rescinding its earlier decision to legalize sports gambling. If the two were indeed related, then that certainly was a good beginning. Now if as the result of their joining the party, UMNO would also declare "money politics" and corruption *haram*, then they truly are on the path of rehabilitating the organization and its members.

The realist in me however, saw something else; a bunch of folks with otherwise unpromising careers seizing an opportunity to advance themselves. I see no difference between them and the many not-too-talented young Malays who, unable to advance on their own prowess, sought the patronage of UMNO.

UMNO is inundated with lawyers who cannot draw up a coherent contract and engineers more adept at building a bridge with more water flowing over than under it. This latest crop of recruits is no different. Google their names; their meager scholarly output becomes apparent. As for their *khutba* (sermons), those too are canned, produced by a committee at headquarters.

Just as these ulama are using UMNO to advance their careers, so too is UMNO exploiting them to enhance the party's tarnished Islamic image, what with its unwise earlier decision to allow betting in sports. These ulama are there to sanitize UMNO. "Whitewash" is the more appropriate term.

These ulama ought to be reminded that exploitative relationships, personal as well as political, rarely endure.

The game that UMNO is engaged in, and where these ulama are only too-willing participants, is a very old one. Throughout history, locally and elsewhere, the powers-that-be had successfully co-opted willing ulama. Ulama, like other mortals, can be bought; only the price varies. For some, the promise of a steady salary, government-issued car and quarters would do it; for others, an impressive title. However, whether the price is a penny or a pot of gold, a hooker is still a hooker.

Prime Minister and UMNO President Najib is well attuned to these corrupt relationships. Consider his bald statement during the recent Sibu by-election, "You help me, I help you!"

In Malaysia, the market for ulama is saturated. Seen in that light, their eagerness to join UMNO is understandable. They are certainly doing themselves some good, at least in this world, but whether they are also doing the community any good is another matter.

These political ulama, whether in UMNO or PAS, are a far cry from those illustrious earlier ones for whom the prophetic saying, "Scholars are the heirs of the Prophet!" was apt. Likewise, today's Islamic states, Malaysia included, are a far cry from those earlier ones, which Feldman describes as "so Islamic that they did not need the adjective to describe themselves."

No wonder Malaysian Prime Ministers from Mahathir to Najib are obsessed in calling Malaysia an Islamic state. They have to, for Malaysia has nothing to show for it but the label.

June 27, 2010

"UMNO is Malay; Malay, UMNO" Myth Forever Shattered!

While UMNO apologists and sycophants in academia, blogosphere, and the mainstream media quibbled over such minutia as the number of participants at last Saturday's massive KL112 (January 12, 2013) rally, two facts are indisputable. First, that peaceful and largely Malay demonstration, the largest the nation had ever witnessed, forever shattered the myth that UMNO is Malay, and Malay, UMNO. Second, given a modicum of respect by and without provocation from the authorities, Malaysians are quite capable of partaking in peaceful rallies.

On this second point the authorities, specifically the police under its new leadership, are finally learning that water tankers, personnel with anti-riot gears or tear gas canisters, and other crude displays of power often precipitate rather than prevent violence. The earlier BERSIH 3.0 rally demonstrated that point very clearly.

The size and orderliness of this KL112 rally, together with the bravery and determination of the participants, was reminiscent of the transformative event of over 66 years earlier, the opposition to the Malayan Union Treaty. That altered the course of Malaysia's history. *Insha' Allah* (God willing), last Saturday's rally will too.

The power imbalance between those demanding change and those in power back in 1946 was enormous. Then it was mostly illiterate and unsophisticated Malay peasants facing the much superior and more formidable colonial authorities. Yet in the end, right won over might, and justice prevailed!

Today, while the UMNO Government is detested to the same degree as the old colonials, if not more so, it is nowhere as sophisticated a wielder of power as the British. Meanwhile, those clamoring for change are far more worldly, more committed, and in far greater numbers than their adversary–UMNO and its supporters. More importantly, unlike the colonials, today's UMNO government is crippled with corruption and incompetence while also crude wielders of power. All the more we should expect that right and the truth, as well as justice, will again prevail.

National Literary Laureate Samad Said's stirring reading of his poetry *"Di Atas Padang Sejarah"* (On This Field of History) last Saturday at Merdeka Stadium prompted me to make that comparison with the anti-Malayan Union Movement. He is old enough to remember and may have even participated in that historic protest.

"Di atas padang sejarah," Pak Samad asserted in his poetry, *"pantang kita mungkiri janji."* (We must not renege on our promises.). Today, the successors to those who brought us Merdeka over 55 years ago have betrayed that promise, and demonstrated no remorse or shame.

While Pak Samad's gray hair and rousing poetry reading lent an air of history and gravity to the moment, the Blue Gang's Ito Mohammad and his song *"Ubah Sekarang"* (Change Now!), specifically composed for the occasion, gave the gathering a certain hip! There was no mistaking however, the seriousness of his message.

"Ubah sekarang," Ito belted out in his trademark rhythm and blues beat to the cheers of thousands, *"Kita cari kebenaran*! (We seek the truth!) *Ubah sekarang/Teggakkan Keadilan* (Uphold justice!)" Then to the roar of the crowd, he added, *"Ubah Sekarang* / Send-off Barisan!"

Ito is a talented performer and a committed crusader with a definite mission, in the mold of Bono. Ito is for truth and justice, to give meaning to

Merdeka, for the sake of our children and grandchildren. One thing is certain: Ito is no *carma* (contraction for *cari makan*–hired hand) artist.

The 1946 anti-Malayan Union Movement was led by the charismatic, farsighted and savvy Datuk Onn; so too KL112 in the person of Anwar Ibrahim. In many substantive ways Anwar is a far more formidable and superior leader. Onn meekly obeyed the commands of his sultan in the sycophantic manner of Hang Tuah, and was banished to Singapore; Anwar in the chivalrous tradition of Hang Jebat had the courage to take on a man far more powerful (at least then) than the sultans or King–Mahathir. Anwar paid a severe price, physically and in many other ways for his defiance but in the end he prevailed, unlike Jebat. Last Saturday was proof of that victory. Meanwhile his old nemesis Mahathir was left to rant in his blog.

Far more important than leaders are the commitments of their followers. UMNO could not have organized a rally a fraction of the size of KL112 without resorting to bribes, outright giveaways, or having their *carma* artists, academics and journalists singing high praises for its leaders, plus the establishment's usual hired crowd.

There was a pathetic attempt, no doubt by a bumbling UMNO operative, at a Facebook posting calling those rally participants to collect their fees! That posting bombed as it was immediately exposed for the hoax that it was. Those UMNO hired hands were not even sophisticated enough to pull a cyber stunt!

Anwar commits to ten goals, the top being free and fair elections. Elections must not only be fair and free but more importantly, be seen as such. Our Elections Commission (EC) lacks credibility, both on conducting elections as well as maintaining the integrity of the electoral rolls.

It is too late to change the personnel at EC. Besides, that would not make any difference. They have been indoctrinated to believe that their agency is just another electoral instrument of Barisan instead of an independent agency answerable to the King and thus the citizens. At this stage the only credible way to ensure fair and free elections would be to invite external observers.

Free and fair elections should be the priority. The responsibility for maintaining the integrity of the electoral process extends beyond the EC and Election Day. We must never let or tolerate the 2008 post-election fiascoes of Perak and Selangor to recur. In Selangor, the hooliganism and vandalism of the staff, condoned by its outgoing UMNO Chief Minister Khir Toyo, stood in marked contrast to the civility and orderliness in the transfer of power between Gerakan and DAP in Penang. This being Malaysia, the races of the protagonists at both events (Malays in Selangor and Chinese in Penang) did not escape notice. Toyo was later convicted of corruption. He epitomizes UMNO's rotten core.

Meanwhile in Perak, the permanent establishment including the sultan (who should have been the stabilizing and buffering element) were themselves hopelessly entangled in another mess. They too did not shine.

We must also never allow the prostituting of government agencies and departments as Barisan's election machinery. I have no problem with *The New Straits Times* and *Utusan Melayu* continuing as UMNO newsletters and their "journalists" as UMNO propagandists; after all both are owned by UMNO. I take issue when taxpayer-financed agencies like Bernama, Radio

Television Malaysia (RTM), and Biro Tata Negara (National Civic Bureau) doing likewise.

Ito's rhythmic *ubah sekarang* is not, as UMNO leaders would like us to believe, changing horse midstream rather letting an old lame and tired one to pasture. Our culture is kind; we do not send our old horses to the glue factory even though that would turn them from revenue consumers to producers.

On that August 31, 1957 and at the same Merdeka Stadium, a second past midnight Tunku Abdul Rahman declared Merdeka for our new nation. He brought home from England our Declaration of Independence. He gave our new nation hope and all the promises implied with our sovereignty. Today, Tunku's successors in UMNO Baru, through their venality, have betrayed that solemn covenant. They have, in Samad Said's poetry, *mungkiri janji*. It is time we reclaim that promise and our dream.

Last Saturday, when Anwar repeated "Merdeka" seven times in the manner of the late Tunku, he had begun that process of reclaiming. Tunku brought the document of Declaration of Merdeka; more than half a century later Anwar will give meaning to its words in our everyday lives.

Ubah sekarang! Tolak mereka yang memungkiri janji! Change now! Remove those who have betrayed us!

January 5, 2013

Mahathir's Continuing Burden Upon The Nation

Mahathir is the only prime minister who had devalued the *ringgit*, the very symbol of Malaysia's sovereignty. If that were his only negative legacy, the nation could bear it. Unfortunately the man has burdened (and continues to burden) Malaysia with many more. He has also devalued our culture and institutions. Most of all he has devalued the trust Malaysians have in each other, a vital but scarce asset in a plural society.

On a much lesser scale but no less consequential, and to serve more as a concrete example, the upcoming UMNO leadership convention will be another. With its "no contest" rule now the norm, the convention mocks the very meaning of a leadership election, reducing it to the level of the old Soviet Politburo "elections." This coming event will again expose the party's corruptness and how pathetically bereft it is of talent. The same old tired and tainted candidates will be recycled. It is an exercise less of renewal and rejuvenation, more of an old and leaking sewer treatment plant being given a fresh veneer of leftover paints. The stench remains.

As for the candidates, they would be like desperate monkeys elbowing and clawing each other to the top, their howling preventing them from hearing the cracking branches as the tree was crashing down.

Legally this party is not the original UMNO of the sprit of 1946 that humbled the colonialists, rather "UMNO Baru" (New UMNO), Mahathir's creation after he maneuvered a less-than-honest squeaky victory over his challenger, Tengku Razaleigh, back in 1987. The original UMNO was subsequently deregistered. UMNO Baru is but a pretender to that glorious old party, the spirit of 1946, the one that derailed the Malayan

Union and brought independence to the country. This UMNO Baru bears all of Mahathir's ugly trademarks.

I have never met the man except being in the audience at one of his many public appearances decades ago, and his acknowledgments at having received a few commentaries I sent him while he was a backbencher in Parliament. My analysis of him is strictly based on his policies and performances as a leader. It is not colored by my personal feelings or a show of gratitude. I had not sought any favor from him and he had granted me none, thus sparing me the *"mudah lupa"* (ingrate) epithet.

This *mudah lupa* is a special burden in our culture where one's personal kindness and familiarity could hide and indeed excuse many a sin. Mahathir himself is not spared this burden; hence his being easily hoodwinked by the put-on piety and humility of his chosen successor, Abdullah Badawi. Even Mahathir's earlier enthusiasm for Najib to replace Abdullah was based less on Najib's talent, more an expression of Mahathir's gratitude to Najib's late father for having "rehabilitated" Mahathir into UMNO.

Yes, Mahathir was once kicked out of that grand old party back in 1970, in the aftermath of the deadly 1969 race riots. Those early UMNO leaders were wise and prescient in their judgment of him.

Rehabilitated he was, and with that his quick ascent to the top post. Now the nation and the party bear the burden of his many follies. Malaysia will continue bearing them long after he is gone, such is the damage he inflicted upon the country. The currency devaluation was painful enough, especially to the poor who still bear the burden today.

Judging by past performances, this upcoming leadership contest would again assault the sensibilities of our Malay culture. Forget about *budi bahasa* (graciousness) and *halus* (soft) ways. Those previously found guilty of "money politics" (that's corruption to the rest of us) like Isa Samad and Khairy Jamaludin would again be elected to top positions. So too would former Selangor Chief Minister Khir Toyo, except that he is now serving time for corruption. Incidentally Khir Toyo is regarded as "clean" by his fellow UMNO members. As for Isa and Khairy, the former is now put in charge of the multi-billion ringgit FELDA, the latter, a cabinet minister. That too, is part of Mahathir's legacy.

One might quibble about Khairy for he once bragged about being Mahathir's vocal critic. However, Mahathir's legacy is the overall pernicious culture he fostered in UMNO Baru. In any other culture or jurisdiction, that young man would not even be nominated for dog catcher. That speaks volumes to the degradation of UMNO Baru, Mahathir's legacy. Its destructiveness is pervasive and permanent precisely because it is less obvious.

Mahathir's scathing and relentless criticism of his successor, Abdullah Badawi, cannot hide the obvious fact that he (Mahathir) was responsible for the mess. *He* appointed Abdullah. Similarly, Mahathir was also instrumental in Najib replacing Abdullah. Mahathir's excuse that there being no one else is just that–an excuse. Two successive dud appointments to the highest office of the land, another reminder of Mahathir's ugly legacy!

Mahathir never tires of reminding Malaysians about Petronas Twin Towers, the gleaming highways, and the KLIA, all built during his administration. He also used to brag about Putrajaya, the multibillion-dollar new capital city. Not anymore. Yes, Putrajaya is graced by some futuristic bridges but it must be the only capital in the world that does not have any foreign embassy. As for those bridges, they must be the only ones to be erected where first they had to dig a lake so they could have water underneath those bridges!

It is pathetic that after having served as the nation's longest-serving chief executive, Mahathir could point only to those physical monuments as his legacy. We have to constantly remind ourselves that the deterioration of our institutions (especially our schools and universities), the pervasiveness of corruption, the soiling of our culture (especially Malay culture), and the erosion of the trust we have in each other are the very core of his legacy.

It took the Chinese decades to recognize and then overcome Mao's malignant *feng shui*. It took the Soviets generations to free themselves of the grip of Stalin's ghost. How long will Malaysians, Malays specifically, take to escape the *hantu* (ghost) of Mahathirism? Will we ever?

August 15, 2013

The Future – Blue Chip To Penny Stock

Long before the twin tragedies of Malaysia Airlines (MAS) Flight MH17 (shot down in eastern Ukraine in July 2014) and MH370 (disappeared literally from thin air over the South China Sea earlier that March), the company's shares were already languishing at the bottom floor of the KLSE at around 22 *sen*. Yes, that is *sen*, as in cents, or pennies. Even bottom feeders were shunning the shares.

To think that a decade and a half earlier the Mahathir Administration paid RM8.00 for those same shares! Factoring in for inflation and devaluation, it should be about RM30.00 in today's devalued ringgit. If you add in the expected appreciation as per the KLSE Index, the shares should be trading at around RM50 today.

From RM50 to 22 *sen*! Formerly blue chip MAS now a penny stock; its shares good only to wallpaper your bathroom; they are useless for toilet paper.

MAS shares are an apt metaphor for Malaysia. She too has taken a beating in her values, the consequence of the toxic triad of the leadership of Abdullah Badawi, Najib Razak, and UMNO. I should also add Mahathir; he was also a major factor. However, he is now long gone though still making some loud but ineffective noises. At any rate, Mahathir's many ugly legacies should and would have been ameliorated by now if Malaysia has had competent and diligent leadership.

Alas Abdullah and Najib are neither competent nor diligent, and UMNO, the instrument of their leadership, is a corrupt and sclerotic organization unable to respond to changes. All three are Mahathir's legacy. That is the heaviest burden Malaysia has to bear.

The drop in the value of MAS shares is readily apparent and easily quantifiable, with the burden borne exclusively by its unlucky but willing shareholders. In contrast, the devaluation of Malaysia, while also readily apparent to citizens, has yet to register on her leaders. They still delude themselves as leading a blue chip nation. The weight of the nation's devaluation is borne not by them but by those least able to bear it, the poor. Again let it be said so those self-proclaimed champions of the Malays in UMNO and elsewhere can hear it loud and clear, Malays are overrepresented in that class.

Nor has the full magnitude of the nation's devaluation been appreciated or quantified. Consider my old high school The Malay College, dubbed "Eton of the East" by its proud old boys. In the 1960s it prepared its students well for universities. Today it is but an expensive glorified middle school; its students have to go elsewhere to matriculate. This sorry state was reversed only recently with the introduction of its International Baccalaureate program.

On a more general level, in the 1980s there were still many Chinese parents who enrolled their children in national schools. Today even Malays are shunning that stream in ever increasing numbers, with both opting for Mandarin schools instead.

In the 1980s I could still gather a few Malays at Stanford to invite them to my home for Hari Raya celebrations. Today at elite campuses Malays are as rare as clean public toilets in Malaysia.

In late 1990s a young Malay doctor, a graduate of the University of Malaya (UM), did well in her US Medical Licensing Examination to be accepted at a top American hospital for her specialty training, a reflection of her superior undergraduate medical education. Today, the British Medical Council had long ago withdrawn its accreditation of UM's medical faculty. Yet that did not stop the university's leaders from deluding themselves that their institution could be among the top global 100 within a few years. Not to be outdone, the vice-chancellor of another Malaysian public university bragged about his institution aspiring to be the "Harvard of the East," within a decade!

As is apparent, Malaysia has no shortage of her Walter Mittys, or his local counterpart, the Mat Jenins.

That is only the education sector. For the greater economy, in the 1970s Malaysia was able to finance its ambitious and highly successful rural development schemes like FELDA, as well as expand her schools, without resorting to any borrowing, local or foreign. Today, public and private debts threaten to sink the nation and its citizens.

As for FELDA, Malaysia brags about floating the biggest global IPO with its Felda Global Holdings (FGH), bigger in valuation than even Facebook. For a reality check, visit a FELDA settlement. The roads are still unpaved while the homes lack electricity and potable water. The schools are an embarrassment. Oil palm, the foundation cash crop, is still being harvested in the old back-breaking and neck-stretching labor-intensive ways of the 1960s. There is little or no innovation; no hydraulic lifts or mechanical harvesters to relieve the onerous and treacherous human burden.

In the 1970s the Malaysian ringgit was on par with the Singapore dollar. Today the ringgit vies with the *rupiah* and *rupees*. Soon Malaysians would be trading in millions just for their daily bread. I suppose that is one way for the nation to brag about having many millionaires.

As for security, Malaysian homes are now fortified fortresses, with armed guards at road entrances. Malaysians are well advised not to don expensive watches or wrist bracelets if they value their hands. Malaysian borders are as porous as fishing nets. At least those nets trap the big fish; Malaysian borders let them in and out, their pathways greased by the devalued ringgit.

I am belaboring a point here. These are all painfully obvious to the average Malaysian. My doing so is merely to illustrate in tangible and graphic terms readily comprehensible by kampong folks the devaluation of Malaysia that is the consequence of the toxic trio of Abdullah, Najib, and UMNO. They will continue to spew their lethal brew onto Malaysia at least until the next general election, due no later than June 2018. For those now burdened by their poisonous potion, that is a long time away. In nation-building however, that is only a blink of the eye. I am optimistic that positive change will come with that election *if* the process can be kept honest. Then Malaysians will have a chance for change.

One of the triad, Abdullah, is already gone and no longer sullying the nation. As for UMNO, despite being the largest and ruling party at the federal level for over the past half a century, it never gets a foothold in Sarawak. Of the nine states in the peninsula, UMNO is now permanently wiped off in Penang, Kelantan, and Selangor. If the federal territory of

Putrajaya and Kuala Lumpur were also a state, UMNO would be wiped out there too. At one time it was also out in Perak, Kedah, and Trengganu.

That leaves only Najib. My earlier prediction of his premature ending as prime minister notwithstanding [see "Priority of Packaging Over Performance'" page 118], he is now secure at the helm of the UMNO rickety ship. However, to be the unchallenged skipper of the *Titanic* is no job security; it could very well undermine your wellbeing.

I am not disheartened for I am always amazed at the ability of one person to initiate transformational changes. Often those individuals are the ones we least expect. There is no rhyme or reason for such leaders to emerge except that they somehow appear at the right time and place, with all the right people to help them to do the right thing in the right manner; in short, the confluence of all the elements and the alignment of all the stars.

In the 1990s Indonesia was threatened to be ripped apart by its bewildering centrifugal forces. Today it celebrates its peaceful democratic transition with a new and promising leader in Joko Widodo. Further east, who would have predicted back in the 1970s that a diminutive, uninspiring and uncharismatic Deng Xiaoping would dismantle the horrific legacy of the colossal but destructive Mao Zedong?

Further east across the Yellow Sea, in the 1950s the South Koreans depended entirely on the spending of the hundreds of thousands of American GIs stationed there. Then came General Park; today Samsung, Hyundai and LG are global household brand names.

At the same time I do not underestimate the ability of one idiot to wreck untold damage upon a nation while its citizens stand by and let it happen. Nearby there was Indonesia's Sukarno, further away Zimbabwe's Mugabe, and in the not-too-distant past, Iraq's Saddam.

Thus I do not underestimate Najib to do likewise to the great nation of Malaysia if Malaysians let him. I hope they would not.

Two Black Swans and Many More Dark Crows

Malaysia suffered through the two horrific man-made disasters in the span of just a few months in 2014. The disappearance of Malaysia Airlines Flight 370 over the South China Sea remains a mystery. While we know what happened to Flight 17, the question remains of why a MAS plane? After all, a Singapore Airlines jet had earlier flown a similar route while an Air India one was only a few kilometers away.

As an interesting cultural and social observation, the Air India crew tried to contact the ill-fated Flight17, but was unsuccessful. Meanwhile Singapore Airlines was tooting right after the accident that it was now avoiding that route.

When a "black swan" (rare, unpredictable) event occurs, it is predictable for some to look beyond the realm of the rational for an explanation. This is not an affliction of only the uninformed and poorly educated. In part this reflects the universal recognition that there is a greater power governing us all that we have as yet to fully comprehend.

When 9-11 struck, many religious leaders insensitive to the pain of the victims' relatives and friends called it divine retribution for America's tolerance of homosexual ways; likewise when Katrina broke the levees of New Orleans.

At the other end of the world, when the Asian tsunami hit northern Sumatra on the eve of Christmas 2004, the iconic image that was seared into everyone's memory was of the lone mosque standing forlornly and unscathed amidst the sea of destruction around it.

Those with even an inkling of science knew that the tsunami was caused by a shift in the earth's tectonic plates deep in the floor of the Pacific Ocean off the coast of Sumatra. That knowledge has profound consequences; it led to the creation of ocean sensors that could detect those earth and giant wave movements well ahead to warn those that may be affected. Along the coast of Japan and western North and South America there were already early warning systems and clearly marked evacuation routes. Indonesia did not have them.

The science-challenged Indonesian peasants saw things differently. To them, the lone standing mosque was Allah sending them a message. The peace treaty that ended the generations-long civil war in Aceh was signed soon after. Their metaphysical interpretation of events too had a beneficial consequence.

Before we dismiss or belittle the Indonesians' belief, there is still the question of why the tectonic shift had to occur there and at that particular time and not at some remote uninhabited part of the Pacific. That defies science, at least as we know it. Modern science offers only probabilities.

So when Malaysia suffered through two eerily similar "black swan" tragedies in the two passenger jet crashes (both were Boeing 777), it was not a surprise that many looked for explanations beyond science. To be sure, a plane disappearing or crashing is not a black swan event, but Flight 370 disappeared without leaving any trace, incredulous in this day of round-the-clock ubiquitous satellite surveillance. That tragedy still baffles everyone. As for the ill-fated MH17, while we knew what happened (it was shot down), still the question remains *why* a MAS plane was the unfortunate victim.

When an obscure village alim says that the calamities were caused by MAS serving alcohol onboard, he can be scoffed at or be ridiculed. By that theory Emirate Airlines would have been a top casualty. However, when thoughtful commentators like Kadir Jasin, the former editor-in-chief of *The New Straits Times*, and Zaid Ibrahim, a former cabinet minister and successful corporate lawyer, alluded to *bala* or divine retribution, then we are compelled to pause and reflect. This is especially so when their views resonated with the general public.

In reality, many had taken figurative pot shots at MAS in the past. Stated differently, long before those two black swans, the airline had had many dark crows. MAS would long ago have been grounded, and many times too, had it not been for the government's repeated expensive bailouts.

Profitable units of the airline, like catering and maintenance, had been siphoned off to UMNO cronies, with MAS forced to buy back those services at inflated prices, converting what were once revenue-producing units into revenue-draining ones. On another front, instead of pampering its customers, MAS was coddling its employees, from ramp handlers to top executives, with board members on weekend jaunts to London on their free passes. They were happily hogging the company's trough at customers' expense, with taxpayers footing the bill.

While other airlines were getting substantial discounts for their new planes and passing those savings back to their companies, MAS was paying full retail price, with the discounts going into the pockets of crony middle men "consultants" in cahoots with top executives. Then there was that "brilliant" idea of selling its headquarters in a prime Kuala Lumpur location and then renting space back from its new owner. It's akin to selling your house and then paying rent to the new owner, adding another layer of expense. This was what Pan Am Airlines did in 1970. We all know what happened to that company.

Not to be outdone, there was that wonderful financial engineering dubbed WAU (Widespread Asset Unbundling) where MAS sold its planes and then leased them back. Again it was like selling its headquarters. Not owning your own planes is a smart and effective strategy for a start-up airline as it conserves capital that could be diverted to expanding your market. It is a dumb move for an established company to do so as that would only add another layer of costs. The only ones wowed by that WAU scheme were the new owners of the planes and the investment bankers who arranged the deal.

If MAS shares were a metaphor for Malaysia, then MAS the company was a mirror to the country. Previously reliable services like power and water that were provided by competent public entities are now privatized, sold at heavily discounted prices to favored political cronies. Those ersatz capitalists, pseudo entrepreneurs, and rent seekers came out like bandits, but the pipes often run dry, and when they do flow, the water is not fit to drink. Likewise with electrical supplies; they are erratic and with ever escalating prices.

The government cannot forever protect MAS from the reality of an increasingly competitive world. The price for bailouts keeps escalating and is no longer sustainable. For MAS the skid was greased by the entry of Air Asia at one end, which cannibalized MAS on the domestic and regional fronts, and Singapore and other Asian airlines like Cathay Pacific that chipped away at MAS's long-haul destinations.

Likewise, Malaysia cannot forever protect its citizens from external realities like globalization, or local ones like the increasing competitiveness of those (mainly non-Malays) *not* dependent on government.

The first black swan, disappearance of MH370, exposed the incompetence of Malaysian leaders on the world stage. Malaysians do not need to be reminded of this. These leaders could not even handle simple queries from journalists and the public. The astute political cartoonist Zunar captured well the bumbling Najib. His biting cartoon depicting a "Too Weak" Najib "Two Weeks" after MH370 was carried by *The Washington Post*.

Like MAS, Malaysians too have been exposed to the reality of a highly competitive globalized world. They now realize that the "education" they had received at local institutions has been nothing more than indoctrination. Their low English proficiency and abysmal communicating skills and critical thinking faculties do not serve them well in the new marketplace.

I hope Malaysian leaders would heed the wisdom of Zaid Ibrahim and Kadir Jasin, that is, treat the two black swan events as the Indonesians treated their black swan of the Asian tsunami. Keep the Malaysian house pure and in good order, free of what displeases Allah, not to please Him but to please Malaysians.

Malaysia is burdened with the toxic leadership of Abdullah, Najib, and UMNO. Abdullah is now gone though he is still costing the taxpayers a bundle, for apart from his generous pension he is also "double dipping" as head of a government agency. That leaves only Najib and UMNO.

Rudderless Najib changes with the slightest shift in current. That's at least twice a day with the tide. The man is without conviction or principles. Convincing him is not the problem, making him commit to it, is. Whoever has his ear last gets him. Allah's will excepting, his position in UMNO is secure.

As for UMNO, the *kucing kurap* (scabrous cats) have taken over. They are so consumed with scratching themselves and each other such that even the meekest mouse has full run of the house. Or to use a more familiar metaphor, the lunatics have taken over the asylum. The party's recent election (October 2013) saw only a few bright faces; there were more seeds in a pea pod. All six new vice presidents were "half-past-six," two were previously guilty of "money politics." The 25 members of the Supreme Council were no better.

As president Najib could appoint an additional 17 to the Supreme Council, enough to elevate its caliber and alter the dynamics. Instead, his choice reflects and aggravates the sorry state of UMNO.

As party members have not seen fit to change UMNO's leadership, Malaysians are duty bound come the next election to remove them and their party the privilege to lead the nation.

Acknowledgments

Except for the introduction and conclusion (The Future–Blue Chip To Penny Stock), these essays have been posted earlier in various blogs. I thank Raja Petra Kamarudin who has been most generous with his *Malaysia Today* (mt.m2day.org) in carrying my commentaries right from the inception of his very popular website. I am also grateful to Lim Kit Siang (blog.limkitsiang.com) and Din Merican (dinmerican.blogspot.com) for carrying these and other of my essays. More recently I have also contributed to *The Malaysian Insider*. These online portals are popular with different segments of Malaysians, so I am pleased to have the opportunity to present my views to such a diverse group.

Again my wife Karen helped me go over the manuscript and picking up the errors that had been missed earlier.

Index

About The Author

Bakri Musa is a surgeon in private practice in Silicon Valley, California. Malaysian-born and Canadian-trained, he left his native country in 1963. He keeps a close track of the social and political developments in Malaysia, including a 30-month stint as a surgeon there from 1976-78.

He has given presentations on Malaysian affairs at Stanford University's Shorenstein Asia-Pacific Research Center, The Woodrow Wilson International Center for Scholars in Washington, DC, The University of Buffalo, and Rochester Institute of Technology. Apart from scientific articles in scholarly journals, his lay commentaries have appeared in mainstream Malaysian papers *The New Straits Times* and *The Sun Daily*. He was a long-time columnist for the on-line portal *Malaysiakini* (Malaysia Now) and a regular contributor to *Malaysia Today* and *The Malaysian Insider*.

Beyond Malaysia, his Op-Ed pieces have appeared in *The New York Times*, *International Herald Tribune*, and *The Far Eastern Economic Review*. He has also appeared on National Public Radio's "Marketplace." All eight of his previous books have been on Malaysian socio-political affairs, the latest, *Liberating The Malay Mind*, was released in 2013.

He is now completing his memoir, *Cast From The Herd. Memories of Matriarchal Malaysia*, chronicling growing up there. He maintains a blog that also serves as a repository of his essays at www.bakrimusa.com, and www.bakrimusa.blogspot.com as well as on Facebook.

www.ingramcontent.com/pod-product-compliance
Lightning Source LLC
Chambersburg PA
CBHW030419290526
45786CB00001B/55